SONATA FRAGMENTS

MUSICAL MEANING AND INTERPRETATION
Robert S. Hatten, *editor*

SONATA FRAGMENTS
Romantic Narratives in Chopin, Schumann, and Brahms

Andrew Davis

Indiana University Press

This book is a publication of

Indiana University Press
Office of Scholarly Publishing
Herman B Wells Library 350
1320 East 10th Street
Bloomington, Indiana 47405 USA

iupress.indiana.edu

© 2017 by Andrew Davis

All rights reserved

No part of this book may be reproduced or utilized in any form or by any means, electronic or mechanical, including photocopying and recording, or by any information storage and retrieval system, without permission in writing from the publisher. The Association of American University Presses' Resolution on Permissions constitutes the only exception to this prohibition.

♾ The paper used in this publication meets the minimum requirements of the American National Standard for Information Sciences—Permanence of Paper for Printed Library Materials, ANSI Z39.48-1992.

Manufactured in the United States of America

Library of Congress Cataloging-in-Publication Data

Names: Davis, Andrew C., 1973– author.
Title: Sonata fragments : romantic narrative in Chopin, Schumann, and Brahms / Andrew Davis.
Description: Bloomington : Indiana University Press, 2017. | Series: Musical meaning and interpretation
Identifiers: LCCN 2017008807 (print) | LCCN 2017013823 (ebook) | ISBN 9780253025456 (e-book) | ISBN 9780253025333 (cloth : alk. paper) | ISBN 9780253028938 (pbk. : alk. paper)
Subjects: LCSH: Sonata—19th century. | Chopin, Frédéric, 1810–1849—Criticism and interpretation. | Schumann, Robert, 1810–1856—Criticism and interpretation. | Brahms, Johannes, 1833–1897—Criticism and interpretation.
Classification: LCC ML1156 (ebook) | LCC ML1156 .D38 2017 (print) | DDC 786.2/18309—dc23
LC record available at https://lccn.loc.gov/2017008807

1 2 3 4 5 22 21 20 19 18 17

For Corey

Contents

Acknowledgments — ix

Introduction: Romantic Musical Discourse, or, a Rhetoric of Romantic Music — 1

Part I. Fragmentation and Atemporality

1 Fragmentation: Aesthetics of Nineteenth-Century Romanticism — 19

2 Atemporality in Narrative and Music — 34

Part II. Structural and Rhetorical Strategies in Music with and without Text

3 Music with Text: Two Slow Movements by Brahms — 51

4 Music without Text: Forms of Atemporality — 82

Part III. Brahms's Piano Sonatas

5 Treatment of the Medial Caesura — 125

6 Treatment of the S-Space — 132

7 Treatment of the Development and Recapitulation — 155

8 Treatment of the Slow Introduction and Coda — 168

Conclusion — 177

Selected Bibliography — 179
Index — 199

Acknowledgments

I THANK THE UNIVERSITY of Houston for a Faculty Development Leave in fall 2012, during which I wrote most of the initial draft of the manuscript.

The Moores School of Music and then director David Ashley White consistently provided generous support for travel to professional conferences, domestically and internationally, during my many years on the Moores School's music theory faculty.

Many individuals have contributed to this project in meaningful ways; any omissions here are unintentional, and any shortcomings that remain in the final product are entirely my own. Robert Hatten read and commented extensively and incisively on all aspects of the manuscript. Michael Klein offered invaluable suggestions for focusing my arguments and refining my interpretations. James Hepokoski read portions of the manuscript and generously lent his time critiquing the work via e-mail, telephone, and during a short residency at the University of Houston in spring 2013. And the staff at Indiana University Press was exceptionally professional and a pleasure to work with in every way.

Finally, I extend my deepest gratitude to my wife, Corey Tu. It is hard to overstate the extent to which her brilliant performances of and insights into the music of the Romantic period have informed my own thinking about this repertoire.

SONATA FRAGMENTS

Introduction: Romantic Musical Discourse, or, a Rhetoric of Romantic Music

There is a moment in the transition of the first movement of Chopin's Piano Sonata in B minor, op. 58 that raises difficult questions. As shown in example 0.1, the movement opens with what seems to be a structurally unproblematic, if weighty, eight-bar primary theme (P) that ends by tonicizing its own dominant (F♯ minor) in m. 8. The transition (TR) then begins immediately (m. 9), opening with a restatement of the P idea on the subdominant E minor and continuing in a normative fashion. The rhetoric suggests tonal and motivic dissolution—as would be expected in a sonata transition—before we eventually reach a dominant pedal in the bass in m. 14. The pedal is on an F♯ dominant of the original B minor, which appears to signal that this transition is of the nonmodulating variety—one that never leaves the tonic key. None of this is necessarily unusual.

The first sign that this transition may not continue in the most normative fashion—the first sign of trouble, perhaps—appears in m. 17, when the F♯ pedal seems to be abandoned in favor of a rather surprising half-step move downward in the bass, to F, a pitch staged as the dominant of B♭ major. This emergent B♭ major veers immediately, in the very next bar, toward its own relative minor, ultimately aiming at a dominant-seventh chord in that key (g:V7) at the end of m. 18 and, one would assume, a G-minor local tonic triad on the downbeat of m. 19. Thus, obviously, mm. 17–18 introduce a chromatic tonal shift into the TR. But even this move is not necessarily unusual, and there may well be no reason at all for surprise: perhaps this is a sonata transition that appears to be openly rethinking or reconsidering its original (nonmodulating?) tonal course; or, more broadly, perhaps this TR is exceptionally developmental and chromatic—not surprising, after all, in a piece that employs a typically mid-nineteenth-century chromatic harmonic language.

Whatever one chooses to make of the events in mm. 17–18, the movement's rhetoric becomes even more strained and the questions more numerous at the downbeat of m. 19. Here, the dominant seventh from m. 18 b. 4, instead of resolving as expected onto a G-minor triad, crashes onto a jarring, *sforzando*, fully diminished-seventh chord of the E-G-B♭-C♯ variety, which in turn gives way to material that initially seems rhythmically fragmentary and then, shortly afterward, appears to become tonally disoriented. Measures 20–21 point toward but never successfully stabilize E♭ (is this a "tonic" that was foreshadowed by the earlier

Example 0.1. Chopin, Piano Sonata in B minor, op. 58, i, mm. 1–45.

Example 0.1. (*Continued*)

"dominant," B♭, major? And is this E♭ major or minor?); mm. 23–27 point toward a D minor that is equally ambiguous with regard to its large-scale function (should we regard the earlier E♭ as a Neapolitan? And should we regard this D minor as parallel to D major, itself the relative of the movement's home key?); and m. 28 implies a dominant of G minor (is this a return to the tonal implications of mm. 17–18?) that resolves deceptively, in m. 29, onto an E♭-major triad (is this, finally, a realization of the E♭ implications from a few measures back?).

At this point, thankfully, the transition (surely we must still be in the sonata's transition?) becomes somewhat more coherent and easier to explain: m. 33 arrives on a dominant pedal in D major (the original nonmodulating transition has become a modulating one), which in turn leads unproblematically to a half cadence in m. 39 (the exposition's medial caesura [MC]) and, finally, in m. 41, to a typically Chopinian secondary theme (S)—a lyrical nocturne in D major.

Exactly what do we make of these events, structurally and expressively? What do we make of the diminished-seventh chord in m. 19 and the music that follows? Is this all part of an exceedingly developmental transition that we should accept as representative, within the expanded tonal-formal language of the mid-nineteenth century? Is it possible that we have no "transition" at all in this piece, and that instead we have a lengthy, exceptionally developmental P-theme that modulates and cadences (in m. 39 or m. 41), and that as a whole obviates the need for a Classical sonata transition—all in the name of achieving "unity" and "organic" growth typical of nineteenth-century musical style and aesthetics? Or is it possible that all these events together manifest Chopin's struggles with how to build a coherent, large-scale form such as a sonata, and that they confirm the long-standing critical notion that he may have been better served by working in the smaller genres—character pieces and other kinds of salon music—in which he had found so much success?

* * *

A similar problem, articulated a bit differently in the surface musical details, emerges in the first movement of Brahms's Piano Sonata in F♯ minor, op. 2. This movement opens as shown in example 0.2, with another relatively unproblematic, eight-bar P-theme—a typically Brahmsian theme, in that it appears to spin out of itself continuously rather than fit comfortably within a Classically conceived notion of period or sentence rhetoric. P yields at m. 9 to the TR, which opens (as in Chopin's op. 58) by restating the initiatory motive from P, on the tonic F♯ minor. The module then veers almost immediately toward the relative major, A major, with predominant harmony (A:IV) in mm. 11–12 leading normatively to a dominant in m. 13. Measure 13 falls, via a descending arpeggiation through the dominant-seventh chord, toward what one surely must assume is an impending III:HC MC, probably at m. 14 b. 1. But, in a most surprising move, m. 14 appears to reconsider, moving away from the b. 1 dominant via parallel, descending stepwise motion—essentially backing up, it seems, to the subdominant (A:IV, middle of m. 14) before settling on an equivocal C♯-major triad at the downbeat of m. 15. Should we regard the m. 15 downbeat as a half cadence, and an MC, in the original tonic, F♯ minor? Should we regard the transition as having reconsidered its tonal direction, as did Chopin's? Is this even the end of the transition at all?

None of these questions are answered by what happens next, at m. 16. Here, the sonata descends into music that appears to be completely separated from what precedes it, in multiple parameters—among them register, texture, and dynamic level. What are we to make of the large-scale structural function of this music? The half cadence in m. 15 might have suggested that we should expect S at this moment, but are we really expected to accept m. 16 as an S-theme? This music refuses to leave the tonic (mm. 16–19 compose out tonic-dominant motion in F♯ minor); it refuses to relinquish the P idea, which creeps back in, mysteriously and in A major (!), at m. 23; and its rhetoric, far from engaging with what we might normally expect of a Romantic, Brahmsian, lyrical S, instead suggests equivocation and indecision. Surely, there can be no question that S itself arrives later, at m. 40 and in the minor dominant (C♯ minor), following what appears to be a half cadence in C♯ minor at m. 38.

Example 0.2. Brahms, Piano Sonata in F♯ minor, op. 2, mm. 1–46.

Example 0.2. (*Continued*)

Should we understand the transition as having continued beyond m. 15 all the way to m. 38, which we should regard as the exposition's real MC? Should we understand this as an exposition in which an apparent MC fails to give way to a normative S—certainly not unusual, even in the Classical style? Should we then understand this movement as an example of the young Brahms engaging with sonata procedures that are essentially borrowed from Haydn, Mozart, and Beethoven? Or should we (again, as in the Chopin example) understand the situation as evidence of a more Romantic Brahms seeking a larger sense of organicism and unity within the sonata structure?

* * *

Finally, the first movement of Schumann's Piano Sonata in F♯ minor, op. 11 raises similar issues. Here, a typical Schumannian sonata exposition, given in example 0.3, comprises cyclic repetitions of a theme that is itself built on internal cyclic repetitions of its own (smaller subrotations within larger rotational cycles, as it were). In this case, Schumann formats the P-theme as a sentence, with an eight-bar presentation (mm. 55–62) that moves sequentially, up a step from F♯ to G♯, or from tonic up to supertonic in F♯ minor; a twelve-bar continuation follows (mm. 63–74) and ends on the dominant in F♯ minor. A varied repetition of this entire structure ensues in mm. 75–94. TR then opens in m. 95, with yet another statement of the P-idea, still in the tonic, F♯ minor; this initiates what should be understood (retrospectively, perhaps) as a dissolving TR-type similar to those heard in the Chopin op. 58 and the Brahms op. 2. This one begins to dissolve beginning around m. 99,

Example 0.3. Schumann, Piano Sonata in F♯ minor, op. 11, mm. 53–175.

Example 0.3. (*Continued*)

Example 0.3. (*Continued*)

10 | Sonata Fragments

Example 0.3. (*Continued*)

where the dynamic shifts to a sudden and unexpected *piano* and the G♯-minor portion of the original sentential presentation expands into an eight-bar sentence of its own, with a four-bar presentation (mm. 99–102) and a symmetrical, four-bar continuation (mm. 103–106). The latter sentence proves rather puzzling: it ends with a quizzical fermata in m. 106, on a B-major triad (dominant of E?), as if openly wondering what just happened and where all these events might be leading. Is this a medial caesura? Should we expect S to follow? And should we expect S in the key of VII, E major?

As at m. 19 in Chopin's op. 58 and m. 16 in Brahms op. 2, what follows comes as a complete surprise and effectively signifies a break from whatever sonata rhetoric might have been operative up until this moment. In startling fashion, Schumann transforms the dominant of E major from m. 106 into an E♭-minor triad in $^6_4$ position in m. 107, accepts this E♭ minor as the new tonic, and proceeds into a twice-repeated eight-bar sentence (mm. 107–14 and 115–22) sounded entirely over a dominant pedal in the new key. The next sixteen bars are literally shouted, *passionato*, at a *fortissimo* dynamic. What are we supposed to make of these events? Are we supposed to accept the shift from m. 106 to 107 as a typical, unsurprising, nineteenth-century chromatic common-tone shift in which the B-major triad of m. 106 becomes an enharmonic ♭VI in E♭ minor? Or is this an equally unsurprising (again, within the nineteenth-century chromatic language) Riemannian *Leittonwechsel* operation that maintains two common tones against a half-step shift downward in the bass? Should we assume m. 107 is an S-theme, one in a highly unusual and distantly related E♭ minor (or D♯ minor?) and one that never stabilizes a root-position tonic and never secures a cadence? Should we assume such procedures reveal a Schumann-the-tonal-progressive straining the boundaries of Classical sonata practice and prefiguring the avant-garde of Liszt and others? Even if so—even if we accept these events as such—what should we then make of what happens at m. 123, which appears to backtrack to a sequential idea last heard in mm. 95–98? This initiates another transition? Or resumes the previous transition? This material modulates, by m. 135, to the key of the relative major, and from there, it drives with characteristic aggression toward what appears to be an MC (a second MC?) in mm. 144–45. Another theme promptly ensues at m. 146, this time a much more typically Romantic, lyrical S-theme in A major that eventually secures a perfect authentic cadence, at m. 168.

Are we supposed to accept these events as typical, in the context of the sonata procedures of Schubert and, later, Brahms himself? Is this perhaps a "three-key exposition" with a "double second group," one that situates Schumann squarely within normative nineteenth-century sonata practice? (Can we even identify what normative nineteenth-century sonata practice looks like?) Or do all these events again reveal—as with Chopin, perhaps—the insurmountable difficulties a large-scale sonata might have posed for a composer who many regard as more comfortable in the smaller genres (character pieces, songs, and the like) characteristic of the period?

* * *

Finding answers to such questions requires situating them within the broader aesthetic and narrative traditions informed by early-nineteenth-century Romantic ideology. This book sets out to do just that, first by considering, in part I, aspects of Romantic aesthetics—especially the aesthetic of the Romantic fragment—and their implications for understanding structure and expression in music of the period; then, in part II, by examining the specific technical procedures—formal ruptures, digressions, and other rhetorical-narrative devices—through which Romantic composers realized fragment aesthetics in musical terms; and then, in part III, by applying the methodological approach thus developed in an interpretation of portions of the three piano sonatas by Brahms from 1853–54, opp. 1, 2, and 5.

The book is narrowly focused, both musically and theoretically. Musically, I have chosen to limit the repertoire under consideration to the piano sonatas of Chopin, Schumann, and Brahms. This serves at least two practical purposes. First, these three composers provide points of departure through which I can develop an interpretive methodology. These are composers of standard, nineteenth-century Romantic repertoire who are often viewed in terms of their formal or tonal-harmonic "progressivism" rather than (especially when it comes to their sonata output) as figures who were at once in dialogue with Classical conventions and, at the same time, representative of the contemporary, Romantic-aesthetic environment in which they were working—the environment of Friedrich Schlegel and others on the literary avant-garde. The approach could then be developed and extended: with appropriate modifications, it might be productively employed to explain aspects of the music of Mendelssohn (both Felix and Fanny), Liszt, Tchaikovsky, or, even later, Mahler, Bruckner, Strauss, Rachmaninoff, and others. Second, the piano sonata itself is one of the early-nineteenth-century genres most obviously indebted to the Classical tradition—unlike, say, the nineteenth-century character piece, which is often considered one of the most characteristic genres of the post-Beethoven era but which was also largely a new genre at that time, rather than one that directly extended Classical practice. As such, the piano sonata provides one of the most readily accessible ways of investigating what became of the eighteenth-century Enlightenment aesthetics that we find manifested in the sonata form itself—by common consent the representative musical form of the Classical age—when subjected to the aesthetic forces of nineteenth-century Romanticism.

Theoretically, the book (especially part III) is grounded in the *Sonata Theory* of James Hepokoski and Warren Darcy.[1] Sonata Theory provides a tool with which—or a lens through which—to examine structural and expressive procedures in nineteenth-century sonatas and their relationship to the procedures found in Classical sonatas. This is a subject Hepokoski and Darcy have already begun to explore, both in their 2006 book and in other related publications before and since.[2] I seek neither to adopt Sonata Theory wholesale, without modifications, nor to rewrite the theory entirely or even in part; rather, I aim to offer a limited, circumscribed expansion of the methodology so as to accommodate within it what I hear as some of the most characteristic, yet most idiosyncratic and anti-Classical, features of the sonata in the Romantic era. My expansions of the theory are related mainly to a particular view of how the Romantic sonata fractures and fragments the largely cohesive, linearly directed temporality that we can understand as a hallmark of the Classical sonata form; these expansions lead, for example, to interpretations of Romantic sonatas as temporally multidimensional works—analogous to novels or films—in which some of the music in any given sonata movement lies "inside," but other music lies "outside," what Sonata Theory would define as the sonata-space proper.

My methodology also seeks an interdisciplinary angle in which I look beyond current approaches in music theory. In this spirit, aspects of my theoretical apparatus as well as my approach to musical interpretation more broadly are grounded in the disciplines known as structural narratology and rhetorical narrative theory. According to Gérard Genette, the term *narratology* originates with Tzvetan Todorov in 1969, and it refers specifically to the study of how a narrative is constructed— how a narrative may be assembled, as it were, from various formal-structural pieces.[3] Such concerns grow out of a distinction, long recognized in narrative theory, between the *content* of the story (the *what*: the chain of events in the narrative plus its "existents"—characters or settings, for example) and the *mechanics of storytelling* (the *how*: "the means by which the content is communicated," or "the mechanism by which the story world is rendered").[4] This distinction has been rendered in various ways: the Russian formalists characterized it as the difference between *fabula* and *sjuzhet*; the French tradition distinguishes between *histoire* and *discours*; and in English, the difference is usually rendered in terms of (following from the French) *story* versus *discourse*.[5]

Rhetorical narrative theory grows out of the Chicago School of literary criticism. Most writers trace its origins specifically to Wayne C. Booth and his 1961 book, *The Rhetoric of Fiction*.[6] For Booth, *rhetoric* refers specifically to how authors use language to guide or control readers, or lead a reader through a narrative and to a fuller understanding thereof—where here *narrative* is understood as an intentional act in which "somebody tells someone else on some occasion and for some purpose(s) that something happened."[7] Thus, the concern in rhetorical narrative theory is for the specific techniques, strategies, and procedures with which authors create "a successful ordering of [their] reader's view of a fictional world."[8] What devices must one recognize in an author's language in order to be able to successfully interpret that author's narrative, its content, its contexts and purposes, and its meanings? Rhetoric in Booth's sense, moreover, has two facets: the first is narrower and concerns the rhetoric *in* narrative—the specific technical, syntactic, or linguistic devices an author uses to communicate, which we sometimes think of as the "rhetorical conventions" in a language; the second is broader, and concerns narrative *as* rhetoric—the narrative as a "total act of communication," or the whole art of storytelling as rhetorical.[9] Both are important for my approach.

In the broadest sense, then, my approach aims to examine what might be thought of as a narratology for Romantic music—that is, the mechanics of musical storytelling within a specific slice of the common-practice repertoire, with particular attention to what those mechanics tell us about the specific expressive features of this music that make it *Romantic*. Exactly how do Romantic musical narratives go about organizing and telling their tales? In this regard, I am not so much concerned in this book with whether music *is* or *is not* a narrative form.[10] I address this issue in more depth in chapter 2, but in general, I rely on the assumption that, at the very least, certain musical forms constitute *narrative forms*, in the specific technical sense of that term: they are organized so as to tell tales, or so as to imitate the telling of tales, in the sense that they *emplot* a series of events in time such that those events acquire meaningful relationships among one another (where I think of *emplotment* in terms of what Peter Brooks describes as "a structuring operation peculiar to those messages that are developed through temporal succession, the instrumental logic of a specific mode of human understanding").[11] I am more concerned with how the musical narrative is organized, in a structural and a temporal sense. To address this issue, I have borrowed specifically from the methodology developed by Gérard Genette in his 1972 *Discours du récit*—or *Narrative Discourse,* in the 1980 English translation—in particular his account of the central role that temporality plays in narrative structure. Following Genette, in my view Romantic musical narratives comprise multiple levels or streams, where some of these streams are *temporal* (in the sense that their primary function is to articulate the tale being told) but others of them are *atemporal* (in the sense that they convey content interjected from outside the story proper—often authorial commentary or reflection, for example). One might thus wish to think of the present book as if it were titled, if not "Narrative Discourse," then "Romantic Musical Discourse," concerned as it is with the discourse of the narratives found in Romantic music. Such a title would be far too broad and ambitious to accurately describe the project I offer here, but it does point toward a general sense of the fundamental concerns underlying my approach.

At the same time, I am just as concerned with the content of the musical narrative, especially, again, as a window onto exactly what features of this music make it *Romantic*. Exactly what tales might Romantic musical narratives be telling? In this regard, I am interested in the specific rhetorical means through which the music communicates its content—the technical strategies, devices, procedures, or conventions that we can recognize in Romantic music in order to successfully interpret its stories and the ways in which these stories are conveyed in the musical rhetoric. Thus, perhaps the book could even be titled, instead of Booth's "The Rhetoric of Fiction," "A Rhetoric of Romantic Music" (or maybe "A Rhetoric of Romantic Musical Narrative"), although again such a formulation would certainly be much too ambitious. But in suggesting it, I do intend to make two rhetorical moves of my own: first, in replacing Booth's "Fiction" with "Romantic Music," I mean to make explicit my premise that we can think of the most representative examples of Romantic music not only as *narrative* per se but also first and foremost as *narrative fiction* (in that they tell a fictional story, rather than recount specific historical or biographical events—although certainly in some instances, these two functions may bleed into one another);[12] and second, in replacing Booth's definite article "The" with an indefinite "A" ("A Rhetoric" instead of "The Rhetoric"), I mean to acknowledge those who have criticized Booth for implying that his way is the only way (much like some of Allen Forte's critics took him to task for implying that his was the one and only—"The"—structure of atonal music)[13] and to suggest that my interpretive approach may well be only one of a number of productive ways of reading (hearing) what I regard as some of the most structurally and expressively complex music in the Western tonal tradition. I regard my approach as open to expansions and modifications, just as I also think it will dovetail neatly with other existing approaches in music analysis and interpretation—including, but going beyond, Sonata Theory. I have sought not to replace any of the currently available methodologies but rather to build upon them, in the spirit of explicating structure, rhetoric, narrative, and, ultimately, expressive meaning in Romantic music.

Notes

1. Hepokoski and Darcy, *Elements of Sonata Theory*.
2. For example, Darcy, "Bruckner's Sonata Deformations"; Hepokoski, "Monumentality and Formal Processes."
3. See Genette, *Narrative Discourse Revisited*, 7.
4. Chatman, *Story and Discourse*, 19 ("the means by which"); Chatman, *Coming to Terms*, 142 ("the mechanism by which").
5. For a helpful summary and discussion of the issues, see McQuillan, "Aporias of Writing."
6. Booth, *The Rhetoric of Fiction*.
7. Phelan, *Experiencing Fiction*, 3.
8. Booth, *The Rhetoric of Fiction*, 388.
9. Ibid., 415–16.
10. The body of literature on this question is large. See especially Newcomb, "Schumann and Late Eighteenth-Century Narrative Strategies"; Newcomb, "The Polonaise-Fantasy and Issues of Musical Narrative"; and Klein, "Chopin's Fourth Ballade as Musical Narrative."
11. Brooks, *Reading for the Plot*, 10. My assumptions regarding music as narrative are similar to those of other recent authors, including Monelle, *Linguistics and Semiotics in Music*; Monelle, *The Sense of Music*; McDonald, "Silent Narration? Elements of Narrative in Ives's *The Unanswered Question*"; and Monahan, "'Inescapable' Coherence and the Failure of the Novel-Symphony in the Finale of Mahler's Sixth." See also Monahan, "Mahler's Sonata Narratives," esp. 14–16; and Monahan, "Action and Agency Revisited."
12. Rhetorical narrative theory is not concerned with only narrative fiction. Booth in particular makes the point that his approach to rhetoric applies to any kind of narrative, including "histories, myths, journalism, reports of dreams, gossip, lies, hoaxes," or perhaps many others. In fact, Booth at one point even considered titling his book *The Rhetoric of Narration*; see Booth, *The Rhetoric of Fiction*, 407–8.
13. Booth responded to such criticism as only Booth could: "I would now call the book 'A Rhetoric of Fiction,' or perhaps something like '*Some* Notes toward an *Introduction* to a *Possible* Way of Viewing *One* Aspect of the *Many* Rhetorical Dimensions of Narrative, with Special Emphasis on *Some* Limited Kinds of Fiction" (*The Rhetoric of Fiction*, 402). For the criticism of Forte, see Browne, "Review of *The Structure of Atonal Music*."

PART I

FRAGMENTATION AND ATEMPORALITY

1 Fragmentation: Aesthetics of Nineteenth-Century Romanticism

ADDRESSING QUESTIONS SUCH as those posed in the introduction requires considering the constellation of Romantic aesthetics and ideologies pervasive among European artists in the first half of the nineteenth century. These are normally understood as being marked by a skepticism toward older, Classical forms and procedures, the employment of which in music, literature, or other of the arts would have been viewed by the Romantics as something of an exercise in form—as the replication of older procedures for the sake of conformist repetition, as an endorsement of Enlightenment ideals that had long since become outdated. One of the clearest articulations of such a view appears in the literary and cultural criticism of one of the chief spokespersons for German Romanticism, Friedrich Schlegel, who remarked that "The customary divisions [that is, genres] of poetry are only a dead framework for a limited horizon";[1] another appears in writings of one of the movement's principal musical emissaries, Robert Schumann, for example in his oft-cited observation that, since the founding of his *Neue Zeitschrift für Musik* in 1834, "Isolated beautiful examples of this genre [that is, the sonata—although we are invited to think that any of what Schumann saw as the traditional Classical forms, including the symphony and the concerto, might have served the point just as well] might certainly appear here and there, but on the whole it seems as though the form has run its life course, and this is to be sure in the order of things, for we should not repeat the same things for another century but rather be mindful of seeking out the New."[2] Both views jibe nicely with the understanding of European Romanticism that has taken shape over about the last century of literary criticism, in which the movement has been described as unified by its favoring the new over the old, and innovation over tradition, in all aspects—materials, forms, styles—of the arts.[3] In literature, furthermore, in explaining Romanticism critics have normally given special emphasis to the centrality in the movement of the individual, of personal experience and expression, and of the deepest reaches of the visionary artist's own imagination in the creation of an artwork—the act of which, Wordsworth wrote in 1800, was to be the result of a "spontaneous overflow of powerful feelings."[4] More specifically, many have pointed to the importance of nature as an artistic topic: in Romantic literature, nature becomes both thematized within the work as well as the deeper stimulus, the source of inspiration, for the bold, new ideas of the artists themselves; such thinking is an important part of what some view as a certain kind of collapse (or a "mystical union") of subject and object characteristic of Romantic art.[5]

Many such features of the Romantic movement—indeed, the very movement itself—are products of a larger trend in nineteenth-century thought, one that has been explicated by Michel Foucault as an epistemic shift that occurred approximately in the years 1775–1825.[6] The shift was one in which knowledge and worldviews ceased to be organized within their eighteenth-century, taxonomic forms (Foucault: "the great circular forms in which similitude was enclosed")[7] concerned with enumeration and identification of individual, observable elements in a system, but rather came to be governed by a way of thinking concerned with the complex, hierarchical, often invisible relationships between, and functions of, the organic components of such systems. Such thinking has numerous ramifications for the organization of knowledge in a wide range of disciplines, including the arts; it gives rise to, among other consequences, a situation in which the interior, unobservable facets ("the dark, concave, inner side")[8] of a being or a system—those facets that lie beyond pure empirical observation and representation—rise to the level of a central interest for inquiry; individual components (organs in an animal, words in a language) become pieces or fragments of a larger, organic whole, subject to the complexities of their own relationships and to their own interior temporal associations rather than independent, autonomous features subject to description and definition purely on their own terms. A taxonomic organization of knowledge concerned with description, observation, and representation thus gives way to a narrativized form concerned with identity, subjectivity, and being.

All such features of Romanticism and nineteenth-century thought, moreover, account well for certain prominent stylistic features of the movement as manifested in literature and music—especially those having to do with an enhanced sense of subjectivity and self characteristic of Romantic artworks. First, Romanticism tends to involve narratives focusing on the "common man" and "common life," rather than the aristocratic upper classes. Again Wordsworth: "The principal object then which I proposed to myself in these poems [*Lyrical Ballads*] was to chuse incidents and situations from common life, and to relate or describe them . . . in a selection of language really used by men"; and it is, furthermore, in "low and rustic life" that "the essential passions of the heart find a better soil in which they can attain their maturity."[9] These concerns stem directly from the movement's rejection of Classical or Enlightenment values and attitudes. Second, the movement is marked by an attraction to the supernatural, nonrational, marvelous, or fantastical; such emphases grow out of its concern for the inner reaches of the artist's soul or consciousness, which the Romantics would have regarded as beyond the reach of—that is, unexplainable within—traditional eighteenth-century Enlightenment, taxonomic forms of logic. And third, the movement is often characterized by a preference for heroic, revolutionary, salvational, questing, or (especially in music) pastoral narratives. All such generic preferences follow from what the early nineteenth century would have viewed as the promise of the French Revolution and the crisis of confidence that resulted from the abdication of that promise. All such narrative types, furthermore, tend to invite readers to identify the protagonists in a narrative either with themselves or with what the Chicago School of literary criticism would call the narrative's *implied author*: the author whose skills, values, preferences, ideologies, and aesthetics are revealed to readers through the rhetorical choices that readers observe the implied author making as they read a given text.[10]

The last of these five narrative types—the pastoral narrative—is especially important in Romantic music. (Note that my concern here is with the pastoral as a specific narrative paradigm or plot framework and not necessarily as a *topic* governing stylistic and expressive gestures in the music, although certainly the two issues overlap to some extent.[11]) Recent literary criticism has suggested that pastoral narratives can be either narrowly or broadly defined.[12] The narrower definitions refer to a literary form that derives from Greek and Roman poems about the beauty of life in the country; until the early seventeenth century, moreover, the pastoral was defined as an idyll concerned mainly with shepherds living in a primeval natural environment. In the seventeenth century and after, the form begins to appear in dramas and, later, in novels; the shepherds often disappeared, while the landscapes and natural environments in which they had existed remained a central focus. Such narrower definitions are essentially those invoked in specific musical instances of the pastoral such as Monteverdi's *Orfeo,* Haydn's *Creation,* or Beethoven's Symphony no. 6 in F major, op. 68 ("Pastoral"). Wider definitions of the form refer to mythical narratives of wish fulfillment, in which the central concerns are broadly drawn oppositions between, for example, humans versus nature, urban versus rural, or generally anything conceived as idealized (and unattainable) versus something else understood as less than perfect (human frailties, urban environments, or a present-day, complex world fraught with distress and anxiety). Themes of retreat and return are characteristic and, indeed, critical in pastoral plots: retreat and return in this context are normally metaphorical, but generally speaking, they take the form of a retreat from some sort of flawed, present-tense site or state of being into a simpler, more innocent, venerated, and always intentionally fictitious time or place that came to be known by the generic name *Arcadia*—perhaps an escape from the city to the country, from the real to the unreal, or from the conscious to the unconscious mind. There follows an eventual return to the original point of departure, lessons having been learned.[13]

As these examples suggest, Arcadia itself comes in various shapes and sizes in pastoral narratives; in fact, it is best understood as a generalized abstraction rather than specifically as some kind of pristine natural environment or scene—even though the latter may describe well the form in which it often appears in pastoral artworks (including, for example, in Romantic landscape paintings or in musical examples such as the Pastoral Symphony).[14] Pastoral narratives, furthermore, normally adopt a celebratory attitude toward their constructions of the Arcadia image: the retreat to the imagined paradise is actively yearned for and desired, even while it remains fictitious, distanced and unreal, and ultimately lost and unrealizable. And most literary constructions of Arcadia invoke a shift in tense, where the escape is from a problematic present into a more perfect past; that is, the fictional paradise, in whatever form it may take, is typically framed in the narrative as the product of a wishful, hopeful, reminiscent look backward—one tinged with lament, loss, and regret—into a lost golden age unspoiled by the inadequacies of modern life. At the same time, such narratives also imply, paradoxically perhaps, a concern for the future: the nostalgia for a lost past simultaneously suggests the presence of a vision for a better, freer, more blissful life yet to come, and thus it is possible to think of pastoral narratives as concerned with such oxymoronic constructions as "Utopian Arcadias" or "Arcadian Utopias." The multiply directed historical temporalities implied in such formulations can be understood as the product of larger a cultural trend, one in which the clear teleology inherent in Enlightenment thinking (all events "progress" toward a better future) breaks down in favor of a greater awareness of a subject's moment in historical time as well as that subject's relationship with both the future and the past.[15] Such trends are consistent with the epistemic shift discussed in Foucault, from which, as mentioned, there emerges in the nineteenth century a greater awareness of historical and cultural subjectivity.

Pastoral narratives broadly construed comprise a central focus—one of *the* central concerns—of the art, literature, and music of eighteenth- and nineteenth-century European Romanticism, especially in England and Germany. That this is true follows from the concern in the Romantic movement with subjectivity and with themes of limitless imagination and emotion, dissatisfaction and restlessness, and infinite longing or yearning for a better past or a better future in which the imperfections of modern life will be cast off and left behind. For the Romantic, art was responsible in part for creating modern civilization, but it was also responsible for cutting off humankind from its original, unspoiled, simplistic state; the re-creation of the pastoral paradise was thus one of the most pure of all artistic endeavors. A number of critics of Romantic literature have emphasized this aspect of the movement: one of the best examples is Northrop Frye, who defines Romantic narratives as those that are marked by a concern for the "world of original human nature, now a lost paradise or golden age," which, in the Romantic imagination, became "a better and more appropriate home for man than his present environment, whether man can regain it or not."[16] Interpreting such narratives involves attending to the various ways in which they construct their fundamental opposition between perfect and imperfect; as Terry Gifford writes, interpretations of the pastoral need to stem from "alert readings that are capable of making critical judgments about their inner tensions, their contextual functions, their multiple levels of contradiction."[17]

Such views of Romanticism, while certainly capturing some of the most important, prevailing artistic tendencies of the period, also have the effect of suppressing some of the movement's other important stylistic features—especially those backward-looking features that connect Romantic art more directly to its Classical antecedents. To simply map the movement onto a neat, coherent, linear narrative in which the past is rejected in favor of inexorable progress toward the future is a reductive oversimplification of reality—as are most such attempts at a teleological telling of history, whether in the arts or elsewhere. Notwithstanding René Wellek's description of a unified Romanticism (in which he found an underlying coherence, writing that an examination of Romantic literature "all over the continent" reveals "throughout Europe the same conceptions of poetry and of the workings and nature of poetic imagination, the same conception of nature and its relation to man, and basically the same poetic style, with a use of imagery, symbolism, and myth which is clearly distinct from that of eighteenth-century neoclassicism"),[18] the movement may also be understood in terms that foreground its competing strands of ideologies, its internal contradictions, and, indeed, its links to older, Enlightenment ideals (something like what Arthur Lovejoy may have had in mind when he described "a *prima facie* plurality of Romanticisms, of possibly quite distinct thought-complexes," rather than Romanticism as "the heaven-appointed designation of some single real entity, or type of entities, to be found in nature").[19] These kinds of conceptions of the movement have the effect of foregrounding its links to the past: that is, Romantic artists, rather than—as many of the artists themselves would have us believe[20]—absolutely abandoning their past in favor of revolutionary new modes of expression (abandoning, as Friedrich Schlegel's brother August Wilhelm put it, the Classical "poetry of perfection" in favor of the Romantic "poetry of infinite desire"),[21] instead engaged in a provocative, reflexive, intertextual, and self-critical dialogue with the artworks of the past.

These are important features of Romanticism that manifest specifically in the dialogue in Romantic art with the wide, complex system of stylistic and generic norms that dates from the eighteenth century and before and within the direct or indirect commentary, often found in Romantic artworks, on their Classical forebears. They suggest a view of Romanticism not as a movement that rejected Classicism outright but rather joined a Classicism-in-progress—where the Romantic movement explored and fully realized the implications of (even while it also questioned) Classical and Enlightenment values. And such views are not inconsistent with contemporary aesthetic positions: for example, even in many expressions of the Enlightenment worldview—in, for example, "the vitalism of Diderot, the passion of Rousseau, and the skepticism of Hume"[22]—one can see a critical attitude toward the indiscriminate application of cognitive reason above shared human feelings, a concern for the role of individual emotion and imagination, and a preoccupation with natural purity and simplicity, along with an effort to reject the complexities of a rapidly advancing society. All are often understood as fundamentally Romantic concerns, or at least, within Enlightenment thinking, as harbingers of Romanticism. Likewise, on the other side of the coin, artists who identified with the Romantic movement were also much slower to reject Enlightenment rationality than is often thought: literary criticism has recognized for some time now that the "spontaneity" to which Wordsworth referred in his description of Romantic poetry is probably best understood not in the sense of "irrational" or "unpremeditated" but more in the sense of "free"—in the sense, that is, of a "voluntary" expression of the artistic and intellectual predilections of the inner self, where that expression is fully developed in dialogue with past precedents rather than one that stems simply from indiscriminate adherence to some externally imposed, contemporary ideals. This is one reading, perhaps, of Wordsworth's notoriously enigmatic statement that "Poems to which any value can be attached, were never produced on any variety of subjects but by a man, who being possessed of more than usual organic sensibility, had also thought long and deeply. For our continued influxes of feeling are modified and directed by our thoughts, which are indeed the representatives of all our past feelings."[23]

I find that this view of Romanticism as fundamentally engaged in a dialogue with Classical precedents is critical for a full understanding of the expressive potential of Romantic music. This position is one of the primary motivating factors in my choice of the sonata—as mentioned, the representative genre in the Classical era—as the genre through which to examine Romantic structure and expression and its relationships to musical Classicism. That is, the Romantic sonata follows directly from, but also transforms, the Classical sonata, and a good deal of its expressive potential is rooted in a listener's understanding of its dialogue with an array of Classical sonata-rhetorical procedures. To not account for such a dialogue in the Romantic sonata is to render unavailable a good deal of the genre's musical meaning. The analyses and interpretations that follow all build upon these basic premises.

* * *

Just as important for an understanding of musical Romanticism is an understanding of the central importance in Romantic art of the treatment of space, time, and temporal relationships—where these strategies stem directly from the shift in episteme at the turn of the nineteenth-century toward one that emphasizes interior, internal relationships among parts of a whole and thus allows for the expression of new forms of subjectivity and consciousness. Northrop Frye's account of the revolutionary use of spatial imagery in Romantic literature is directly relevant here: "What I see first of all in Romanticism is the effect of a profound change, not primarily in belief [that is, political, religious, social, artistic, or others], but in the spatial projection of reality."[24] For Frye the central feature of this change—a feature suggested both in Wordsworth's use (as mentioned) of "spontaneous" and in the emerging nineteenth-century epistemic concern for the role of individual consciousness—was a kind of turning inward toward the soul, an interiorization of Romantic metaphorical and allegorical structures in which those structures tended to "move inside and downward instead of outside and upward" not only for the inspiration and creative resources of the artist but also for the imagery in the artworks themselves.[25] Thus, in Romantic poetry "the creative world is deep within, and so is heaven or the place of the presence of God. . . . In the Romantic construct there is a centre where inward and outward manifestations of a common motion and spirit are unified, where the ego is identified as itself because it is also identified as something which is not itself."[26] Elsewhere he writes, similarly, that

The mechanical being characteristic of ordinary experience, it is found particularly in the world "outside"; the superior or organic world is consequently "inside," and although it is still called superior or higher, the natural metaphorical direction of the inside world is downward, into the profounder depths of consciousness.

If a Romantic poet, therefore, wishes to write of God, he has more difficulty in finding a place to put him than Dante or even Milton had, and on the whole he prefers to do without a place, or finds "within" metaphors more reassuring than "up there" metaphors.[27]

Recent critiques have noted, furthermore, that Frye's view of Romanticism resonates with Harold Bloom's. Bloom has proposed understanding the movement in terms of an "internalization" of one of the narrative types mentioned earlier: the "quest" narrative, which he characterizes as a subtype of the Romance genre—which itself dates from the Middle Ages and comprises plots involving knights, warriors, castles, and all the associated themes of chivalry and exaggerated, impossible passions.[28] According to Bloom, one of the most important contributions of early-nineteenth-century Romanticism was to take the norms and patterns of an existing genre and interiorize them—that is, personalize them, or transpose them from the exploits of fictional, idealized characters onto the personalities and lives of the artists themselves. Redemption, a characteristic feature of the quest-romance and often granted therein by some higher, supernatural, or spiritual power, thus derives, in the genre's interiorized form, not from outside the narrative subject but from within that subject's own consciousness—from the free-ranging imagination of a prophetic, heroic artist-creator.

These views of Frye and Bloom on the characteristic Romantic sense of interiority resonate in interesting ways with other important formulations of Romantic art. Among the English Romantics, for example, Wordsworth's poetry has been described as intimate, mysterious, and as emanating from the center of the poet's innermost soul.[29] Perhaps even more important in this regard is German Romanticism, in which similar themes emerge especially in the aesthetics of Friedrich and August Wilhelm Schlegel.[30] Friedrich Schlegel's Romanticism in particular is often understood today in the counterrevolutionary sense I described above, as he overtly rejected the rationalist aspects of the French Revolution—which he and his brother regarded as the central motivating event for most of the period's cultural history—and adopted a certain spiritual tilt, grounding much of his philosophy in a Christian-theological mysticism.[31] From these features of Schlegel's thought there coalesces an emphasis on a deep, isolated introversion and personalized interiority—an inward-looking, self-critical aesthetic ideology in which he seemed to require of Romantic artists (including himself) a historical consciousness that both acknowledged and *questioned* Classical precedents; a critical attitude toward themselves and the present state of their art; and an unflagging hope that even in the face of the deepest despair, the imperfections of the present hold within them the seeds of a more perfect future.

For Schlegel, these views were not (or should not be) hidden within the Romantic artwork; rather, he seems to have thought it was crucial that they be manifested outwardly and obviously. Thus his aesthetic position—key to my own interpretive approach—that what may be interpreted by some as disintegration and decay in Romantic art may also be the very raison d'être of the Romantic artwork itself. For, according to Schlegel, in such disorder and illogic—in the fracturing, illogical ordering, formal clefts, and other ruptures characteristic of Romantic art—lies the potential for the artist to express in the very form and structure of the work the self-reflection and interiority vital to the Romantic ordering of time, space, and image. Indeed, for Schlegel the best or most Romantic artworks are those that (perhaps paradoxically) find the most creative, vivid, and imaginative ways of composing out their own interiorized self-criticism through a distinctly anti-Classical formal fracturing and dissolution. Writing in 1795–96, Schlegel averred that "[The beautiful] is so little the guiding principle of modern poetry that many of the most excellent works of recent times are actually representations of the ugly, so that one is forced to admit, though reluctantly, that the representation of disorder in all its abundance and despair in all its strength, as opposed to the representation of abundance and strength in complete harmony with one another, demands creative energy and artistic prudence to an equal if not higher degree."[32]

Thus a central feature of Schlegel's criticism becomes a preoccupation with the ways in which such formal fracturing might be outwardly manifested in Romantic poetry.[33] Related is a concern for the ways in which such apparent formal disorder can be positively valued in critical approaches to Romantic art. Following John Daverio's illuminating study of German Romantic ideology and its relevance for understanding music of Schumann, Brahms, and others, I will focus here on two of Schlegel's critical concepts—only two within a larger system of critical categories he developed: the *arabesque* (Ger. *Arabeske*), and the *fragment*. Schlegel appropriated the arabesque from eighteenth-century art theory, in which it describes (in Greco-Roman or Renaissance painting, for example) an ornamental style wherein long, flowing, curving lines create a kind of grotesquerie, or a formal distortion, where in the most extreme cases the arabesques themselves threaten to obscure, or overwhelm, the main image.[34] Schlegel used the concept specifically as it implies a disruption in an orderly arrangement of events, using it as such to describe certain episodic structural features that he found especially characteristic of the modern novel, or the *Roman*: in this regard, he essentially equated the arabesque with the technique, definitive in Greek comedy, known as *parabasis* (Ger. *Parekbase*), a structural or rhetorical device in which the chorus effects a suspension of the narrative's orderly progress by interrupting the proceedings with commentary from outside the drama, often as if spoken from the poet himself. Schlegel found similar strategies—digressions and interruptions that suspend the narrative flow—in the novel or the *Roman,* especially in, for example, Cervantes's *Don Quixote*, itself episodically organized and a central influence on Schlegel's view of Romantic structural tendencies. For Schlegel, in fact, the very term *romantic* (Ger. *romantisch*) is a *generic* term meaning, literally, "in the manner of the *Roman*" or "in the manner of a novel"—which, practically speaking, translates to "characterized by parabasis or arabesques" (Schlegel: "The *Roman* tends toward parabasis," or, elsewhere, "In the fantastic novel, the elements of parabasis should be constant").[35] Daverio has observed that Schlegel's entire theory of Romanticism can thus be understood as a theory of the novel itself—where for Schlegel, the *novel* was a new genre comprising works (either poetry or prose) that were, as Daverio describes it, "fantastically formed and generically ambiguous"; and, more broadly, the novel was the prototypical literary form for the narrativized organization, expression, and exploration of knowledge in nineteenth-century epistemology. Such conceptions underlie Schlegel's view of the Romantic artistic enterprise at the broadest levels: he wrote in 1797 that "All works [that is, artworks] should be novels; all prose should be novelistic," and "All products of the imagination should novelize, should approximate the novel as closely as possible."[36]

It is important to note here that Schlegel's idea of the arabesque, as Daverio has discussed, actually goes somewhat further than simply a straightforward equation with "narrative digression" or "interruption." For Schlegel, it implies a certain *intentionality* on the part of the artist who employs it.[37] That is, an arabesque, in the best Romantic art, is deployed with the aim of making an aesthetic statement specifically from a stance that Schlegel characterized as imbued with *Romantic irony*: the arabesque deliberately fractures an otherwise coherent, "perfect" form and allows for an introduction into that form of a distanced, objectified, overtly self-critical attitude in which the author of the work, or even the work itself, questions the very possibility of the work's existence or the possibility of the work's own future.[38] In this sense, Schlegel's notion of the arabesque captures his broader conception of Romanticism itself (especially its interiorized self-reflectivity) but also goes further, linking aesthetically to the second of his critical categories: the fragment.

Like the arabesque, the fragment is not so much Schlegel's own concept (though as Daverio has pointed out, he liked to refer throughout his writings, oxymoronically, to his "system of fragments")[39] but rather a literary genre comprising works of poetry or prose published in partial rather than intact form—where the partial, incomplete work would be understood as representing either a larger work of which we have only a broken remnant, or a work begun but not yet completed, or perhaps even (if the work is presented as having a formal ending but no beginning) a work finished but not yet begun.[40] The form grows out of the Romantic aesthetic interest, mentioned earlier, in seeking freedom from the constraints of the older Classical genres. As such, in its earliest forms the fragment typically took the form of a portion, or a remnant, of one of the Classical genres; Goethe's tragedy *Faust*, first published as a fragment in 1790, is representative in this regard.[41] But the pervasive use of the form, especially among the British Romantics (Coleridge, Keats, Byron, and others) and the German Romantics of the Jena School (among others, Ludwig Tieck, Novalis [Georg Philipp Friedrich Freiherr von Hardenberg],

Wilhelm Heinrich Wackenroder, and the Schlegel brothers themselves), produced a large number of exemplars that, taken together, can be understood as comprising a genre in their own right—indeed, one of the characteristic generic products of the Romantic era.[42]

These exemplars themselves take various forms: some are in the form of short, pithy aphorisms, as in the fragments of the Schlegel brothers;[43] others are works that are formally complete but that nevertheless maintain in one or more dimensions a certain semantic ambiguity or open-endedness. Works of the latter type were said by Schlegel to exhibit a "hedgehog" effect (in the sense that they have no beginning or ending: "A fragment must like a small work of art be quite separated from the surrounding world and complete in itself like a hedgehog");[44] any sense of completeness one might find in such works is but a surface feature, a completeness resulting not from conventional structural or narrative mechanics but rather from an ending (or a beginning) asserted by the author in the face of the work's own signification of infinite formal or semantic openness. Conceived even more broadly, the fragment manifests August Wilhelm Schlegel's definition of the beautiful in art, in which "The beautiful is a symbolic representation of the infinite, for from this formulation it becomes clear how the infinite can appear in the finite," as well as his conviction that "Romantic poetry . . . is the expression of the secret urge towards the chaos that is constantly laboring to bring forth new and wonderful creations, and that is hidden beneath, indeed within, the orderly universe."[45] This last dictum in particular intersects in interesting ways with the late-eighteenth- and early-nineteenth-century fashion for ruins, as does Friedrich Schlegel's notion of the fragment itself: that is, Romantic fragment forms can be understood as Classical forms intentionally subjected to decay and deterioration. The aesthetic motivation would be something like that which motivated the eighteenth-century landscape architects who became fond of adding ruins to landscape sites, even when those sites may have been without ruins to begin with.[46] Ruins became a standard symbol in Romantic landscape prose, poetry, painting, and literature, where in literature especially (and, as I will argue, in music as well) the fragments Schlegel valued so highly can be understood as fractured remnants of Classical genres—specimens of architectural ruins, as it were, wrecked not literally by the forces of nature but by the forces of the Romantic artistic spirit.

* * *

This discussion suggests that regardless of the specific form taken by any of the genre's exemplars, the fragment as a critical category is rich with potential as an avenue into the aesthetics of Romantic art. In the most immediate sense, it is directly relevant for how we formulate the expressive dialogue (as I described that dialogue above) between Romantic artworks and their Classical precedents: the idea of the fragment, and the related idea of fragmentation in a work of art, becomes a means of positively valuing features of an artwork that might otherwise be evaluated negatively—as problematic or deficient, or as products of artistic accidents, failures, or other kinds of shortcomings. Thinking for a moment specifically in terms of music, Schlegel's sense of the fragment makes possible a music criticism that goes beyond notions of composers (Romantic composers who wrote structurally ambiguous sonata movements, for example) being "unable" to achieve what might be viewed as minimum standards of unity and coherence—standards that are derived from the demands of a Classical genre that the Romantic composer might be judged as incapable of meeting.

In a much larger sense, the fragment becomes the paradigmatic form that manifests the Romantic doctrine of an individualized, ironized, self-critical, original expression. As fundamentally anti-Classical and modern, it manifests the Romantic desire for rebellion against inherited forms. And it captures the Romantic view of history, in which the present is imperfect specifically because it is incomplete—a fragment of a grand historical trajectory in which the present always looks backward toward an idealized past and forward toward a better future. Even the arabesque, considered specifically as a narrative strategy in Schlegel's sense, manifests the aesthetic of the fragment: the arabesque interrupts, and thus it produces a formally fragmented space. In the most extreme cases arabesques can be so intrusive and so proportionally prominent that they threaten to overwhelm the very identity (and, with it, the "coherence") of the works they ostensibly embellish. Finally, the fragment speaks to the Romantics' faith in the power of the individual imagination. In Schlegel's view, the imagination is the source of such apparently contradictory forces as creation and destruction, optimism and skepticism, or euphoria and misery;[47] the fragment form liberates the artist to embrace this inherent irrationality, illogic, and ambiguity, freeing that artist from an uncritical acceptance of the rationality, logic, and clarity that are definitive in Classical conceptions of form and structure. Thus, the fragment becomes a formal emblem, representative of the Romantic worldview that embraces the utter futility of expressing the inexpressible, ineffable nature of one's innermost being.[48]

Notes

1. "Die gewöhnlichen Einteilungen der Poesie sind nur totes Fachwerk für einen beschränkten Horizont"; Schlegel, *Athenäum Fragmente* no. 434, in *Charakteristiken und Kritiken I*, 252 (translated in Janowitz, "The Romantic Fragment," 447). Schlegel also wrote, similarly, that "Romantic poetry is a progressive universal poetry.... It has the potential for the highest, most manifold evolution by expanding not only outward but also inward, for each thing destined to be a whole entity is organized uniformly in all its parts, so that the prospect is opened up of a boundlessly developing Classicism" ("Die romantische Poesie ist eine progressive Universalpoesie.... Sie ist der höchsten und der allseitigsten Bildung fähig; nicht bloss von innen heraus, sondern auch von aussen hinein; indem sie jedem, was ein Ganzes in ihren Produkten sein soll, alle Teile ähnlich organisiert, wodurch ihr die Aussicht auf eine grenzenlos wachsende Klassizität eröffnet wird"); see Schlegel, *Athenäum Fragmente* no. 116, in *Charakteristiken und Kritiken I*, 183 (translated in Furst, *European Romanticism*, 4–5).

2. "Einzelne schöne Erscheinungen dieser Gattung werden sicherlich hier und da zum Vorschein kommen und sind es schon; im Uebrigen aber, scheint es, hat die Form ihren Lebenskreis durchlausen und dies ist ja in der Ordnung der Dinge und wir sollen nicht Jahrhunderte lang dasselbe wiederholen und auch aus Neues bedacht sein." Schumann, "Sonaten für das Klavier," 134 (reprinted in Schumann, *Gesammelte Schriften über Musik und Musiker*, vol. 3, 80). Cited in Daverio, *Nineteenth-Century Music and the German Romantic Ideology*, 21, and (partially) in Hepokoski, "Beethoven Reception," 427. The translation given here is Daverio's.

3. What follows draws on the definition of Romanticism given in Abrams and Harpham, *A Glossary of Literary Terms*, 213–15.

4. Wordsworth, "Preface," 291 ("For all good poetry is the spontaneous overflow of powerful feelings") or 307 ("I have said that poetry is the spontaneous overflow of powerful feelings").

5. Daverio, *Nineteenth-Century Music and the German Romantic Ideology*, 2. On the Romantic conception of nature and its role in the creative process, see also Lawrence Kramer, "The Strange Case of Beethoven's *Coriolan*"; and Monelle, *The Musical Topic*, esp. 202–6. See also Rosen on the treatment of landscape in Romantic art, in *The Romantic Generation*, 116–236 (esp. 123–35). On the collapse of subject and object in Romantic literature, see Wimsatt, "The Structure of Romantic Nature Imagery"; and Abrams, "Structure and Style in the Greater Romantic Lyric." Both are discussed in Day, *Romanticism*, 94–100.

6. Foucault, *The Order of Things*, 217–49.

7. Ibid., 217.

8. Ibid., 237.

9. Wordsworth, "Preface," 289–90.

10. Booth, *The Rhetoric of Fiction*, passim. Note that according to Booth, the implied author is not the *real author*—the flesh-and-blood author who penned the text—but rather the author that readers make the real author become as they read. Some implied authors may be conflated to some degree with their real authors, but in other cases, the real author and the implied author may be incompatible—or at least their compatibility may not be verifiable. Cone's *The Composer's Voice* is largely an examination of Booth's implied-author concept from a musical point of view: Cone's "virtual persona" is roughly analogous to Booth's "implied author," and Cone himself acknowledges his debt to Booth as early as page 2 in his book. I have chosen to retain Booth's phraseology in referring to, in a musical context, an "implied composer" instead of Cone's "virtual persona." For critiques of the implied-author concept from a musical point of view, see Maus, "Agency in Instrumental Music and Song"; and Monahan, "Action and Agency Revisited."

11. On markers of the pastoral as a topic and, eventually, as an *expressive genre*, see Hatten, *Musical Meaning in Beethoven*, 91–111; and Monelle, *The Musical Topic*, 207–71. Hatten, *Interpreting Musical Gestures, Topics, and Tropes*, 56–65, moves toward adopting the pastoral as a broader *mode* of interpretation but stops short of my treatment of the pastoral as a prescription for plot trajectory. See also endnote 13.

12. The following summary draws largely on Gifford, *Pastoral*; and Monelle, *The Musical Topic*, 185–206. See also Hatten, *Interpreting Musical Gestures, Topics, and Tropes*, 53–67; Klein, *Intertextuality in Western Art Music*, 68, 70–71; Klein, "Chopin's Fourth Ballade as Musical Narrative," 48–51; Rosen, *The Romantic Generation*, esp. 41–236; and Hepokoski, "Beethoven Reception," esp. 438.

13. The name *Arcadia* dates from the poetry of Virgil, in which it refers to the traditional home among the Peloponnese mountains of Pan and other simple peasants. See Monelle, *The Musical Topic*, 186. On forms of retreat and return in pastoral narratives, see Gifford, *Pastoral*, 45–115, esp. 81–82, where he makes the point that the return from the fictional Arcadia to reality is critical in order for the narrative to avoid being escapist. For a musical consideration especially of this last point, see Klein, "Chopin's Fourth Ballade as Musical Narrative," 49. My definition of the pastoral as a plot paradigm also departs somewhat from Robert Hatten's sense of the pastoral as an expressive genre, exemplars of which begin and end in Arcadia and are thus more positively

inflected in an expressive sense. My own conception, in foregrounding themes of retreat (to an idealized Arcadia) and return (to an imperfect present), is more negatively inflected and lies more within what Hatten would define as a *tragic* expressive genre (Hatten, *Musical Meaning in Beethoven*, 67–90). See also endnote 11.

14. On the broader definition of Arcadia, see esp. Gifford, *Pastoral*, 13–44; and Monelle, *The Musical Topic*, 186–87, 190–94, and 196–98. On the connection of the Arcadia concept with the Romantic view of nature, see esp. Monelle, ibid., 202–6.

15. This is the subject of Koselleck, *Futures Past*.

16. Frye, "The Drunken Boat," 80.

17. Gifford, *Pastoral*, 12.

18. Wellek, "The Concept of 'Romanticism' in Literary History: II," 147. Cited in Day, *Romanticism*, 4. See also the comments in Daverio, *Nineteenth-Century Music and the German Romantic Ideology*, 2.

19. Lovejoy, "On the Discrimination of Romanticisms," 235–36. See also the discussion in Day, *Romanticism*, 184–85. For a somewhat different reading of Lovejoy, see Daverio, *Nineteenth-Century Music and the German Romantic Ideology*, 2.

20. McGann has cautioned against an uncritical acceptance of the Romantics' own unitary and notoriously polemical descriptions of their artistic aims and achievements—including their emphasis on the uniqueness and individuality of their creative works and their claims to an organicism that pervades both their art and their lives. See his *The Romantic Ideology: A Critical Investigation*; see also the comments in Daverio, *Nineteenth-Century Music and the German Romantic Ideology*, 6.

21. This is Wellek's characterization of August Wilhelm Schlegel's view of Romanticism; see Wellek, "The Concept of 'Romanticism' in Literary History: I," 6–7. On the role of August Wilhelm Schlegel in the dissemination of Romantic ideology, and on the relationship of his writings with those of his brother Friedrich's, see Daverio, *Nineteenth-Century Music and the German Romantic Ideology*, 11.

22. Gay, *The Rise of Modern Paganism*, x (quoted in Day, *Romanticism*, 59). The present discussion draws on Day, ibid., 57–70, which takes Gay as its point of departure.

23. Wordsworth, "Preface," 291. See also the discussion of Wordsworth (as well as Blake and Gillray) in Butler, *Romantics, Rebels, and Reactionaries*, 39–68; and see Day, *Romanticism*, 67–70.

24. Frye, "The Drunken Boat," 78.

25. Ibid., 85. See also Kramer, "The Strange Case of Beethoven's *Coriolan*," esp. 259–60, on "the elevating appropriation of the inner through the outer, of the self through representation of (or in) the world." Monelle traces this interiorizing impulse to the very beginnings of the Romantic movement itself: "The greatest pastoral dramas, Poliziano's *Orfeo* and Tasso's *Aminta*, are allegories of the inner life, fables of the soul, in which the pastoral figures are merely emblems" (*The Musical Topic*, 197–98).

26. Frye, "The Drunken Boat," 86.

27. Ibid., 79–80.

28. Bloom, "The Internalization of Quest-Romance." Day links Frye and Bloom in *Romanticism*, 93–94.

29. Monelle, *The Musical Topic*, 203–6.

30. What follows draws on the discussion of the Schlegels' Romanticism in Daverio, *Nineteenth-Century Music and the German Romantic Ideology*, esp. 1–88.

31. See, for example, Day, *Romanticism*, 135–39 and 179.

32. "[Das *Schöne*] ist so wenig das herrschende Prinzip der modernen Poesie, daß viele ihrer trefflichsten Werke ganz offenbar Darstellungen des *Häßlichen* sind, und man wird es wohl endlich, wenngleich ungern, eingestehen müssen, daß es eine Darstellung der Verwirrung in höchster Fülle, der Verzweiflung in Überfluß aller Kräfte gibt, welche eine gleiche wo nicht eine höhere Schöpferkraft und künstlerische Weisheit erfordert, wie die Darstellung der Fülle

und Kraft in vollständiger Übereinstimmung." Quoted and translated in Daverio, *Nineteenth-Century Music and the German Romantic Ideology*, 13–14. The original appears in Schlegel, *Die Griechen und Römer*, in *Studien des Klassischen Aletertums*, 219.

33. Portions of what follow have previously been published in Andrew Davis, "Chopin and the Romantic Sonata: The First Movement of Op. 58." *Music Theory Spectrum* 36, no. 2 (2014): 247–69.

34. Daverio, *Nineteenth-Century Music and the German Romantic Ideology*, 19–47. On the relationship of the arabesque and the grotesque, see Kayser, *The Grotesque in Art and Literature*, esp. 19–20.

35. "Der Roman tendenzirt zur Parekbase"; "Die Parekbase muß im F[antastischen] R[oman] permanent sein." Schlegel, *Fragmente zur Literatur und Poesie* nos. 137 and 463, in *Fragmente zur Poesie und Literatur*, 96 and 123. Translated in Daverio, *Nineteenth-Century Music and the German Ideology*, 29.

36. "Alle Werke sollen Romane/alle Prosa romantisch sein"; "Alle Geisteswerke sollen romantisiren d[em] Roman s[ich] möglichst approximiren." Schlegel, *Fragmente zur Literatur und Poesie* nos. 590 and 606, in *Fragmente zur Poesie und Literatur*, 134 and 136. Translated in Daverio, *Nineteenth-Century Music and the German Romantic Ideology*, 3–4 ("All works") and 230n10 ("All products").

37. Daverio, *Nineteenth-Century Music and the German Romantic Ideology*, 20–21. For more on this point, see also Blackall, *The Novels of the German Romantics*; and Polheim, *Die Arabeske* (both cited in Daverio, ibid.).

38. "Romantic irony . . . is the simultaneous operation in literary productions of creation and destruction and joy and skepticism" (Janowitz, "The Romantic Fragment," 448). For a musical consideration, see Longyear, "Beethoven and Romantic Irony"; and Hatten, *Musical Meaning in Beethoven*, 172–88.

39. Daverio, *Nineteenth-Century Music and the German Romantic Ideology*, 54.

40. On fragment aesthetics generally, see, from the musical literature, Daverio, *Nineteenth-Century Music and the German Romantic Ideology*, 49–88; Rosen, *The Romantic Generation*, 41–115; and Satyendra, "Liszt's Open Structures and the Romantic Fragment." From literary criticism, see Janowitz, "The Romantic Fragment"; Levinson, *The Romantic Fragment Poem*; and McFarland, *Romanticism and the Forms of Ruin*.

41. Goethe, *Faust: Ein Fragment*.

42. On this point, and on the wider issue of genre in Romantic literature, see Levinson, *The Romantic Fragment Poem*, 5–59.

43. A number of these have been cited already. Rosen cites more in *The Romantic Generation*, 48–50 and 94–96. Furst, *European Romanticism*, offers a helpful anthology of fragments by the Schlegels and others.

44. "Ein Fragment muß gleich einem kleinen Kunstwerke von der umgebenden Welt ganz abgesondert und in sich selbst vollendet sein wie ein Igel." See Schlegel, *Athenäum Fragmente* no. 206, in *Charakteristiken und Kritiken I*, 197 (trans. McFarland, *Romanticism and the Forms of Ruin*, 45). For more on the hedgehog analogy, see Rosen, *The Romantic Generation*, 48. On the paradoxical, closed-yet-open structural nature of the fragment form, see Rosen, ibid., 50–51; and Satyendra, "Liszt's Open Structures and the Romantic Fragment," 193–94.

45. "Das Schöne ist eine symbolische Darstellung des Unendlichen; weil alsdann zugleich klar wird, wie das Unendliche zur Erscheinung kommen kann"; "Die romantische . . . ist der Ausdruck des geheimen Zuges zu dem immerfort nach neuen und wundervollen Geburten ringenden Chaos, welches unter der geordneten Schöpfung, ja in ihrem Schosse sich verbirgt"; August Wilhelm Schlegel, *Vorlesungen über dramatische Kunst und Literatur*, in August Wilhelm Schlegel, *Kritische Schriften und Briefe*, vol. 6, 81–82 and 111–12. The translations are from Furst, *European Romanticism*, 94 and 112. For further discussion, see Janowitz, "The Romantic Fragment," 447–49.

46. On ruins, see Rosen, *The Romantic Generation*, 92–94 and (on the aesthetic of ruins in Romantic landscape painting) 142–50. See also the historical discussion and musical application in McKee, "Alternative Meanings in the First Movement of Beethoven's String Quartet in E♭ Major, op. 127."

47. Janowitz, "The Romantic Fragment," 448. See also endnote 37 and the associated text on Romantic irony.

48. See also McFarland, *Romanticism and the Forms of Ruin*, 3–55.

2 Atemporality in Narrative and Music

THIS CHAPTER SETS out to construct a theory of structure and expressive meaning in the nineteenth-century Romantic sonata, within the view of Romanticism articulated in chapter 1.[1] The theory will focus particularly on the problematized moments of formal and expressive ambiguity characteristic of that genre. I first consider what we might mean by *narrative* or *narrative forms* in music, continue by examining issues related to time and temporality within those narrative forms, and finish by proposing ways that some of these (mainly literary) concepts might map onto music.

* * *

While the theory draws largely on structural narratology, I find that recent musicological literature provides a helpful point of departure. In particular, Karol Berger has drawn a distinction between two types of forms (where *form* is a vehicle for the expression of content): the *narrative* and the *lyric,* forms that underlie a wide array of arts and genres, from literature to architecture, painting to music.[2] Berger's narrative-lyric opposition can manifest in various ways in the arts: some art describes or depicts (narrative), whereas other art reflects (lyric); some art signifies motion in time (narrative), whereas other art signifies temporal stasis (lyric). For Berger, the distinction has its roots in the long history of narrative theory, dating from Plato's differentiation between *diegesis* (telling) and *mimesis* (showing), two modes in which a poetic narrative transmits its content: in Plato, the diegetic mode entails a narrator speaking directly to an audience, while the mimetic mode entails a narrator communicating indirectly—usually through characters resident in the drama itself. Diegesis and mimesis were for Plato among the principal determinants of poetic genres, of which he thus named two: the epic, characterized by diegesis, and the dramatic, characterized by mimesis. Seventeenth-century narrative theory added a third genre that Plato himself never considered: the lyric, defined as poetry concerned with the ideas and sentiments, rather than the stories and actions, of a narrator. And the resulting tripartite division remained standard through the nineteenth century and beyond, even while Friedrich Schlegel himself added a fourth genre to the mix: the *Roman,* or the "novel," defined as a mixture of all three genres, "fantastically formed and generically ambiguous."[3] Schlegel, thus, as mentioned, gave rise to one of the specific meanings of the word *Romantic* (Ger. *romantisch*): literally *novelistic,* in the specific sense of *fragmentary* with regard to form and genre. For Schlegel, it was the novel that "[colored] the whole of modern poetry";[4] it was the novel and its *romantisch* features that were key to the entire modern artistic enterprise.

Berger argues that the standard tripartite categorization scheme—epic, dramatic, and lyric—invites confusion. The confusion is rooted in a confounding of a genre's mode of presentation and the nature of its content—where the confounding is made possible by the fact that the principal distinction between epic and dramatic genres lies in the mode of transmission of content (diegetic or mimetic, respectively) and the distinction between epic and dramatic genres and the lyric genre lies instead in the nature of the content itself (epic and dramatic genres both contain plots, while lyric genres do not). To remedy this situation, Berger proposes removing the mode of delivery from the equation and differentiating among the types solely according to the nature of the content: the natural consequence is that *lyric* becomes one category, while epic and dramatic are folded into another, which Berger suggests we can call *narrative*.[5] The two new categories, according to Berger, constitute forms, not genres, in that they distinguish ways of organizing narrative content into intelligible relationships between the smaller parts and the larger whole. Narrative forms impart causal ("one motivates another") or reactive ("one follows from another") relationships onto what would otherwise be unmotivated, ad hoc arrangements of rhetorical event modules, and in so doing, they foreground the order of events in time as an essential facet of those events' identities and expressive potential.[6] Lyric forms, on the other hand, represent not actions but rather thoughts, mental states, emotions, or situations (not "the actions one does" but "the states one finds oneself in"[7]), none of which depend on a quantitative conception of time, and as such, lyric forms allow events to occur in any order, or even simultaneously, without changing either those events' meanings or the expressive outcome of the form as a whole.

One of my central concerns is with the ways in which narrative content can be arranged structurally within a narrative form defined as such. The discipline that concerns itself with questions about the structure, or the *discourse,* of the narrative—the telling of the story, rather than the story itself—is known as structural narratology. Recent work in structural narratology has made a number of important contributions to our understanding of narrative structure: among these, one of the most important for my purposes is the recognition that even in a narrative form that depends for its expressive meaning on the ordering of events in time, not all of these events must participate in the narrative structure in exactly the same way with regard to their temporal-significative value. That is, some of the events, or some of the formal modules, may be presented to a reader out of order, may be disclosed to a reader at varying rates of speed, or may be repeated multiple times, without necessarily affecting the actual content of the story itself or the temporal mechanics of the fictional story world that they are meant to represent. That this is possible stems from the fact that, as Gérard Genette has explained, any narrative, whether oral, written, or cinematic, necessarily exists within a kind of temporal duality.[8] It engages simultaneously with two temporal spaces: that of the narrative's content and that of the actual act of narration. The former is known as the *erzählte Zeit*—literally "narrated time" or, in Genette's rendering, "story time" (*temps de l'histoire*); this is the time that passes within the world of the story itself. The latter is known as the *Erzählzeit*—literally "narrative time" (*temps du récit*); this is the time of the narrative act, or the time it takes to recite or otherwise tell the story, and from the point of view of narrative theory it must be, according to Genette, regarded as a "quasi-fiction" or a "pseudotime" ("a false time standing in for a true time").[9] This distinction between story time and narrative time overlaps with what some writers in musical semiotics have recently characterized as *time* versus *temporality*, where, broadly speaking, temporality constitutes *time signified:* time is what many would think of as "real time" or "clock time," which is normally an absolute, natural condition—forward vectored, continuous, and irreversible—of the "real world" in which we move and in which our narratives occur; temporality, on the other hand, is the time denoted, or the time meant, by various signifiers within the narrative text, whether that text is a film, novel, narrative poem, or some other.[10]

For a reader to assume that all rhetorical events or formal modules in a narrative text participate in that narrative in temporally equivalent ways is to confuse ("naïvely," says Genette) different facets of this temporal duality.[11] That is, to assume as much confuses the syntagmatic presentation of the events in a narrative (within the world of narrative time) with the actual temporal function, or the signified temporal value, of those events within the narrated content (within the world of story time). That the two do not necessarily coincide is one of the most basic aspects of Western literary narratives in all their forms, as Genette has compellingly argued. In fact, he traces the beginning of the Western narrative tradition to the *Iliad*, which, as he explains, opens *in medias res* with the quarrel between Achilles and Agamemnon before very shortly thereafter backing up in time—flashing back about ten days—to recount, in a longer, retrospective passage, the cause of the quarrel itself.[12]

Genette's temporal duality can produce a number of different relationships between the story time and the narrative pseudotime.[13] He discusses a number of possibilities, of which two are especially relevant here: relationships concerning duration (*durée*) and those concerning order (*ordre*). With regard to duration, events in the story time may occupy a duration that does not directly and consistently correlate, absolutely or proportionally, with their duration in narrative pseudotime. This is because narrative time can accelerate or decelerate with respect to story time (the events of a few years might be related in just one paragraph, while a conversation lasting just a few minutes may take several pages to unfold). But the issue is complex, largely because it may not always be clear just how to measure narrative time: in a written or an oral narrative, it might be the length of the text needed to tell a particular story, or it might be the time it takes a reader to read or tell that story. But these measurements raise a number of additional questions: How does one measure the "length" of a text? How does one compare the length of one text to another? How does one compare the speeds at which individual readers read? In film or in music, these questions may seem a bit more straightforward (e.g., the length of time needed to view a film never changes), but complications nevertheless remain: in music, for example, how would one account for the varying durations of different performances of a piece? Genette's theory sidesteps these and other related complexities by concerning itself not so much with narrative time measured as an absolute value but rather with the pace at which the events of the story are delivered within the narrative time: this pacing is a property of the narrative discourse that he calls the *narrative rhythm* (*rythme du récit*).[14] Any narrative, he says, will have in its structure a *referential* narrative rhythm or a "zero reference point" ("*le point de reference, ou degré zero*")[15] against which deviations can be perceived. The referential narrative rhythm is thus established internally, as an immanent feature of the narrative itself. It is often useful to locate it in those parts of the story where the internal temporal flow approximates the flow of real time. Changes in the story's pace—accelerations or decelerations—as measured against the referential narrative rhythm are known as *anisochronies* (*anisochronies*).

With regard to order, as in the *Iliad* example, the sequence of events in the story may not coincide with the sequence in which they are presented in the narration. That is, the story can be told in a nonlinear or nonchronological fashion.[16] This gives rise to several possible categories and subcategories of features in the narrative discourse. For example, an event or passage in the narrative may refer forward or backward, to a time later than or earlier than its actual location in the story. Or it may be stripped of any explicit temporal reference, such that it is not possible for a reader to place it in an unambiguous temporal relationship with what surrounds it. Genette calls the first of these categories the *anachrony* (*anachronie*), within which are several possible subcategories, including the flashback, or *analepsis* (*analepse*), and the flash-forward, or *prolepsis* (*prolepse*).[17] Genette calls the second category the *achrony* (*achronie*): events in this category are, according to Genette, *atemporal* (*intemporel*), in the sense that they remain dateless, ageless, isolated from, and independent of the larger narrative structure.[18]

These distinctions lead to one of the fundamental features of narrative discourse as Genette defines it: the presence of a linearly directed, temporally unified narrative *stream*, flowing at a uniform rate and with uniform (normally chronological) order, thus anchoring the story by providing a foundation along which it progresses through time in a forward-vectored fashion. Genette calls this stream the "first temporal level" of the narrative, or simply the *first narrative* (*récit premier*).[19] Together with the story time–narrative time duality characteristic of all narratives, Genette's concept of first narrative implies the possibility of a binary opposition at the largest structural level of the narrative discourse. First, some of the events in a narrative may occur within the first-narrative stream. Such events may be identified according to either chronological or durational criteria: that is, these are the events in which story time and narrative time coincide, or these are the events that establish the referential narrative-rhythmic pace. I will call this the narrative's *primary temporal stream*, or simply its *temporal stream*. Second, some other events in the narrative may occur outside of, or off, the first narrative—outside the temporal stream. Again, either chronological or durational criteria may be invoked:

these might be events presented out of chronological order or events that comprise extranarrative authorial commentary or reflection, with no precise chronological relationship to the story proper; or they might shift rhetorically into delivering the story with a markedly accelerated or decelerated rate of speed relative to the referential narrative rhythm. Borrowing language from Genette, I will regard such events as located within any number of possible *atemporal* streams, where here "atemporal" means "not on the temporal- (first-) narrative level." This opposition of temporal versus atemporal streams proves useful as a point of departure for the analysis of narrative discourse in Romantic music, even though it is obviously oversimplified to some degree. In reality, the relationships among temporal levels in a narrative can become much more complex: the content of an atemporal achrony, for example, might itself function as an independent, localized first narrative, and it might contain its own atemporal digressions, deflections, or deviations.

* * *

In sum, three fundamental principles of narrative forms have emerged: a narrative form can be regarded as any form that depends for its expressive meaning on an event sequence ordered in time; any narrative form will engage with a temporal duality in which narrative pseudotime (or discursive time) moves independently from story time; and any narrative form is capable of producing an opposition between temporal and atemporal (first-narrative and non-first-narrative) streams. All this applies just as well to novels, narrative poetry, films, and, indeed, to pieces of music.

The definition can be further delineated with regard specifically to music. Some musical forms should be understood as *narrative forms* precisely because they depend for their expressive meaning on an ordered presentation of events in time. This seems true whether we choose to accept the wider premise that music itself, as an art form, is *narrative* in the strictest possible sense, with diegetic narrating voices, past tenses, and other features often thought to be minimal in any definition of narrative. If some musical forms are narrative, or at least analogous to narrative, it follows that they have the capacity to engage with Genette's temporal duality and, as a result, that they have the capacity to engage with the opposition of temporal versus atemporal streams, as I have defined them here.

Perhaps the most obvious example of a narrative form in music is the sonata form. The sonata form and, ultimately, the entire structural and rhetorical apparatus within which a sonata constructs its expressive meaning, depends fundamentally on temporal order: the sonata is premised on a cogent, ordered succession of musical-rhetorical events and affective or expressive states, all of them staged by the composer as unfolding in forward-driven, linearly directed time. This central aspect of the sonata's identity is perhaps best understood within the structural and hermeneutic framework provided by the Sonata Theory of James Hepokoski and Warren Darcy.[20] Sonata Theory understands the sonata in a temporal-narrative sense, and at the most basic level, it concerns itself with questions such as "What does it mean to have *this* musical module situated *there* (as opposed to elsewhere)—and following, say, *that* module?"[21] In the Sonata Theory view, a sonata narrative unfolds on top of a formal foundation based on multiple passes, or multiple ordered cycles or *rotations,* through a series of structural stations or formal zones. These zones are conceived not as musical "themes" or "groups" thereof, but as *action spaces* inhabited by what we might think of as musical-narrative agents, among which meaningful causal or reactive relationships accrue as the narrative unfolds in time.[22] Such agents may take the form of themes in the more traditional sense or, more generally, musical-rhetorical modules of varying shapes and sizes. The action spaces themselves comprise the sonata-formal zones known traditionally as, in order of appearance, the primary theme (P), transition (TR), secondary theme (S), and closing (C). Within these spaces, the musical rhetoric has a fundamentally teleological quality in which it aims at certain structural objectives or punctuation marks, the most important of which include the Medial Caesura (MC, normatively occurring at the end of TR-space), the Essential Expositional Closure (EEC, occurring at the end of the S-space in the first rotation or *exposition*), and the Essential Structural Closure (ESC, at the end of the final full rotation or *recapitulation*). The order of these events' presentation within the sonata rhetoric is central to the sonata's immanent meanings as well as, mentioned above, to the expressive outcome of the work as a whole. Note that Sonata Theory relies on a concept of *rhetoric* that overlaps with Wayne Booth's, in which rhetoric refers to the specific technical features of the language (literary or musical) that an author (or composer) uses to guide a reader (listener) through a story (again, literary or musical); rhetoric comprises the particular strategies and procedures through which authors, or composers, create "a successful ordering of [their] reader's [listener's] view of a fictional world."[23]

Given this sonata-as-narrative framework, it follows that Genette's concept of a temporal duality in narrative forms as well as my own conception of a temporal-atemporal opposition therein will apply to the sonata form in music. To rephrase two earlier points in musical terms, we might now say that a sonata may contain certain musical-rhetorical modules, not all of which necessarily participate in the sonata narrative in exactly the same way with regard to their temporal-significative value; and, likewise, that some of the events in a sonata may occur within what can be regarded as the "first sonata narrative" or the temporal stream of the sonata proper, while other of its events may occur outside of, or off, this first-narrative level and thus within any number of possible atemporal streams. The result is a view of sonatas as constituting an assemblage of various formal modules, some temporal and others atemporal, where not all of these contribute to the sonata structure in temporally equivalent ways.

The concept of a temporal-atemporal opposition within the sonata intersects in various ways with musical concepts of epic, dramatic, and lyric forms. As in Genette's narratology or Booth's rhetorical narrative theory, we can think of the multiplicity of temporal meanings within a sonata's various formal modules as producing a narrative populated by multiple "voices," any of which may adopt different modes of delivery as they contribute to the narrative. Some of these voices might be musically analogous to those of characters in a drama, for example, and thus might "speak" mimetically, as in a dramatic form. Others might be analogous to various forms of narrating voices that speak diegetically, from outside the space of the story, and in a past tense, in which the story is something that already happened; these might be something like the voice of the narrator in an epic poem, for example, or that agent in a narrative that some have called the "narrating survivor"—one who lives on to speak of a tale in the past tense.[24] The musical content purveyed by any of these voices might be temporal or atemporal—inside or outside the first narrative. This raises complex issues that are best considered in the context of specific musical examples, but for now, to put it as simply as possible, when the musical content proceeds in an unproblematized fashion—according to the norms and expectations operative on any given structural or generic level—that music can generally be regarded as located within the narrative's principal temporal stream (the first narrative). As such, the temporal elements in the sonata will often include its principal rotational modules (P, TR, S, and C), normatively presented—that is, sounded in the normative chronological order and at the normative narrative-rhythmic pace, such that story time (understood now as sonata-story time: the time passing within the world of the sonata) and narrative time (the time in which the sonata is conveyed aurally to the listener) can be understood as coinciding. When such norms and expectations are disturbed by certain types of *rhetorical gestures* comprising expressively *marked* discontinuities or other disruptions that encroach on the music's normative, forward-vectored flow, that music can signify a shift outside the first narrative and into an atemporal stream.[25] All such atemporality would be understood as disengaging story time from narrative time. The possibilities may be numerous, but its forms might include musical modules that audibly accelerate or decelerate the narrative rhythm and thus produce musical analogs for what Genette would regard as anisochronies; others might be regarded as out of order (in the sense of "out of place") with respect to the music that surrounds them and thus may comprise musical analogs for anachronies (proleptic, if they are perceived as occurring too early in the narrative, or analeptic, if they are perceived as occurring too late); and others may have no audible or immediately verifiable temporal relationship with the ongoing musical trajectory and thus may comprise musical achronies.[26]

Musical achronies are particularly important features of the Romantic sonata, in which they often take the form of modules interpolated (perhaps illogically or otherwise problematically) into the structure that appear to immobilize, suppress, arrest, or suspend the generically obligatory forward-vectored progress through the first-narrative stream. In many cases, such interpolations can be interpreted as musically analogous to narrative detours that invoke a lyric, as opposed to a mimetic or diegetic, mode of delivery—something like the lyric idylls of Romantic poetry, which are "extended moments of lyric reverie" comprising forms of authorial commentary, description, or reminiscence by a lyric subject or agent, all carried out within a "realm of subjectivity, intimacy, and phenomenological temporality."[27]

* * *

More broadly, this opposition of temporal and atemporal streams is one of the chief concerns—one of the foremost genre-defining features—of Romantic music and specifically of the sonata in the Romantic era. The interpretive model that I seek to develop from this principle is one that ultimately provides a means of mapping Schlegel's concept of the *Roman* and the *romantisch* directly onto music—one that provides, indeed, a way of identifying the very features of the Romantic repertoire that make it *Romantic* in the contemporary, nineteenth-century sense of that word. In this regard, my analytical approach overlaps most directly with precedents in which commentators have sought to account for Schlegel's notion of the Romantic era as one defined by a certain *novelizing* (or *Romanticizing*) of various literary genres. I have already mentioned John Daverio's contributions to our understanding of these aspects of Romantic music and the history of the Romantic period. Others who have addressed similar concerns include Anthony Newcomb, who has framed the issues specifically in terms of understanding the differences between eighteenth- and nineteenth-century music and the narrative strategies therein, and who has proposed that one of the ways of coming to terms with the idiosyncrasies in music of Schumann is to compare its structure and rhetoric to novels of Novalis, E. T. A. Hoffmann, and Jean Paul (Johann Paul Friedrich Richter); and Janice Dickensheets, who recently wrote a doctoral dissertation focusing in part on ways in which "novelistic" features in Schlegel's specific sense of that term can be brought to bear on an interpretation of music of Brahms (specifically the Piano Sonata in F♯ minor, op. 2, portions of which I will address in part III).[28]

My approach also overlaps with those of other writers on musical narrative and semiotics who have sought to develop ways of accounting for expressively marked structural and rhetorical discontinuities and the temporal, narrative, or expressive implications thereof—especially in music of late Beethoven and after. William Kinderman, for example, finds that such discontinuities can produce what he calls "parenthetical enclosures"—essentially interpolated episodes that fragment the musical structure and, very importantly, its temporal space (effecting the "enclosure of one time within another");[29] these are similar to the atemporal interpolations that I will propose fragment the sonata structures in the piano sonatas of Brahms and others. Carolyn Abbate, in her theory of nineteenth-century musical narrative, has claimed that nineteenth-century operas comprise multiple voices, not all of which engage in the music's narrative structure in parallel ways; only some may be specifically *narrative*, where for Abbate a narrating voice (i.e., a lyric agent) requires the presence of a disjunction—similar to the discontinuities that Kinderman emphasizes in Beethoven—that sets it apart from the ongoing, unmarked musical discourse.[30] And Abbate's conception of such disjunctions overlaps, in turn, with what

Robert Hatten has described in terms of *shifts of level of discourse*: these are shifts in which we can hear, in music, a distinction between the dramatic and the epic, or the mimetic and the diegetic, in the sense that certain disjunctions or other sharp, abrupt, expressively charged changes in the musical discourse can be understood as constituting musical analogs for shifts from "direct discourse to indirect discourse or narration."[31] Such discursive shifts can be signaled by marked changes of musical style or topic, or, more generally, certain kinds of extreme ruptures in one or more dimensions of the musical fabric (texture, dynamics, register, etc.): these might include forms of expressively marked non sequiturs (interrupted themes, deflected or rhetorically charged harmonic progressions or modulatory schemes, stalled developmental procedures, sudden or unusual tonal shifts, etc.); shifts of stylistic level (especially those that suggest some kind of expressive reversal); and various forms of direct or self-quotation, intertextual importations, or other stylistic allusions. As mentioned, Hatten's approach invokes both temporality and implications of agential presence: he describes some discursive shifts as effecting "disruptions of the temporal norm" or, more specifically, as moments of phenomenological temporality that reveal the presence of a lyric subject.[32] All such shifts have the potential to signify the presence of a Romantic-ironic stance in the work.

And my approach resonates with certain poststructuralist narratologies positing that a text is something other than a linear entity that reveals its meaning in a unidirectional fashion, from beginning to end, in a single utterance and at a uniform rate. Roland Barthes, for example, is well known for having touched on the concept of multiple voices within a text by proposing a reading of Balzac according to an array of multiple interrelated *codes* (hermeneutic, proairetic, semic, symbolic, referential, etc.), with the aim of foregrounding the idea that a text comprises a network of different "levels of meaning," any of which may be interrelated in various ways.[33] Mikhail Bakhtin touched on similar concepts, in particular in his notion of *dialogism*—the theory of the interrelation in a text among multiple languages or multiple modes of speaking, all of which are themselves constituent components of a deconstructed literary world the "base condition" of which is what Bakhtin calls *heteroglossia*.[34] Dialogism and heteroglossia are central to Bakhtin's theory of the novel and to what he regards as novelistic features of other works of literature: for Bakhtin the novel is defined by a unity of diversities of speech types, individual voices, and, indeed, of genres themselves, all of them socially and ideologically heterogeneous, such that the novel's own generic features resist consistent codification.[35] Obviously, such conceptions overlap in significant, striking ways with Schlegel's theory of the novel—as digressive, "fantastically formed," and "generically ambiguous"—and Schlegel's notions of what constitutes the *romantisch* in literature.[36]

And while these resonances from the poststructuralist literature may seem rather general, there is at least one concept from that tradition that intersects with my own approach in a more direct and especially engaging way. This is Bakhtin's concept of the *chronotope,* which foregrounds the possibility of a latent *spatiality* in the various temporal threads embedded in a nineteenth-century novelistic narrative.[37] The concept as Bakhtin presents it is exceedingly complex, but in the broadest sense, it overlaps specifically with how I conceive of temporality in the Romantic sonata narrative. The chronotope (literally "time-space") is essentially a *site* (understood with varying degrees of abstraction, from, for example, a specific location, to a generalized setting or milieu, to an even more generalized plot premise) in which temporal and spatial aspects of such a narrative structure intersect; the concept tries to capture "the intrinsic connectedness of temporal and spatial relationships that are artistically expressed in literature."[38] Bakhtin proposed a typology of chronotopes that govern narrative forms in the novel, among them the "road," the "castle," the "parlor," and the "encounter." Depending on the type, either the temporal or spatial dimension will exist in the narrative in higher or lower degrees of intensity. One of the two dimensions will be primary and the other will be subordinate; within the primary dimension, the subordinate dimension will assert its influence in various ways. For example, in the parlor, space is primary: the parlor is a room, literally—a space with fixed, visible boundaries. A narrative situated within it is thus fundamentally spatially conceived. But within that narrative, various event sequences that are conceived temporally might emerge: dialogue may occur among characters, for example, where within that dialogue, there may unfold various kinds of intrigues, encounters, negotiations, or denouements. Such episodes may carry their own (linearly directed, temporal) plots or subplots; in them, "time, as it were, thickens, takes on flesh, [and] becomes artistically visible."[39]

In the road chronotope, on the other hand, time is primary. One way of thinking of the road is as a temporally vectored, forward-moving "site" on which events of the narrative are situated in time. Such a narrative is fundamentally temporally conceived, and the temporal trajectory of the road governs the narrative's large-scale temporal-structural framework. But at various points along the road, there may occur spatially conceived episodes: these can include encounters among characters, descriptions of landscapes or other scenes, or various other kinds of narrative or nonnarrative sequences. Within such spatial episodes, the narrative's primary level of linear-temporal motion (analogous to Genette's "first narrative") appears to momentarily cease its movement along the road, as if pausing to wait for an internal episode to expand and unfold before resuming its course and continuing on to its next structural station. First-narrative temporality stops (or perhaps momentarily slows) in order to allow for a more purely spatial expansion: "space becomes charged and responsive to the movements of time, plot, and history";[40] a more pure form of Enlightenment teleology gives way to a nineteenth-century form of multiply directed temporalities, allowing for a more focused expression of subjectivity. Such imagery parallels very closely my image of the Romantic sonata: like the road, the sonata constitutes a linear, forward-vectored "site" in which, by definition, a primary temporal level (the first sonata narrative) moves or progresses through time, from one structural station to the next. Occasionally, atemporal modules—analogous to spatially conceived episodes along the road—intrude upon and suspend or otherwise disrupt the motion of the first narrative in favor of various kinds of musical subplots, reflections, commentaries, or other (again, narrative or nonnarrative) events.

* * *

All of these issues speak directly to what defines musical Romanticism. Note in this regard that just because a narrative form might engage with the binary opposition that I have constructed here of temporal versus atemporal, it does not necessarily follow that such a narrative must be modern, innovative, unconventional, or possessive of any other qualities that necessarily set it apart from the norm, however the norm may be defined within some regulating interpretive framework.[41] On the contrary, the degree to which a given narrative is inclined toward the use of disjunctive procedures—or, more specifically, the degree to which a narrative is inclined toward exploiting anachronic structures and the duality of temporal and atemporal narrative stream as I have defined them—seems best understood as a matter of style or, in some cases, genre. Certain stylistic movements and certain genres may be predisposed toward atemporality more so than others: Genette has observed that in folklore narratives, for example, the narration normatively conforms ("at least in its major articulations") to the narrative content with respect to the chronological ordering of its constituent events.[42]

In music, the Classical sonata (following Berger's basic premises) is a genre normatively concerned with linear teleology to such an extent that its formal structure remains in most respects fundamentally different from the kind of temporally fragmented structure I have envisioned here. The Romantic sonata, on the other hand, appears to be preoccupied to a much greater extent with the musical expression of multiple temporal streams and a concomitant structural fragmentation—indeed, as mentioned, it appears to be concerned with these features to such an extent that we might say they are its central aesthetic concerns, or its chief, definitive features. (Berger has suggested as much, writing that "music had no sooner acquired its 'classical' ability to represent linear time, than it began 'romantically' to undermine and question that ability by exploring moments of timelessness."[43]) This view accounts for the abundance of highly problematized moments of structural and expressive ambiguity typical in this repertoire, several examples of which I highlighted at the outset of this book. It foregrounds the very structural and rhetorical features of the style that at once lend the music its Romantic identity—where the Romantic sonata is understood as a deeply discontinuous, fragmented, metaphorically "ruined" Classical sonata structure, a Classical form broken apart by the forces of the Romantic aesthetic spirit and the Romantic concern for fragmentation as a self-conscious, self-critical evaluation of the state of one's own art. This kind of deliberate structural and temporal fragmentation realizes in music the fractured, ruined forms that Schlegel and others in the Romantic movement sought in poetry and other literary genres. Exactly how it can be signified within the musical rhetoric of the Romantic piano sonata is the concern of parts II and III of this book.

Notes

1. Portions of this chapter have previously been published in Davis, "Chopin and the Romantic Sonata."
2. This discussion draws on Berger, "Narrative and Lyric." This article clearly shaped Berger's later book (*Bach's Cycle, Mozart's Arrow*), although his examination of the narrative-lyric distinction does not appear in the book.
3. On Schlegel's conception of genres, see Daverio, *Nineteenth-Century Music and the German Romantic Ideology*, 3–4 and 24–34.
4. Daverio, *Nineteenth-Century Music and the German Romantic Ideology*, 3; the original is reprinted in Schlegel, *Charakteristiken und Kritiken I*, 188.
5. Berger's interpretive move ("Narrative and Lyric," 454–57) draws on Ricoeur, *Time and Narrative*, vol. 1, 32–45. According to Ricoeur, the aim of all narrative poetry, epic and dramatic alike, is the representation of action, or the *plot*—what Aristotle called *muthos*; the mode of representation, whether *diegetic* or *mimetic*, does not affect emplotment, and thus the modal distinction can be ignored in favor of a categorization that relies more strictly on content.
6. Berger, "Narrative and Lyric," 458. Berger also notes (459) that most narrative forms contain numerous nonimmediate and long-range relationships among phases of the narrative; the relationships of *causing* and *following from* are not restricted to immediately adjacent phases. See also endnote 21.
7. Berger, "Narrative and Lyric," 459.
8. Genette, *Narrative Discourse*, 33–34. Genette draws on Christian Metz, for whom a narrative is a "doubly temporal sequence" in which "there is the time of the thing told and the time of the telling (the time of the significate and the time of the signifier)"; "this duality ... invites us to consider that one of the functions of narrative is to invent one time scheme in terms of another time scheme." See Metz, *Film Language*, 18 (cited in Genette, ibid., 33).
9. Genette, *Narrative Discourse*, 33–35 ("Nous devons ... prendre au mot la quasi-fiction de *l'Erzählzeit*, ce faux temps qui vaut pour un vrai et que nous traiterons, avec ce que cela comporte à la fois de réserve et d'acquiescement comme un *pseudo*-temps"; see Genette, *Discours du récit*, 78). Genette takes *erzählzeit* and *erzählte Zeit* from Müller, "Erzählzeit und erzählte zeit (1948)."
10. Monelle, "The Temporal Image," 81. Monelle borrows the notion of "clock time" (while admitting its oversimplification) from Langer, *Philosophy in a New Key*.
11. Genette, *Narrative Discourse*, 85.
12. Ibid., 25–27 and 48–49.
13. What follows draws on ibid., 86–112.
14. Ibid., 86–95.
15. Genette, *Discours du récit*, 122.
16. What follows draws on Genette, *Narrative Discourse*, 33–85.
17. Ibid., 35–36; see also 48–67 (on analepses) and 67–79 (on prolepses).
18. Ibid., 83–84.
19. Ibid., 48. The concept is similar to what Byron Almén calls the "primary narrative level"; see Almén, *A Theory of Musical Narrative*, 163–64.
20. Hepokoski and Darcy, *Elements of Sonata Theory*. For an introduction to the Sonata Theory concepts and terminology invoked in this paragraph, see ibid., 9–22. For further discussion specifically of the sonata-as-narrative view latent in Sonata Theory, see esp. Monahan, "'Inescapable' Coherence and the Failure of the Novel-Symphony"; Monahan, "Success and Failure in Mahler's Sonata Recapitulations"; and Monahan, "'I Have Tried to Capture You ...': Rethinking the 'Alma' Theme from Mahler's Sixth Symphony."
21. Hepokoski and Darcy, "Monumentality and Formal Processes," 218. I will adopt throughout the book Hepokoski's term *module*, which is "a flexible term covering any of a number of small building-blocks within a work," ranging from the smallest formal units to "any slightly

larger unit without strong inner contrasts," or to what many would think of as a "phrase"; see Hepokoski and Darcy, *Elements of Sonata Theory*, 69n10.

22. Note that here Berger's ("Narrative and Lyric") view of narrative forms may be a bit too restrictive in that he focuses closely on rhetorical relationships defined by causality ("one event motivates another") at the expense of reactivity ("one event follows from another"). For a Sonata Theory view of *reactive modules* and their importance in sonata narratives, see Hepokoski, "Monumentality and Formal Processes," 230. I thank Professor Hepokoski for drawing my attention to the problem.

23. Booth, *The Rhetoric of Fiction*, 388.

24. Abbate, *Unsung Voices*, 230. See also Klein, "Chopin's Fourth Ballade as Musical Narrrative," 25–26 and 35–44; Karl, "The Temporal Life of the Musical Persona"; Karl, "Structuralism and Musical Plot"; and Monahan, "Action and Agency Revisited," esp. 365–66.

25. *Markedness* refers to the principle that the meaning of one term or sign in a binary opposition is weighted, or *marked*, with respect to the other (Hatten, *Musical Meaning in Beethoven*, esp. 34–63; Hatten, *Interpreting Musical Gestures, Topics, and Tropes*, esp. 11–16). *Rhetorical gestures* in music are "those highly marked musical events that direct our attention to some aspect of the ongoing musical discourse, perhaps dramatically redirecting our path through the form or genre" (Hatten, *Interpreting Musical Gestures, Topics, and Tropes*, 164).

As will be clear here, my interpretive approach also relies heavily on the concept of *stylistic* (or *generic*) *competence* in the interpretation of musical meaning (see Hatten, *Musical Meaning in Beethoven*, 10–11, 269–72, and 288, esp. the glossary entry "Competency") and on what has recently been called "deformation theory." Regarding the latter, I will use *deformation* in the sense in which it appears in the work of Hepokoski, who borrows the concept from reader-response theory and genre theory—in which "the normative thing that does not happen, or that is kept from happening (what the literary critic Wolfgang Iser called the 'minus functions' of a text) can be as important as what does occur" (Hepokoski, "Beethoven Reception," 447). *Deformation* thus refers to "the stretching of a normative procedure to its maximally expected limits or even beyond them—or the overriding of that norm altogether in order to produce a calculated expressive effect. . . . The expressive or narrative point lies in the tension between the limits of a competent listener's field of generic expectations and what is made to occur—or not occur—in actual sound at that moment" (Hepokoski and Darcy, *Elements of Sonata Theory*, 614–15). Closely related is the term *normative*, which is used here in the sense of *expected in context*: the context, or the norm, is established by "principles of pattern organization, the syntax of particular styles, and typical schemata," any of which may be actualized as specific musical events in a variety of ways (Meyer, *Explaining Music*, 14). Normative events derive from the "background constellation of standard or traditional options (norms)" in a *genre*, which itself "furnishes an ongoing horizon of expectations for the receiver. All genres (indeed, all familiar actions) involve systems of norms and guidelines, typical and expected procedures," which, in music, are "grounded in increments of elapsing time" (Hepokoski and Darcy, *Elements of Sonata Theory*, 614–21 [616]). Interpreting a musical event as normative should not be assumed to carry aesthetically charged undertones (see Hepokoski and Darcy, ibid., 615n9). Likewise, *deformation* does not connote aesthetic defectiveness, imperfection, ugliness, structural unattractiveness, or misguided compositional execution; it should be understood, rather, as a technical term that allows for the interpretation of a generic expectation and the expressive treatments thereof.

26. This interpretive approach overlaps somewhat with that of Hatten (*Musical Meaning in Beethoven*, 172–88; and "On Narrativity in Music"), who regards discontinuities such as those I am describing here as potentially producing shifts among separate voices or, more generally, as producing what he calls *shifts of level of discourse* (see endnote 30), which, in turn, he reads as musical evidence for forms of narrative commentary—including Schlegel's *Romantic irony*.

27. Hatten, *Interpreting Musical Gestures, Topics, and Tropes*, 54.

28. Daverio, *Nineteenth-Century Music and the German Romantic Ideology;* Dickensheets, "The Nineteenth-Century Sonata Cycle as Novel."

29. Kinderman, *Beethoven,* 240. For a discussion, see ibid., 239–42 and 270–73.

30. Abbate, *Unsung Voices.*

31. Hatten, *Musical Meaning in Beethoven,* 172–88. See also Hatten, "The Expressive Role of Disjunction"; and Hatten, "Expressive Doubling, Topics, Tropes, and Shifts in Level of Discourse."

32. Hatten, *Musical Meaning in Beethoven,* 202 ("disruptions"); Hatten, *Interpreting Musical Gestures, Topics, and Tropes,* 54 (on lyric subjectivity). For an interesting discussion of these same issues as applied to the interpretation of film, see Metz, *Film Language,* especially his distinction between cinematic *narration* (a communicative space marked by a temporal signifier and a temporal signified) and *description* (marked by a temporal signifier and an atemporal signified). According to Metz, intrusions of one type of space into the other are immediately evident to a competent viewer by virtue of the disjunctive force required to make the change: "Within the narrative, the descriptive passage immediately reveals itself: it is the only one in which the temporal concatenation of the signifiers . . . ceases to refer to the temporal relation (whether consecutive or not) among the corresponding significates, and the order it assigns to their signified elements is only one of spatial coexistence (that is to say, of relationships supposed to be constant whatever moment in time is chosen). From the narrative to the descriptive, we pass through a *change of intelligibility,* in the sense in which one speaks of a change of gears in automobiles" (ibid., 19–20, emphasis original).

33. Barthes, *S/Z.* Barthes identifies other codes in other of his writings, as in, for example, "Textual Analysis: Poe's Valdemar (1973)." For another musical consideration of the issues involved, see also McCreless, "Roland Barthes's S/Z from a Musical Point of View."

34. See the glossary definition of "heteroglossia" in Bakhtin, *The Dialogic Imagination: Four Essays,* 428.

35. Bakhtin, "Discourse in the Novel," in *The Dialogic Imagination,* 259–422.

36. In this regard, see also Michael Holquist's comments on Bakhtin's theory of the novel in his introduction to Bakhtin, *The Dialogic Imagination,* xv–xxxiii. Dickensheets draws the same connection in "The Nineteenth-Century Sonata Cycle as Novel," in which her approach to "novelistic analysis" also relies heavily on Bakhtin, dialogism, and heteroglossia.

37. What follows draws on Bakhtin, "Forms of Time and of the Chronotope in the Novel," in *The Dialogic Imagination,* 84–258 (the "Concluding Remarks," 243–58, are especially helpful).

38. Ibid., 84.

39. Ibid.

40. Ibid.

41. Genette's reference to the *Iliad,* mentioned above (endnote 11), is relevant here, in that it was aimed at pointing out that the use of anachronic structures is characteristic of the entire history of Western narratives, and that such structures date from the origins of the tradition itself.

42. Genette, *Narrative Discourse,* 36.

43. Berger, *Bach's Cycle, Mozart's Arrow,* 340 (293–352 for the full discussion).

PART II

STRUCTURAL AND RHETORICAL STRATEGIES IN MUSIC WITH AND WITHOUT TEXT

3 Music with Text: Two Slow Movements by Brahms

THE SLOW MOVEMENTS of Brahms's Piano Sonatas in C major, op. 1 and F♯ minor, op. 2 comprise text-based variations sets. In each, a poem motivates structure—stanzas of the poems correspond to variations in the music—and expression—each movement should be understood as Brahms's own reading of the associated poem—in what amounts to a song without words. This feature proves helpful in interpreting certain of these movements' structural and rhetorical devices, especially the most idiosyncratic among them: that is, the potential meanings of such features can be ascertained by considering their possible relationships to the underlying text. Such meanings can then inform interpretations of a broader range of repertoire: the strategies that appear in these text-based movements can be thought of as implying a similar range of meanings, even when the text is no longer present; the correlations that emerge can then be used to interpret other, non-text-based movements in Brahms's piano sonatas as well as sonatas of Chopin and Schumann—in which strikingly similar rhetorical strategies also appear.

§1. Brahms op. 1/ii

The C-minor Andante second movement of Brahms's Piano Sonata in C major, op. 1 comprises a twelve-bar theme, three variations, and a coda, as outlined in table 3.1. In it, Brahms "sets" the poem "Verstohlen geht der Mond auf" (table 3.2), one of the *Niederrheinisches Volkslieder* published—as a text plus a melody, the latter of which Brahms uses as the set's theme—in a two-volume collection (1838–40) edited by Anton Wilhelm Zuccalmaglio and August Kretzschmer.[1] The poem narrates the moon's secret rise into the night sky to observe a woman—apparently the narrator's beloved—through a small window in the Löwenburg castle. The poem comprises four quatrains, each with an abac rhyme scheme. Each stanza contains two lines (the first and third) that appear to comprise the main narrative and two more lines (the second and fourth) of a recurring choral refrain that comments cryptically on a "little blue flower" and one "most beautiful Rosa"; the poem thus immediately suggests the possibility of multiple voices in its narrative discourse. Its entire trajectory, furthermore, can be read as conveying the emotional journey of a narrator, where the moon is a signifier for that narrator's inner hopes, desires, and fears. The narrator searches for (or perhaps longs to search for, or wishes he could find a way to search for) his beloved; he questions whether he will ever find her; and he fears he will never find her (or perhaps he finds himself unable to summon the emotional

52 | Sonata Fragments

Table 3.1. Formal summary, Brahms, Piano Sonata in C Major, op. 1, ii.

measures:	1–12	13–26	27–56	57–72	73–85
musical form:	theme	variation 1	variation 2	variation 3	coda
text form:	stanza 1	stanza 2	stanza 3	stanza 4	(untexted)

Table 3.2. "Verstohlen geht der Mond auf." August Kretzschmer and Anton Wilhelm von Zuccalmaglio, *Deutsche Volkslieder mit ihren Original-Weisen*, 2 vols. (Berlin: Vereinsbuchhandlung, 1838, 1840), I:56–57. Translated by George Bozarth (1990, 344–78).

1	Verstohlen geht der Mond auf,	Stealthily the moon rises,
2	Blau, blau, Blümelein!	blue, blue little flower!
3	Durch Silberwölkchen führt sein Lauf;	Through silver clouds it makes its way;
4	Rosen im Thal, Mädel im Saal, o schönste Rosa!	Roses in the valley, maiden in the hall, o most beautiful Rosa!
5	Er steigt die blause Luft hindurch,	It climbs through the blue air,
6	Blau, blau, Blümelein!	blue, blue little flower!
7	Bis daß er schaut auf Löwenburg;	Until it looks down upon the Löwenburg;
8	Rosen im Thal, Mädel im Saal, o schönste Rosa!	Roses in the valley, maiden in the hall, o most beautiful Rosa!
9	O schaue Mond durchs Fensterlein,	O moon, look through the little window,
10	Blau, blau, Blümelein!	blue, blue little flower!
11	Schön' Trude lock' mit deinem Schein;	Entice beautiful Trude with your glow;
12	Rosen im Thal, Mädel im Saal, o schönste Rosa!	Roses in the valley, maiden in the hall, o most beautiful Rosa!
13	Und siehst du mich und siehst due sie,	And if you see me and if you see her,
14	Blau, blau, Blümelein!	blue, blue little flower!
15	Zwei treu're Herzen sahst du nie;	Two truer hearts have you never seen;
16	Rosen im Thal, Mädel im Saal, o schönste Rosa!	Roses in the valley, maiden in the hall, o most beautiful Rosa!

strength to even begin looking for her). Over the course of the poem—over the course of the moon's journey—the narrator gradually loses his objectivity and detachment and becomes more and more emotionally involved in the narration, finally (in stanza 4) bursting forth with a love song to a woman whose presence or availability the poem never directly confirms.[2]

The narrative's organization can be productively examined using aspects of Genette's narratology. Some of the most notable structural features of the poem are two sudden and striking shifts in the way its content is delivered. One of these occurs at the start of the third stanza, the other at the start of the fourth. At stanza 3 the shift occurs in the dimension Genette calls the *voice* (*voix*): the identity of the source of the narrative enunciation ("who is speaking?").[3] That is, there is no evidence that suggests that the poem's first two stanzas are not delivered by an omnipotent narrator (the third-person omniscient) who remains outside the story and detached from it, and whose purpose is to describe the moonrise and to set the scene for the emotional outburst that follows ("Verstohlen geht der Mond auf" ["Stealthily the moon rises"], "Durch Silberwölkchen führt sein Lauf" ["Through silver clouds it makes its way"], etc.). But at stanza 3, the poem immediately and unexpectedly reveals the explicit presence of a specific lyric subject or voice, divulging, as it were, a previously unseen persona within the tale who no longer has the will to remain hidden and silent. This revealed agent dives into the ongoing story in order to speak to—or issue orders to—the moon: "O schaue Mond durchs Fensterlein" ("O moon, look through the little window"), "Schön' Trude lock' mit deinem Schein" ("Entice beautiful Trude with your glow").[4]

At stanza 4, the shift occurs in the dimension Genette calls the *mood* (*mode*): the "modality of narrative 'representation,'" the point of view "from which the life or the action is looked at," or the point of view through which the narrative perspective is focalized or filtered ("who is seeing?").[5] That is, the narrator shifts from addressing the moon directly to hypothesizing on—or dreaming of—what the moon might see if the narrator's own desires were to be fulfilled: "siehst du mich und siehst due sie" ("if you see me and if you see her"), "Zwei treu're Herzen sahst du nie" ("Two truer hearts have you never seen"). This is an emotional outpouring—focalized through the moon's point of view, not the narrator's own—in which the lyric subject seems to be no longer able to contain himself, turning his concerns away from the moon's activities per se and toward the longed-for union with his beloved.[6]

Brahms's musical setting beautifully captures the emotional journey suggested in the poem, and it introduces rhetorical features that conspicuously betray an aesthetic rooted in Romanticism—especially in the ways it creates a sense of fragmentation, rather than a sense of coherence, in the movement's temporal space.[7] Brahms's theme, shown in table 3.1 and adopted, as mentioned, from the Zuccalmaglio and Kretzschmer collection, correlates with stanza 1 in the poem, and (as shown in the example) it appears in the score complete with the (nonsung) text directly underneath, leaving no question about how the words correspond to the music. The theme immediately exploits the opposition found in each poetic stanza between the two lines of narrative and the two lines of choral refrain: in the music, a bleak, monophonic statement in mm. 1–2 contrasts markedly with an accompanied, homophonic refrain in mm. 3–4. Brahms may have read the refrain itself as foretelling doom (thus linking the beloved herself with doom?) in that every time it occurs, it closes with a dark, foreboding perfect authentic cadence in the tonic C minor. In any case, he seems to have been particularly interested in it, using it as he did to convert the idiosyncratic form of the original poem, as it appears in the Zuccalmaglio and Kretzschmer collection and as shown in table 3.2, into a tidier AAB *Barform* (*Stollen, Stollen, Abgesang*) by adding an additional statement of "Blau, blau, Blümenlein!" that does not appear in the original text (see mm. 7–8).[8] Thus in Brahms's rendering, the theme comprises three modules of four bars each: a *Stollen* in mm. 1–4, another *Stollen* in 5–8, and an *Abgesang* in 9–12, where each module rocks between tonic and dominant before ending with a perfect authentic cadence. Each four-bar module in turn comprises two two-bar submodules, and the entire theme responds comfortably to the modular description 1a–1b, 2a–2b, 3a–3b. The theme's monophonic opening, its minor mode, its bare tonic-dominant oscillations, and its overall harmonic simplicity (especially in its first four bars) all suggest a desolate, forsaken scene that we can interpret as imbued with depression and misfortune. The suitability of such an interpretation stems at least partly from an intertextual relationship with Schubert's bleak "Der Leiermann," from *Winterreise* (1827), shown in example 3.2. Brahms's setting resembles Schubert's in at least three ways: in its composing out of an elaborated, minor-mode $\hat{1}$–$\hat{2}$–$\hat{3}$ ascent—or, in perhaps an even closer resemblance, its $\hat{1}$–$\hat{2}$–$\hat{3}$–$\hat{1}$–$\hat{7}$–$\hat{1}$–$\hat{2}$ contour in mm. 2–3, complete with a variant of Brahms's pickup $\hat{5}$ at the voice's entry in m. 9; in its bare, single-voice melody (supported in the Schubert only by the organ-grinder's open fifths); and in its simplified tonic-dominant oscillation that strips away any sense of normative harmonic motion and leaves an austere, persistent stasis in its place.

Some of the most important musical features of Brahms's setting are his responses to the shifts of voice and mood at, respectively, the beginnings of stanzas 3 and 4. Stanza 3 in the poem corresponds to variation 2 in the music, which opens at m. 27: here, Brahms introduces a countermelody in the right hand in the

Example 3.1. Brahms, Piano Sonata in C major, op. 1, ii, theme (mm. 1–12; text present in the original).

Example 3.2. Schubert, "Der Leiermann" (*Winterreise* no. 24).

form of exquisite descending triplet sixteenths on top of the main theme, which continues to sound in the bass voice. The countermelody appears to be a signifier, either *indexical* or *iconic*, for the moon, in that it may bear a loose musical resemblance to a moon high in the sky (the countermelody is positioned in the song's highest register) looking down (the countermelody descends), perhaps into the window of an ancient castle (which the countermelody seems to suggest is a very old castle, or even an ancient ruin: the line has an antiquated, Baroque flavor that results from its use of mordent figures and its generally Bachian melodic profile).[9] Thus, this moment in the musical setting appears to signify a split: what had been a single voice, the theme, becomes two voices, the theme (which we can correlate with the lyric subject) plus the countermelody (which we can correlate with another presence—another character within the story, namely the moon—to whom the lyric subject speaks). Thus, the musical setting reflects stanza 3's shift of voice and the sudden revelation of separate personas in the narrative. We might even go as far as to say that Brahms has made an additional interpretive move in using the music of the movement's main theme to represent the lyric subject himself: while this may seem like an obvious choice, it is not a necessary one, and it directly links the voice of the lyric subject who emerges in variation 2 (stanza 3) with the voice of the third-person omniscient narrator heard earlier, in the theme and first variation (stanzas 1 and 2). This invites an interpretation in which the poem's first two stanzas are spoken by an agent whom we may have assumed strode onto the stage only at the beginning of the third stanza: the protagonist—the narrated lyric subject—is the very same persona who we heard describing the initial rising of the moon. Maybe this even helps clarify the meaning of the text's enigmatic choral refrain: if the opening monophonic module correlates with the voice of the narrator (*forte*), the refrain (*piano*) may correlate not so much with a "chorus" literally but with a revelation of the narrator's inner desires—what he would see if he held up a mirror to his mind, so to speak. Such an interpretation might imply, in turn, that the images of the "blue flower" and the "most beautiful Rosa" are linked to the beloved herself.

The linkage in the music between the voice of the lyric subject who appears in stanza 3 and the narrative voice heard at the poem's opening helps explain some of the musical gestures that appear prior to the start of variation 3. For example, the Beethovenian "fate" motive—triplets (here sixteenths) that suggest the opening motive from the Fifth Symphony—introduced at the pickup to m. 13 (corresponding to the word "Er" in "Er steigt die blause Luft hindurch"—"It climbs through the blue air") may signify the narrator-protagonist's fear of his own fate (via the Beethoven intertext) or a related fear of impending tragedy (via the figure's reference to a tragic expressive topic); the motive may also signify (as an iconic sign) the narrator's own heartbeat, pulsating with anxiety over what the moon might find when it reaches its destination. Will the beloved be located? Will the lovers be united?[10] The "moon" countermelody's use at m. 27 of versions of these same triplet sixteenths might thus link the moon with the narrator's heartbeat, perhaps indicating that the moon itself has become the objectified representation of the narrator's hopes and fears. This invites a reading in which it is the narrator himself who desires the vantage point high in the night sky from where he might catch a glimpse of his beloved, even though he chooses to couch the story in terms of a moon on a journey to find a woman. By the same token, the recurring, piquant cadential dissonances introduced for the first time at m. 16, at the end stanza 2 line 2, "Blau, blau, Blümenlein!" (see also m. 25), probably signify the narrator's inner anxiety about what the moon may find, or, generally, his anxiety over whether or not what he desires is really attainable. The music indicates that his anxiety at these moments is intense enough to be at least partially debilitating: each time they appear, the dissonances trigger the addition of one full measure to the variations structure and thus seem to momentarily block the music from continuing. (A more structural reading might view these additional measures as composed-out versions of the fermatas present at the parallel moments in the original theme, at mm. 4 and 12.)

At the pickup to m. 18, the sound of the heartbeat is immediately intensified, sounding now in octaves and with portamento markings; the motive sounds like it has been enlarged or expanded spatially, and it sounds like it may be trying to gradually overtake the theme. These gestures seem to foreshadow the movement's first major surprise: the ascending arpeggiation in the bass in m. 19, which overrides the ascending stepwise motion present at this location in the original theme (compare m. 19 with m. 6). The initial B-D motion at m. 19 b. 1, moreover, invites a listener to expect an arpeggiated G-major triad, probably with an upward leap onto G at b. 2. But this expectation is brusquely rejected when the arpeggiation instead overshoots the G and lands on a *sforzando* A♭ instead. The text reveals the expressive motivation: this A♭ occurs at the moment in the poem in which the moon has finally climbed high enough to get a glimpse of the Löwenburg castle (in which the

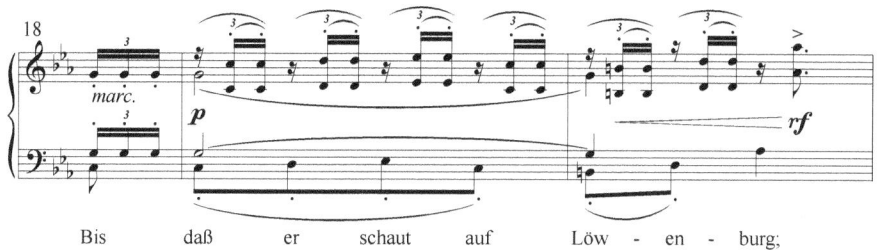

Example 3.3. "Bis daß er schaut auf Löwenburg" (Brahms, op. 1/ii, mm. 18–19; text added).

beloved presumably resides), corresponding precisely, as shown in example 3.3, to the last syllable—"burg"—of "Löwenburg." The narrator's heart has skipped a beat, in response to the moon's having found what it was looking for after its "stealthy" climb, or perhaps in response to a sudden pang of anxiety about what might, or might not, be discovered. This moment of shock is then followed by an extended, composed-out moment of disturbance captured musically in the precadential chromatic deflection in mm. 20–21, to Brahms's preferred key area for such disturbances: the Neapolitan (in this case D♭ major), or, more broadly, a ♭VI–♭II–♯IV/♭V complex.[11] The end of the first variation (modules 3ᵃ and 3ᵇ) soon follows but not before more heartbeat triplets (m. 23, this time preceded on the last eighth of m. 22 by an expressive, syncopated, accented G in the right hand—a gasp for air, perhaps, as the narrator attempts to recover from the shock), another leap to the "Löwenburg" A♭ (last eighth of m. 23), and a striking reversal of this A♭'s normative descending resolution to, instead, an ascending half-step resolution onto A♮ (signifying a striving, or a yearning, for something that may ultimately be out of reach).

Variation 2 (stanza 3 in the poem) ensues. This variation is of central interest with regard to the aesthetics of fragmentation and atemporality. Consider its very first module, module 1ᵃ, shown in example 3.4. The module opens, as mentioned, at m. 27, with the theme in the bass and a countermelody in the upper voice. In m. 28, the theme realizes the upward arpeggiation onto G that had been suggested earlier, in m. 19, but then denied by the startling leap to A♭; the narrating agent has apparently recovered from his shock. But m. 29 introduces a surprise: here, instead of continuing as expected directly on to module 2ᵃ, Brahms instead deploys a varied repetition of m. 28, up a fifth. Module 2ᵃ then begins in m. 30. Measure 29 thus has no direct correspondence with the text: line 9, "O schaue Mond durchs Fensterlein," occupies mm. 27–28, while line 10, the "Blau, Blau, Blümelein" refrain, begins at m. 30. In purely technical, syntactic terms, one might say that m. 29 constitutes a typically Brahmsian form of motivic expansion—one that is not entirely unexpected, of course, here in the middle of a variations form. But the fact that this is the first time in the movement in which the musical setting deviates from poetic text suggests that the gesture is a rhetorical one, and that it holds far more expressive significance. That is, within the definitions of atemporality outlined in

58 | Sonata Fragments

chapter 2, m. 29 can be understood as signifying a shift outside the movement's first narrative proper—its temporal stream—and into an alternative, atemporal stream. Such an interpretation is made possible in part by the text-music correlation (or lack thereof), where in this context, music corresponding directly to the text can be mapped onto the first narrative or temporal stream, while music with no direct textual correspondence can be mapped onto an atemporal stream outside the first narrative. The specific type of atemporality invoked at m. 29, furthermore, is that which is concerned with duration: this is because m. 29 implies not so much a deviation away from the content of the ongoing variation-in-progress (this music is clearly related to that which immediately precedes it) but rather an elongation of that variation—a stretching of its length by one full measure relative to the length of the underlying, twelve-bar prototype.[12] It thus produces a deceleration, in the sense that the variation begins to proceed more slowly, or last longer, than one would have expected, given the internal structural precedents established within the movement's first narrative. I will call this event a *durational atemporality*: in terms of narratology, a durational atemporality in music is analogous to what Genette calls an anisochrony, which involves a change in the speed of the narrative rhythm relative to its referential or zero-reference-point pace—which in this case can be established by referring to the length of the original theme (twelve bars) and the structural rhythms therein (the succession of six two-bar modules).

As in literary anisochronies, the musical analog has the effect of revealing aspects of the narrative structure or narrative discourse. It produces one of Hatten's discursive shifts, in which we move from experiencing the story directly, focalized mimetically through characters and their actions, to experiencing it indirectly, focalized diegetically through the eyes of an external narrating agent (Abbate's "narrating survivor"). The shift makes explicit the fact that what we are reading, or what we are hearing, is a tale that is being told to us rather than a reality in which we are direct participants or to which we are direct witnesses; this is a *novel*, not a dramatic play or an epic poem. In this specific sense, the atemporality

Example 3.4. Brahms, Piano Sonata in C major, op. 1, ii, mm. 25–33.

is directly related to what makes this music *Romantic*: it fragments the first narrative, in this case pulling it apart by slowing it down; and it musically manifests the characteristic sense of interiority found in many Romantic literary narratives. The latter is specifically that turning inward toward the deepest reaches of the imagination or consciousness—in this instance, the consciousness of a narrating agent whom we might even wish to equate with the implied author. We can link the durational atemporality with interiority because it shifts the narrative's pace so as to make that pace correspond not so much to the speed of the events within the story (in the sense of the speed at which those events might unfold in their own story-time world) but rather to the speed at which the narrating agent thinks about or perceives those events. The narrator slows down the story, perhaps adding additional details or commentarial asides, perhaps dwelling on the content a bit longer—thinking about, reflecting on, or questioning (maybe self-critically) what is occurring.[13] Perhaps we can hear in the narrator's voice a reminiscent "if only" sentiment, or maybe we can hear (especially here, given the brooding, minor-mode theme) fear, trepidation, or a reluctance to continue telling the story. In any case, as readers, we begin to move in temporal tandem not with the story itself but rather with the inner workings of the narrator's own mind. We begin to move within the temporal world of the narrator's psychological time, so to speak, instead of within the fictional time world constructed within the story itself. In this case as in many others, the temporal shift can be understood as motivated internally—as foreshadowed by or even caused by certain immanent structural and rhetorical features of the narrative as manifested in music and text. These include the building of anxiety audible in the heartbeat motives (occurring first in m. 12, spatially expanded in m. 18), the pang of anxiety at the sighting of the Löwenburg (the $A\flat$ in m. 19), and the very revelation in the text itself (in the shift of voice at stanza 3 and the concomitant introduction of a countermelody in the music) of a narrating agent and the revelation of a diegetic voice.

Note that durational atemporality in music, as with anisochronies in literature, has nothing necessarily to do with measurements of absolute ("clock") time. The concern is with *temporality*, defined, as mentioned, as *time signified*. Interpreting signified time requires attending to structure and syntax, not measuring absolute time values. In terms of music specifically, this means that even though the absolute number of seconds occupied by a theme or any other formal unit in a given piece of music will obviously vary from one performer to the next, and from performance to performance by the same musician or ensemble, the temporal significance of certain structural and rhetorical events in the music can remain unchanged. This is because the implied composer essentially writes the durational atemporality into the structure of the music. Thus, an event such as Brahms's m. 29, which lengthens a variation by one full measure, can have a consistent temporal meaning regardless of the literal, real-time speed at which that measure or the music around it may be executed in any given performance. Even if a pianist should choose to accelerate through mm. 27–29 in order to play these three measures in the same amount of absolute time as was required to play the parallel mm. 1–2 (or mm. 13–14), m. 29 will still produce a durational atemporality in the sense in which I have explained it here, precisely because the temporal meaning of that measure can be measured by the *implied reader* (or the *implied listener*) in relative structural terms: "what was once two measures is now three measures."[14]

Note also three additional, related points. First, because durational atemporality as I have defined it is a feature of the narrative discourse and not of the narrated story, and because it involves time signified rather than time per se, it follows that the absolute amount of time that passes within a story (even in cases in which that time may be measurable) is not relevant for interpreting that story's signified temporal streams. In the Brahms movement, for example, an implied listener need not be able to measure the amount of time it takes (in stanzas 1 and 2) for the moon to ascend to its position in the sky, or measure the amount of time it takes (stanzas 3 and 4) for the narrator to speak to the moon, in order to interpret (or even experience) the deceleration signified by the durational atemporality in m. 29. The anisochronous effect is an immanent feature of the musical structure, no matter what absolute time values might be embedded within the story. Second, a purely *isochronous* (*isochrone*) narrative—a narrative with no anisochronies, or a piece of music with no durational atemporality—probably does not exist in practice: just as any literary narrative will almost constantly vary the *speed* (*vitesse*) at which it tells its tale,[15] the pace of any musical narrative will likewise vary across the entire musical structure. In music, some of the most common and familiar formal or harmonic strategies may be understood in some sense as contributing to the kinds of temporal layering I have in mind here: these include evaded cadences; phrase expansions; varied restatements or elaborated repetitions of motives or whole formal modules; or elisions, ellipses, or other omissions of expected gestures, whether formal, harmonic, or otherwise. And third, because durational atemporality is an immanent feature of the musical structure, it does not necessarily require the presence of a parallel text such as a poem or a program. Even though a movement (like the slow movement of Brahms's op. 1) that does include such a parallel text might signify certain of its expressive meanings by correlating certain rhetorical gestures in the music with certain features of the text, even music without such textual support can still find ways of signifying the same temporal effects. These might include internal references to its own structural properties, dialogues with the constellation of norms and expectations within a given style or genre, or intertextual allusions and any of the associated arrays of meanings they produce.

Continuing now with the Brahms, observe that the atemporal disruption at m. 29 continues to exert its influence on the next several modules in variation 2. For example, at m. 30 module 1^b (corresponding, as mentioned, to line 10 in the poem) opens in the subtonic B♭ major instead of the tonic C minor as before. This surprising tonal deflection probably connotes a meaning similar to that of the earlier deflection toward the Neapolitan, in mm. 20–21: a psychological disturbance for the narrating agent—a pulling of the narrator further away from reality (further from the tonic) as he anxiously ponders the possibility of either finding (in which case the disturbance may connote a positively inflected mysticism) or not finding (in which case it may suggest an anxiety-induced state of apprehension) his beloved. This problematized move to B♭ major may be the motivation for the suppression of the expected cadence in m. 31 (compare the i:PAC at m. 4 in the original theme, or at m. 16 in variation 1) and for the anisochronous deceleration that results from it: what had been a two-bar module earlier in the movement now becomes a four-bar module occupying mm. 30–33, where these four bars embed within them a miniature antecedent-consequent relationship (aiming at the minor dominant, G minor, in m. 31 and the tonic, C minor, in m. 33). We thus remain in the temporal world of the narrator's psychological time. Modules 2ª (mm. 35–37) and 2ᵇ (mm. 38–41) proceed in exactly the same fashion, although now the narrator speaks even more emphatically: the narrator and the moon now trade registral positions, with the narrator's music (the main theme) moving to the right hand to become higher and more assertive. Module 3ª appears as expected ("on schedule," so to speak) in m. 42 and the referential narrative rhythm (Genette's "zero reference point") resumes anew, even as a striking new tonal profile quickly emerges: the leading tone B♮ expected on the second eighth of m. 42 becomes a surprising B♭ instead, the D expected at m. 42 b. 2 becomes a D♭ (which then becomes, in the next bar, an E♭: see m. 43 b. 2), and the entire module deflects again toward the Neapolitan (with the A♭ major in mm. 42–44 functioning as dominant of the Neapolitan D♭, which appears at m. 44 b. 2). Again the psychological pull of the narrator's beloved exerts its force. Note especially the reaching upward—the hoping for, or striving higher toward, something that may well be unattainable—signified in another nonnormative Neapolitan resolution, this time the ascending D♭-D♮ motion in the inner voice at m. 44 b. 2.

In this context, m. 46 is especially surprising: as shown in example 3.5, instead of moving on to variation 3 following the i:PAC at the end of m. 45 (which should have been the end of variation 2), Brahms instead reopens module 3ª, as if to indicate that something may have been left undone in the previous four bars. This is a form of repetition that can be understood as a larger version of those heard earlier in the variation (mm. 29 and 37, for example), and the same anisochronous effect accrues. The narrative rhythm decelerates via the lengthening of an anticipated structural unit—in this case, the whole variation itself becomes longer—and the narrative discourse again shifts into the atemporal stream of the narrator's interior consciousness. The repetition can also be understood, furthermore, in terms of a related procedure that I will refer to as "resetting the musical clock," which is a specific type of durational atemporality that involves backing up or reverting to an earlier point in the form and subsequently passing through music, or through a part of the musical narrative, that has already been heard once before. The procedure is one that allows the implied composer to rethink, reimagine, or somehow recompose musical events already witnessed, perhaps in order to view those events from a new angle or perhaps in order to propose a solution to a previously unsolved problem (or to propose a new solution to a problem we thought had already been solved satisfactorily). This is an important strategy in Romantic music in general, and many of the idiosyncratic structural features of the Romantic sonata literature may be thought of in these terms. As with other forms of musical atemporality, it has the effect of foregrounding the *erzählte Zeit-Erzählzeit* duality—the independence of story time and narrative time—and, as such, produces a shift in level of discourse and reveals aspects of the narrative discourse, conceived as separate from the structure of the narrated story itself. Use of the strategy can be traced back to the Classical sonata, and especially to the treatment of the genre by Mozart—who, as Hepokoski and Darcy have observed, seems to have been fond of these kinds of effects as a means of lengthening certain formal modules in his sonatas and delaying certain expressively charged moments of anticipated structural closure.[16]

Example 3.5. Brahms, Piano Sonata in C major, op. 1, ii, mm. 41–58.

What follows, moreover, is no simple varied repetition of module 3. Rather, striking discontinuities appear in several musical parameters simultaneously at both mm. 47 and 51. Following a thirty-second-note gap at the end of the first beat in both measures—expressively charged moments of silence that literally set off what comes next from what had been happening before—are a series of thirty-second-note flourishes that involve sudden and conspicuous shifts in multiple parameters, including meter (in each instance, three bars of $^{3}_{16\sharp}$ essentially extend, by four and a half eighth notes, the second quarter notes from mm. 46 and 50), dynamic level (what had been *piano* becomes *pianissimo*, as if trailing away in the distance), register (the lowest pitch in each of the flourishes is three octaves higher than the bass notes that immediately precede them, on the downbeats of mm. 47 and 51), and articulation (both flourishes are marked *molto leggiero*, as if they should be made to float ethereally above the space in which the main movement unfolds). The extremity of these gestures and of the discontinuities they introduce into the formal structure can be said to produce ruptures in the musical fabric, where each rupture has the effect of opening up a fracture, or a fissure, into which can be inserted a parenthetical interpolation. Each interpolation interrupts the movement, seemingly suspending its flow in midstream; the effect is what Kinderman describes as the "enclosing" of "one time within another."[17] The form proper continues to unfold around the interpolations as if they did not exist: m. 50 (second bar of module 3ª) continues from where the first beat of m. 47 left off, before the thirty-second note rest; m. 54 (module 3ᵇ) continues in the same fashion from the first beat of m. 51; and the entirety of mm. 46–55—eight notated measures—constitutes a fragmented, exploded form of what was originally, or what "might have been,"[18] a four-bar formal module (mm. 46-55 = modules 3ª + 3ᵇ, = mm. 42–45, = mm. 9–12). The original four-bar prototype could easily be reconstructed simply by deleting the interpolated material and stitching back together the music left behind. And, in addition to the ruptures, a number of other features of the interpolated music itself underscore that this is material that remains separate and independent from the music around it: this music moves according to its own tonal logic, with the thirty-second-note flourishes composing out IV6–V$^{4}_{3}$ motion in the distant keys of A♭ major (mm. 47–49) and B♭ major (mm. 51–53); both suggest a tonic but never reveal it explicitly (signifying, perhaps, an implied point of arrival that lurks beneath the surface but never materializes); and both feature a harmonic oscillation that creates a sense of musical stasis—a vertiginous sense of tonal nonprogression that replaces the audible teleology and repetitive cadential motion characteristic of much of the rest of the movement.[19]

The interpolations thus can be heard as suppressing an ongoing, normative, forward-vectored trajectory in favor of a distanced, composed-out moment of signified musical time (even while absolute musical time obviously continues to progress in a "forward" direction). The fact that these interpolations are untexted, with no obvious correspondence in the poem, again invites the correlation of texted music with *temporality* and untexted music with *atemporality*. The interpolations are thus *atemporal*, or outside the first narrative. The situation is musically analogous to that in literature in which a measurable duration in the narrative time, delivered exclusively in the diegetic voice of the narrator, corresponds to no duration (a zero duration) in mimetic story time. Genette defines such an event as a *pause* (*pause*), which can take many different forms: descriptive commentaries, reflections, memory-triggered analepses, and so forth.[20] This example also demonstrates the complexity possible within the multilayered, hierarchical temporal world of a Romantic sonata movement: here, m. 46, as mentioned, is already outside the first narrative and thus, in one sense, atemporal in its own right; mm. 47–49 and 51–53 thus comprise digressions within a digression—atemporal interpolations with respect to a local-level first narrative (itself comprising mm. 46–47 b. 1, mm. 50–51 b. 1, and mm. 54–55) which, in turn, is atemporal with respect to the larger first narrative of the variations movement as a whole. Thinking in terms of the precise relationship of the interpolations to the local first narrative that they function to interrupt, the specific form of atemporality here one concerning order, rather than duration: the interpolated music can be regarded as "out of order," or generally "out of place," with regard to its temporal position. The music is interruptive, and it seems not to belong in the location in which it has been placed. I will call this a *ruptured atemporality*, so named because the shift in level of discourse it signifies is almost always cued (as it is here) by severe discontinuities or ruptures on the acoustic surface of the music. In terms of narratology, a ruptured atemporality is a musical analog for what Genette would call either an anachrony or, more generally, an achrony: the interpolated music belongs, in a sense, "somewhere else," whether that location is earlier or later than the actual location in which it appears. If the music seems to occur too early (maybe it foreshadows events that will occur in a more complete form later on), then we have a musical analog for a prolepsis; if it seems too late (maybe it looks back on events we have already heard), we have a musical analog for an analepsis. More often, especially in the abstract world of musical-narrative discourse, it may be impossible to determine the precise temporal relationship between the interpolated music and the music around it; this will be especially true in situations (such as this one) in which the interpolation appears to be almost completely unrelated to any of the music in the rest of the movement. In these cases, we have a musical analog for an achrony. In any event, regardless of how one chooses to define it specifically, a ruptured atemporality, like a durational atemporality, produces a discursive shift that has the effect of focalizing the narrative diegetically, through the eyes of a narrating agent. As such, it belongs not to the structure of the narrated story but to the structure of the narrative discourse, and (in that it musically represents the narrator's own point of view) it can also be understood as musically manifesting a kind of interiority—another signified turning inward toward the narrator's inner consciousness.

Brahms continues, as mentioned, by resuming module 3ᵃ at m. 54. This is a striking moment: one might have expected m. 54 to look like m. 44 (module 3ᵇ), but it does not, and the difference is loaded with expressive implications. Measure 54 reiterates material originally sounded in mm. 32–33 and 40–41, the last halves of the two anisochronous, four-bar versions of modules 1^b and 2^b. Thus, we have a musical statement of the poem's "Blau, blau, Blümenlein!" replacing what should have been a statement of "o schönste Rosa!," and the recomposition can be understood as another of Brahms's own interpretations of the poem's meaning: it confirms the direct connection between the "little blue flower" and the "most beautiful Rosa," where both are almost certainly references to the beloved herself. In the wake of this confirmation—as if all is now clear—variation 3 (stanza 4 in the poem) opens at m. 57 as a beautifully realized musical vision of a modally brightened, C-major paradise—a musical vision, perhaps, of the longed-for-yet-unattainable Arcadian paradise of the Romantic pastoral narrative. Here C minor–C major maps onto an expressive opposition of real-world–dream-world, thus capturing in the music the shift of mood present at this point in the poem: the narrator's emotions burst forth in an exalted, *forte*, major-mode love song, with the upper-register countermelody (*con grand' espressione*) now dominating the texture to such an extent that for some listeners, this may not even sound like a variation at all, even though a version of the main theme continues to sound in the lower voice to anchor the narrator in reality. This last variation also comprises a move back onto the first narrative: the anisochronies disappear and the referential narrative rhythm resumes in that the pace at which the musical structure proceeds now corresponds once again to the pace of the movement's original theme. The effect is powerful, and when considered in light of the entire movement's narrative discourse, it goes much of the way toward explaining the potent expressivity of this exceptionally moving variation: that is, the movement as a whole comprises a trajectory in which its theme establishes the referential narrative rhythm; the narrative maintains that rhythm through variation 1, even as the narrator begins to show signs of losing his emotional detachment; the narrative rhythm then decelerates and eventually stops altogether in the protracted variation 2, in which the narrator becomes so emotionally involved in the story that his voice can no longer be hidden from view; and the narrative rhythm then resumes in variation 3, where the effect is that of the narrator—having dealt with whatever personal, interior emotional crisis might have occurred—diving headlong back into the story and proceeding at the original pace. The last variation may thus be read as an apotheosis of the narrator-as-protagonist—his final attempt to move on, his last attempt to leave behind once and for all the fears and anxieties provoked by his telling of the tale.[21]

The movement's ending is striking, and it contains one more shift into an atemporal stream. Variation 3 continues to exhibit expressively charged disturbances: the Neapolitan continues to exert its pull in mm. 63–64, where a flat-side tilt suppresses the cadence expected in m. 64 (= m. 8, the end of module 2^b) and sets up the onset of module 3 (m. 65, with its return to C major) with an augmented-sixth chord over an A♭ in the bass. Measure 68 likewise suppresses another expected PAC (compare m. 12, the end of module 3^{b}) in favor of a noncadential move back to the tonic C minor. This series of undercut cadences conspicuously implies a spirit of nonclosure that dominates this part of the narrative to the extent that it can be correlated with a large, composed-out expressive gesture of denial: the music thus reveals—as the poem does not—that the beloved will never be found and the hoped-for union never achieved.

Then, it seems for a brief moment at the end of m. 68 that we might hear, at m. 69, not module 3^{b} as expected but instead a reiteration (again) of the anisochronous expansions in mm. 30–33 and 38–41. But instead we are confronted, in mm. 69–71, with new music—Caplin's *expanded cadential progression*—that foregrounds the heartbeat triplet sixteenths.[22] In that this music overwrites music that we expect in its place, it can be correlated with one final discursive shift into the atemporal stream of the narrator's consciousness: a three-bar module replaces what should have been a two-bar module, thus creating one final anisochronous durational atemporality—perhaps in order to stage a recovery operation in the wake of the missed cadential opportunity in the middle of m. 68. The music slows markedly (via *rubato* in m. 69, a *rit. e pesante* in m. 70, and a *molto rit.* in m. 71) as it deliberately tracks through predominant-functioning harmony toward what surely must be the movement's structural dominant, in m. 71—arriving, *forte*, at a cadential 6/4 chord on the downbeat of that measure. But the cadence that is so firmly and decisively forecasted by this gesture fails to materialize, as a result of the most flagrant gesture of denial thus far: m. 72, far from being unambiguously cadential, must be regarded as equivocal at best, if not an outright, staged cadential *failure*.[23] This particular failure involves a typical Brahmsian undercutting strategy in which some of the key voices are deleted from the texture—in this case, all the voices except the lowest—at the moment of the expected cadence. The result is that even though a resolution in the melody onto $\hat{1}$ might be implied at m. 72, that resolution is not present: it has been forcibly denied, suppressed in a final gesture that confirms the impossibility of the narrator's quest. There will be no beloved; she is unavailable, or she is absent altogether. Perhaps she never even existed to begin with. Perhaps the whole story was but a dream of the narrator, who simply imagined someone (or something—the moon) making a quest in his place—a quest that he himself never acquired the emotional tenacity or fortitude to undertake on his own.

A coda—untexted and thus atemporal again, existing entirely in the narrator's imagination—opens at m. 73 with a variation on the head-motive from the main theme in the left hand. The coda comprises one long, plagal extension of the noncadence at m. 72—a cathartic gesture of peaceful resignation in which the narrator accepts the unreality of what has transpired. A structural descent through the C-major scale occurs in interwoven contrapuntal lines that are offset from one another rather than in strict rhythmic unison, signifying that any "uniting of hearts" that may be present here is at best a hazy image in an ill-formed dream, if not simply an impossibility that will never be achieved, no matter how much infinite longing there may be.[24]

§2. Brahms op. 2/ii

The Andante (second) movement of Brahms's Piano Sonata in F♯ minor, op. 2 provides another opportunity to consider some of the most characteristic structural, expressive, and rhetorical strategies in Romantic musical narratives. Again, the variations format and the presence of the text both aid the task of interpretation. In fact, numerous features of this movement's music and text are remarkably similar to features of the op. 1 slow movement, which Brahms had composed only about half a year earlier; the similarities are so striking that we may well be able to surmise that Brahms must surely have noticed the parallel features of the two poems, and must have sought to provide similar musical responses to them. The text in op. 2 is the *Minnelied* "Mir ist leide," by the thirteenth-century Swiss poet Kraft von Toggenburg.[25] As shown in table 3.3, it includes three stanzas rather than the four of op. 1's "Verstohlen geht der Mond auf"; each stanza in "Mir ist leide" comprises two quatrains plus a sestet (similar to the organization of a fourteen-line sonnet), with an aaab cccb deeeed rhyme scheme. "Mir ist leide" exhibits similarities with "Verstohlen geht" in terms of content and—even with one less stanza—structure: it features a bleak tale concerned with a narrator's anxiety over a lost (or at least an unavailable or inaccessible) woman, who in this case is identified specifically in the poem as a "noble lady" of "very high station"; and, while it lacks the shift of voice that occurs midway through "Verstohlen geht" (it openly declares the presence of a narrating agent in the very first line: "Mir ist leide"—"It is painful to me"), it does feature more than one shift of mood, including one in its final stanza (at line 29), in which the narrator turns away from the anxieties of the first two stanzas and toward a much more positively inflected love song. Its last stanza is thus an emotional outpouring parallel to the outpouring in the final (fourth) stanza of "Verstohlen geht," and both are similarly focalized not through the narrator but through another character in the tale: the moon in op. 1, the beloved herself here in op. 2 ("Ich wil singen. / mere vf gvt gedingen. / Sol mir wol gelingen. / das mv[°]s an ir geschehen. / si kan machen. / trurig herze lachen."—"I want to sing more with good hopes, but if I succeed, that must happen through her. She can make sad hearts laugh").

At the same time, one of the major differences between the op. 1 and op. 2 movements is that op. 2 tracks through its poem in a less direct fashion than did op. 1, to the extent that it may be something of an exaggeration to describe it as a "setting" of its poem. Rather than set every word of the poem, as he seems to have done in op. 1, in op. 2 Brahms instead chose to set only portions of it, loosely, leaving other portions without any corresponding music. He also included more music—much more than in op. 1—that has no directly corresponding text. Table 3.4 summarizes the form: the setting comprises an eighteen-bar theme followed by four variations that span both of the interior movements in the four-movement sonata cycle. The sonata's second movement houses the theme and variations 1–3, and the third-movement Scherzo (which I will not comment on here) houses variation 4;

Table 3.3. "Mir ist leide." As transcribed and translated by George Bozarth (1990, 355). German transcribed from Pfaff (1909, cols. 36–37).

1	Mir ist leide.	It is painful to me
2	das der winter beide.	that winter
3	walt vñ ouch die heide.	has made fallow
4	hat gemachet val.	both forest and heath;
5	sin betwingen.	its firm grip allows
6	lat niht blůmen entspringen.	neither flowers to bloom
7	noch die vogel singen.	nor birds to sing
8	ir vil sůssen schal.	their very sweet songs.
9	alsus verderbet mich ein selig wib.	In like manner, a blessed woman destroys me,
10	dú mich lat.	has left me
11	ane rat.	without giving the counsel
12	den si hat.	of which she is possessed;
13	des zergat.	because of this my joy,
14	an frőiden gar min lip.	even my life, has perished.
15	Miner swere.	From my sufferings
16	schiere ich ane were.	I would leave off without hesitation
17	solde ich die seldebere.	if I could see, without feeling pain,
18	schowen ane leit.	the one who brings happiness.
19	dú vil here.	This very noble lady
20	hat schőne zuht vñ ere.	is of high breeding and honor;
21	der wnsch vñ dannoch mere.	any wish, and yet still more,
22	ist gar an si geleit.	is indeed her companion.
23	rose wengel mvndel rot si hat.	Rosy cheeks and a little red mouth has she,
24	val har lang.	full long hair,
25	kele blank.	a white neck,
26	siten kranc.	slender waist:
27	min gedanc.	my thought is
28	an ir vil hohe stat.	of her very high station.
29	Ich wil singen.	I want to sing
30	mere vf gvt gedingen.	more with good hopes,
31	sol mir wol gelingen.	but if I succeed,
32	das mvs an ir geschehen.	that must happen through her.
33	si kan machen.	She can make
34	trurig herze lachen.	sad hearts laugh,
35	grosse sorge swachen.	lessen great worry;
36	des mvs man ir ieheh.	one must grant her that.
37	wurde mir ir werder trost geseit.	If her worthy comfort would be given me,
38	seht fúr war.	see, verily,

Table 3.3. (*Continued*)

39	offẽ bar.	obviously,
40	minú iar.	the rest of my life
41	wolde ich gar.	I would indeed consider
42	mit frőiden sin gemeit.	full of joy.

Table 3.4. Formal summary, Brahms, Piano Sonata in F♯ Minor, op. 2, ii–iii.

movement/measures:	ii/1–18	ii/19–36	ii/37–67	ii/68–87	iii (all)
musical form:	theme	variation 1	variation 2	variation 3	variation 4
text form:	stanza 1	stanza 2	(untexted)	stanza 3	(untexted)

the entire Scherzo is untexted, as is (as I will show presently) variation 2 in the second movement.

The theme, shown in example 3.6, almost seems to overtly declare that intertextuality with op. 1 will be one of the central issues in the movement. Like the theme in op. 1, it opens with an ascending $\hat{1}$–$\hat{2}$–$\hat{3}$ figure in the minor mode—B minor here, C minor in op. 1. There are differences: the op. 2 theme is entirely a Brahms original—there is no extant lied melody for "Mir ist leide," as there was for "Verstohlen geht"—and Brahms formats it as a pair of sentences in a loose, open-ended antecedent-consequent relationship, as opposed to the *Barform* design he used before.[26] But the choice of the sentential period format also underscores a deeper similarity: in using it, Brahms imposed a certain Classical regularity on the theme that is not present in the obviously non-Classical text, just as he imposed a similar regularity on the op. 1 theme by molding it into a *Barform*, even when "Verstohlen geht," like "Mir ist leide," did not suggest such formal tidiness.

Sentence 1 occupies eight bars, with a four-bar presentation (basic idea in mm. 1–2, restatement in mm. 3–4) moving from tonic to subdominant and a four-bar continuation (mm. 5–8) moving first to the Neapolitan C major and then on to the dominant and a terminal i:IAC in m. 8.[27] Sentence 2 expands to ten notated measures before terminating in m. 18 on a i:HC, which leaves the period more open-ended than would a more normative, i:PAC-ending.[28] The theme appears to set every word in the poem's first two quatrains, but it also includes extra, untexted music, and its metric organization does not respect the irregular line structure in the text. Both of these factors, together with the fact that the text does not appear in the score, can make it difficult to know just how to scan the text onto the music. One of the best solutions is probably the one provided by Bozarth and shown below the score in example 3.6:[29] the four syllables of the poem's first line, "Mir ist leide," correspond to the four eighths in m. 1; all but the last word of line 2 (again four syllables: "das der winter") to the four eighths of m. 3; and the last word in line 2,

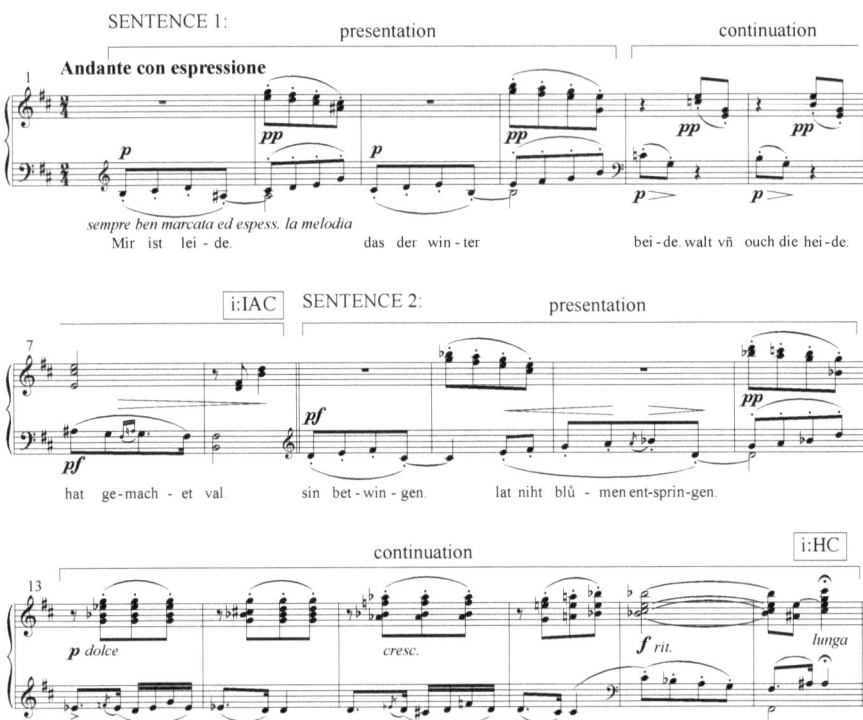

Example 3.6. Brahms, Piano Sonata in F♯ minor, op. 2, ii, theme (mm. 1–18). Text added according to Bozarth (1990, 356). For complete text, see figure 3.4.

plus lines 3–4 (eight total syllables: "beide. / walt vñ ouch die heide"), to mm. 5–8—where the two eighth-note figures in those measures provide clear analogs for the two-syllable groupings in this part of the poem and confirm the presence of one-measure, untexted gaps in mm. 2 and 4.

But even while these opening eight bars may exhibit a basically Classical organization on the surface, they also reveal an underlying, fundamentally Romantic aesthetic. This becomes evident upon considering those one-measure gaps in the text setting: these invite an interpretation in which the theme is understood as embedding within it a Romanticized, fragmented, multivalent temporality. That is, just as op. 1 invites the mapping of a texted-untexted opposition onto a temporal-atemporal opposition, op. 2 similarly invites text-competent listeners to hear mm. 1 and 3 as comprising the main melody or the theme proper—the first narrative, or the temporal stream—and the contrasting, untexted gestures in mm. 2 and 4 as outside the first narrative and in a parallel, atemporal stream. The situation is best regarded, moreover, as a conflation of a durational and a ruptured atemporality: this is a durational expansion with a rupture on top of it—an anisochrony that opens up room for a simultaneous fracture and the shift in level of discourse it connotes. The atemporality is durational in the sense that mm. 2 and 4 can be heard as lengthening mm. 1 and 3 by one bar each—in effect by seizing two moments from those measures (the last eighth notes in each: A♯ at the end of m. 1, B at the end of m. 3—the last syllables of "leide" and "winter," respectively) and freezing them in time by extending them as static pedal tones, momentarily refusing to allow the narrative to continue. Their temporal meaning is comparable to, for example, that of m. 29 in op. 1/ii: they constitute extra, untexted music that elongates a shorter, underlying structural duration and thus signifies a deceleration in a narrative rhythm that would otherwise have proceeded more rapidly. Ruptures are present in the sense that on top of the pedal tones, the upper voices in mm. 2 and 4 both sound an inverted version of the motives from mm. 1 and 3 (in effect turning the movement's head-motive upside down), at a *pianissimo* dynamic (even softer than the *piano* in mm. 1 and 3—as if mm. 2 and 4 are distant echoes), and with a sharp registral discontinuity (in which the upper voices in mm. 2 and 4 are positioned an octave and a half higher than their mm. 1 and 3 counterparts). Thus, these upper voices can be thought of as occupying an atemporal stream that floats figuratively above the stream in which the temporal stream unfolds—very much like the way in which mm. 47–49 and 51–53 in op. 1/ii floated above a parallel first narrative in the voices below. Given the motivic inversions, perhaps we should regard these measures as hazy musical reflections of the narrator's inner consciousness—mirrors onto his mind, so to speak, similar to the mirrors suggested by the choral refrains of mm. 3–4 and 7–8 in op. 1/ii. Given the poem's revelation (in line 10—a line that, notably, is never set directly in the music) that the narrator's beloved has deserted him, perhaps we can also hear in these gestures another form of a Romanticized "if only" sentiment—quick pauses for reflection or reminiscence on a more beautiful past, lost in the loneliness of an imperfect present.

Sentence 2, in mm. 9–18, can be heard as informed by a similar sense of temporal fragmentation. Again, some of the music in these measures must be understood as untexted, as Bozarth has suggested (refer again to example 3.6). The presentation module is unproblematic in this regard: line 5 in the poem maps onto mm. 9–10, line 6 onto mm. 11–12 (including the two eighth-note pickup). But in the continuation module, line 7 maps onto mm. 13–14, while line 8 appears to map onto mm. 17–18 (again including the pickup) rather than mm. 15–16—which are essentially a sequential repetition of mm. 13–14. Thus, mm. 15–16 are left without text, and this invites a reading in which these two bars constitute an atemporal echo of mm. 13–14, similar to the echoes in mm. 2 and 4 of mm. 1 and 3, rather than an integral part of the first narrative itself. This is another durational atemporality in that the echo similarly adds extra material to and thus lengthens a formal unit, slowing down the referential narrative rhythm. A module that should have occupied four bars (hypothetically mm. 13–16) now occupies six (mm. 13–18).

This interpretation brings to light an important aspect of the musical definition of what Genette calls the referential narrative rhythm or the "zero reference point" for a narrative's pace. Mapping such a concept onto music was relatively straightforward in op. 1: there, the theme sounded at the beginning of the movement clearly established a pace against which the temporal meaning of events in later variations (such as those at mm. 29 and 37) could be measured. But in op. 2, if a durational atemporality occurs in mm. 13–18—within the theme itself—then this implies the presence of an unsounding prototype version of that theme (what Rothstein calls an *implied prototype*)[30] that contains the referential pace. Such a prototype would be a more normative version of the theme, one that never appears on the acoustic surface but that is nevertheless available—as a "what might have been"—in the musical imagination of the implied listener, attuned to phrase-organizational norms in Classic-Romantic instrumental music. In this case, the prototype version of mm. 13–18 can be imagined by referring back to sentence 1, and its hypothetical features prove key to interpreting the expressive meaning of the six-bar module as a whole. That is, sentence 1—the eight-bar sentence as a whole, plus the four-bar presentation and continuation modules and the smaller two-bar submodules—sets the referential pace at which the implied listener will expect sentence 2 to proceed. Note that this does not mean sentence 1 is purely mimetic: as mentioned, it already involves a durational atemporality of its own, due to the durational expansions in mm. 2 and 4. It does, however, constitute a zero reference point, locally, for the pacing of the music that follows it. And sentence 2 does indeed open in accordance with the expectations thus established: mm. 9–12 function as a four-bar presentation and signal that the module will be a sentential consequent, the length of which will normatively be the same as that of the foregoing sentential antecedent.

What happens at m. 13 is key in this context. This measure and the music that follows are central to an interpretation of expressive meaning in the rest of the theme; in fact, this music proves central for interpreting expressive meaning later on in the movement. Instead of proceeding with music derived from the parallel mm. 5–8, as the expectations outlined above would suggest it should, m. 13 introduces new material that, in turn, appears to initiate an entirely new sentence—one in which the untexted mm. 15–16 comprise a sequential repetition of the two-bar basic idea in mm. 13–14, and in which a four-bar presentation module (mm. 13–16) leads to a short, two-bar continuation (mm. 17–18). In a strictly technical sense, the introduction of a second, smaller sentence functioning as the continuation module in a larger one is a form of the procedure known as "sentence replication," in which the formal organization on one hierarchical level is repeated on a higher or lower level.[31] These measures are also not "new," strictly speaking, but rather may be regarded as a typically Brahmsian transformation of mm. 5–8: mm. 13–14 compose out a leaping G-D fourth that loosely refers to the descending two eighths figures in mm. 5 and 6; the half-step appoggiatura relationship between m. 13 b. 1 and m. 15 b. 1 (E♭-D) originates in the C-B gesture composed out across m. 5 b. 1 and m. 6 b. 1; and their harmonic progression refers obliquely to the harmony in the original continuation, in that m. 13 deflects to E♭ major (Neapolitan of the D major at m. 9) in the same way that m. 5 deflected to C major (Neapolitan of the B minor at m. 1). But the gesture may be read as a rhetorical one that carries far greater expressive significance than such a purely formalistic analysis might suggest: the anisochrony signals a shift in level of discourse—a shift in the dimension Genette would call the mood—and we thus enter into what may be heard as a digression, or an interjection, by the narrating agent. That agent seems to overtly reject the precedent of mm. 5–8 in favor of a new alternative: the *dolce*, singing-style topic in mm. 13–16 (indexically and iconically signifying the singing birds mentioned in the poem's seventh line) replaces the austere simplicity of mm. 5–6; the confident *crescendo* in mm. 15–16 replaces the diffident *decrescendo* in mm. 7–8. Perhaps the narrator is reluctant to continue moving forward with what we know is a desolate, painful tale: he chooses instead to pause and reminiscence, briefly distracted by the seductive, mesmerizing sound of the birds.

But the tale must continue. Variation 1 commences at m. 19; variation 2 follows at m. 37. As in op. 1, these two variations are central to an understanding of the movement's rhetorical and expressive strategies. First, their large-scale structural profile underscores an important feature of Brahms's text setting in the movement as a whole: as mentioned, he has loosely set only selected portions of the poem. That is, the onset of variation 1 at m. 19 strongly suggests that the musical setting continues at that point not with the closing sestet in the poem's first stanza (lines 9–14) but instead skips directly to the opening of stanza 2: the four syllables of line 15 ("Miner swere") are parallel to the four syllables of line 1 ("Mir ist leide"), just as the music obviously starts another pass through the main theme at m. 19 (note the restatement of the head-motive, B-C$\sharp$-D-A$\sharp$). Thus the main theme comprises a setting of the first two quatrains in stanza 1, omitting the closing sestet. Variation 1 behaves similarly: it corresponds bar for bar with the main theme and thus sets the first two quatrains in stanza 2 (lines 15–22) but, again, not the closing sestet (lines 23–28).

Second, variations 1 and 2 employ specific rhetorical strategies that prove remarkably similar to those that appeared in the corresponding variations in op. 1. Variation 1, for example, again introduces a musical signifier for the interiority of the narrator: the syncopated, persistent pedal tone on an upper-voice G beginning in m. 19. This might be a musical icon for a bell tolling far away in the distance (probably foretelling doom), but it also might be an icon for the narrating agent's heartbeat, parallel to the triplet sixteenths first introduced at m. 13 in op. 1. Here in op. 2, the heartbeat also becomes gradually more audible as the narrator's anxiety level increases—where in this movement the anxiety rises in tandem with the increasingly specific, and increasingly painful, memories dredged up in the poem's second stanza ("Miner swere. / schiere ich ane were. / solde ich die seldebere. / schowen ane leit."—"From my sufferings I would leave off without hesitation if I could see, without feeling pain, the one who brings happiness"). The heartbeat pedal persists throughout the entire variation: the pedal shifts up to B$\flat$ at m. 28 to accommodate the shifting tonality (which touches on G minor and E$\flat$ major in mm. 27–34), then shifts enharmonically to A$\sharp$ at the terminal half cadence in B minor (mm. 35–36).

The op. 1–op. 2 similarities run deeper. In op. 2, variation 2 engages with both the durational and the rupture forms of atemporality, just as did the second variation in op. 1. But the temporal situation in op. 2 is again more complex, as it was in the main theme. Most important is the fact that variation 2 should be understood as entirely untexted, as mentioned earlier and as indicated in table 3.4. This is not immediately obvious, and it must be determined retrospectively. The implied listener will initially assume that variation 2 correlates with stanza 3, in light of the theme-stanza 1, and variation 1-stanza 2, correspondences. But variation 3 opens at m. 68 in a modally marked B major instead of the home key of B minor, and the modal shift at that moment can easily be heard as a musical response to the shift of mood that occurs at line 29 in the poem. The strategy even bears a striking resemblance to the shift from C minor to C major at the last variation of op. 1, in response to the remarkably similar shift of mood in "Verstohlen geht." It follows that variation 2 has no corresponding text and constitutes a single, composed-out moment in time, outside the first-narrative stream—an extended duration in which, although music passes before our ears, the story itself does not advance concurrently. Again, the situation is analogous to a literary *pause*, in which a measurable duration in narrative time (the content of which is delivered entirely in the diegetic voice of the narrator) corresponds to a zero duration in mimetic story time. In terms of my musical categories, this is the form of durational atemporality effected by a resetting of the musical clock: we have here a narrative reversion to an earlier moment in the form followed by a retracing of previously sounded music, with the purpose of rethinking or reimagining events that have already passed by once before. In this case, variation 2 would be understood as reverting to the beginning of variation 1, setting up the opportunity to reimagine variation 1 from a new angle.

This is indeed exactly what happens, and it helps explain a number of idiosyncratic rhetorical and expressive features that appear in this part of the movement. First, right from the beginning, variation 2 is staged as having descended into a dream space, deep in the interior reaches of the narrator's consciousness. This is part of the signified surrounding the variation's refusal to open in the tonic B minor: m. 37 departs, at a mysterious *piano* dynamic, not from the tonic triad (compare mm. 1 and 19) but instead from an elaborated dominant-seventh chord on G. Thus, the very pitch that functioned as the upper-voice heartbeat pedal at the outset of variation 1 becomes a stabilized chord root, shifted to the bass. What was once only a distant glimmer of interiority—the lurking heartbeat—becomes a central, foundational element in the music; the narrative shifts from outward reality to inward fantasy. Second, the atmosphere is tinged with psychological and emotional disturbance. The G7 chord recasts the characteristic head-motive (now sounding in the bass, as D-E-F♯-C♯) in a new light: its first and third notes, far from their former identities as a stable root and third in an implied tonic triad, now become the less stable fifth and seventh of a dissonant dominant-seventh chord. G7, as the enharmonic German augmented-sixth chord in B, also functions as dominant of the Neapolitan (C major) in the original B minor: this again summons up Brahms's preferred tonal location for housing anxious disturbances or moments of contemplation and reflection—especially, it seems, those triggered by ruminations on lost love. The narrator is trying to come to terms with his pain—trying to find a way to "leave off without hesitation" (line 16) from his sufferings. And third, the variation introduces an expressively charged countermelody, notated in the middle staff among the three in use at this point in the score. This is a strategy similar in principle to the one Brahms employed in variation 2 of op. 1; here again, as before, it implies the presence of a separate agent in the narrative. But whereas in op. 1 the countermelody comprised an entirely new contrapuntal line (signifying the presence of the moon, as distinct from the agent who narrates the story), here in op. 2 it comprises a transformed, decorated, chromatic version of the original head-motive, B-C♯-D-A♯. Thus, rather than signifying a completely separate persona, the line instead seems to represent another musical representation of the inner consciousness of the narrator himself. It provides another window, so to speak, onto the narrator's mind, allowing for a view from a different angle or from a different position than before.

    Structurally, variation 2 proceeds normatively through its first sentence—thus retracing lines 15–18 in the poem—maintaining the same eight-bar structure and ending in m. 44 with the same i:IAC as before (mm. 37–44 = mm. 1–8 = mm. 19–26). After this, however, there begins a series of atemporal expansions. The first occurs at the cadence itself: m. 45 adds two extra beats to an IAC that, in its previous manifestations, had occupied only one bar of music (mm. 44–45 = m. 8 = m. 26). Thus, the narrator tarries—lingering on the cadential moment, pausing to reflect before continuing. That this music correlates with line 18 ("the one who brings happiness") suggests that it probably captures the narrator's wondering aloud about whether happiness will ever be possible. The effect is underscored by the hushed *pianississimo* (suggesting thoughts trailing off into the distance) and by the repeated iteration of the $\hat{6}$–$\hat{5}$ (G-F♯) upper-neighbor figure, itself surely a gloomy remnant of the anxious, heartbeat pedal G from variation 1, as Bozarth has also noted.[32] Motion resumes at m. 46, with sentence 2 (line 19: "dú vil here"—"This very noble lady"), but what appears here is not what the implied listener expects: the main theme, which should be in the bass (in accordance with its position in m. 37), has disappeared, and only a pedal point and a version of the countermelody from m. 37 remain. In addition, instead of the bass stepping up a third, from the bleak, minor-mode B of the IAC in mm. 44–45 to a more hopeful, major-mode D (expected in accordance with the precedents in mm. 8–9 and 26–27), instead it reneges, falling instead of rising, settling wearily onto an A♯ in what amounts to a forlorn sigh. The narrator realizes that happiness is but an unrealistic illusion; the "noble lady" will never be found.

    This triggers a complete loss of rationality. The continuation module in m. 50 comprises a complex example of durational atemporality, with multiple accelerations and decelerations, that in this context seems to signify the spinning out of control of a delusional mind. At the downbeat of m. 50, the implied listener expects the E♭-major dotted-eighth-sixteenth figure from the downbeat of m. 13 (or m. 31), but there appear instead four sixteenths parallel to those of m. 13 b. 2. These appear one beat ahead of schedule, so to speak, jumping in ahead of the figure that was due on the downbeat. The harmony at this moment, on the other hand, appears to signify reluctance: it hangs on to G minor (see the triad at m. 50 b. 1) instead of yielding, as expected, to E♭ major (again, compare mm. 13 and 31). In this context, the *forte* dynamic (introduced at the end of m. 49) probably connotes a frustrated outburst—the angst of a desperate lover, discouraged by the inaccessibility of his beloved. What follows only deepens the already-swirling confusion: mm. 50–51 elliptically condense into two bars material (from mm. 13–16) that originally occupied four—a good musical analog for Genette's *summary* (*sommaire*), in which a duration in the narrative time is shorter than the corresponding duration in diegetic story time; the narrator tries to reorient himself by the end of m. 51, at which time the E♭ major that was expected back at the downbeat of m. 50 finally appears—albeit in the form of a major-minor seventh in the 4/3 inversion rather than a stable root-position triad; m. 52 again resets the clock, reiterating in its top voice material from m. 13 instead of continuing on with m. 17; and m. 53 anxiously summarizes in only two beats music that originally occupied four (m. 53 b. 1 = m. 14; m. 53 b. 2 = m. 15). Finally, at m. 54 the bass voice spirals into a sequential descent through a diminished-seventh chord, D♯-B♯-A-F♯, using the sixteenths gesture from mm. 50–53, while the right hand—apparently trying to finish the variation, or at least move forward with the story and break free from the confusion—tries to invoke the lower-voice, cadence-anticipating gesture from mm. 17 and 35.

From these delusional depths comes what is perhaps the most striking gesture in the entire movement: the peroration at m. 56, which has no obviously corresponding text and which seems to intrude from out of nowhere. It introduces striking discontinuities in the dynamic level (now *fortissimo*, the loudest volume indicated thus far in the movement), texture (a fuller, triadic, homophonic, and homorhythmic texture replaces the intricate polyphony that had prevailed at least since m. 46), articulation and expressive indications (the *grandioso* chords, most of them rolled, appear to forcibly overwhelm the searching, introspective quality that pervades much of the rest of the movement), and tonality (the music finally achieves the D major that was rejected earlier, at m. 46, where the bass stepped down to A♮ instead of up to D). The strategy parallels in a number of ways the one Brahms employed late in the second variation in op. 1, in mm. 47–49 and 51–53. First, this is a ruptured atemporality, in which an intrusive musical gesture out of place with respect to the surrounding music in turn ruptures the musical fabric, cues a shift in level of discourse (mimetic to diegetic), and connotes a move into a parallel atemporal stream, outside the first narrative. Second, the rupture immanently signals its own separation or independence from the surrounding material: in this case, forward-vectored musical motion literally ceases in favor of a two-bar prolongation of a D-major triad. And third, the rupture implies a network of similarly hierarchical relationships among the various temporal streams: here, variation 2 as a whole is already atemporal to begin with, so m. 56 initiates a digression within a digression—a narrative excursion that is atemporal with respect to a local first narrative, which in turn is atemporal with respect to the movement as a whole. In terms of expressive content, the event may respond to multiple interpretations, but given the textual evidence, it seems appropriate to hear it as a desperately optimistic cry that follows on the heels of the narrator's spiraling into the depths of despair. Perhaps it musically manifests the "good hopes" to which the narrator refers later on in the poem (see line 30); maybe it provides him a brief respite from his tormented present, in which he can freely imagine the hoped-for union with the beloved. In this specific sense, the event can be thought of as analogous not so much to a literary achrony but more to an anachrony—a prolepsis, to be precise, that refers forward to events in the narrative (or, in this case, to words in the poem) that have not yet occurred. In a broader, Romantic-aesthetic environment (in which a staged conflict between the idealized and the imperfect play a central role), we can also think of an opposition between the brighter, more positive D-major world of the interpolation and the darker, more negative B-minor world around it, where the major-mode world may map onto the unreal, idealized, Romantic-Arcadian paradise and the minor-mode world onto the bleak reality of an inescapable present.

With regard to the relationship between this interpolation and the surrounding music, one feature in particular deserves additional comment. Whereas in op. 1 the ruptures and their associated interpolations appeared for the most part abruptly and without warning, here in op. 2 the interpolation is better thought of as having been entered into gradually, via what I will call a *gateway* passage. A gateway is a module that prefigures a forthcoming discursive shift and warns the implied listener of an imminent disturbance in the narrative. Such is the expressive function especially of the highly anisochronous mm. 50–55. Their strained phrase rhythm foreshadows the more severe structural discontinuity of m. 56; the narrator's delusional confusion anticipates his subsequent outburst. This does not necessarily mean that the gateway music literally foreshadows the interpolated music in any kind of concrete motivic or thematic sense. The concept is more abstract, and it concerns the expressive-narrative trajectory rather than the musical syntax per se: one narrative disturbance—often a durational atemporality—that does not necessarily imply a deviation away from the ongoing story (the narrator hesitates, slows down, adds additional commentary, speaks in a halting fashion, or otherwise embellishes the story) yields to another that implies a cleaner break with the tale in progress (the narrator momentarily abandons the story in favor of an extended commentary, reflection, reminiscence, or some other excursus). The gateway strategy is a common one in the nineteenth-century sonata repertoire, in which some of the most severe discursive shifts tend not to be a total surprise but rather tend to be entered into in stages, with other rhetorical signals foreshadowing their impending arrival.

The concept of a highly idealized Arcadia and the associated notion of retreat and return common in Romantic pastoral narratives probably motivates this movement's ending. If the central climax of the movement—the D-major peroration—concerns a momentary retreat into an Arcadian paradise, then the rest of the movement concerns the required return to reality. Reality calls forth almost immediately, in fact: the head-motive booms forth in a *fortissimo, pesante* D minor at mm. 58 and 60, in an apparent attempt to restart the normative teleological motion, beckoning the narrator out of the dream world in order to reenter the principal temporal stream. The narrator tries to hang on to the beauty of the dream, responding in mm. 59 and 61 with common-tone, fully diminished-seventh exclamations. One more deliberate statement of the head motive in m. 62, now *molto* (!) *pesante*, requires the narrator to yield, and the next five bars essentially continue variation 2 from where it left off earlier, in the middle of its second sentence (around m. 16 in the prototype theme): mm. 63–65 can be heard as an expansion of m. 17, with its cadence-anticipating descending bass (a gesture at which m. 54 also hinted); and mm. 66–67 comprise an expansion of the terminal half cadence from m. 18. Thus, the second variation gives way to the third—the love song, or the apotheosis (as in op. 1), of the narrator-as-protagonist. In one final structural parallelism with op. 1, in variation 3 the anisochronies disappear and the referential narrative rhythm resumes; variation 3 is disrupted by no more deviations from the first narrative (other than a lingering on its final cadence). Reality returns; Arcadia dissolves in unsustainability.

Notes

1. The original lied, with a ten-bar melody and the text of the complete four-verse poem, appears in Kretzschmer and Zuccalmaglio, *Deutsche Volkslieder mit ihren Original-Weisen*, I:56–57. The theme and the text are reproduced in Bozarth, "Brahms's *Lieder ohne Worte*," 350–51. Parmer ("Brahms, Song Quotation, and Secret Programs," 178) calls Brahms's setting a "transcription," where that composer "appropriates and transforms much more of the song source" than would be the case with a more traditional "setting" or an "allusion." Brahms was apparently fond of this lied and used its melody again much later in his career, as no. 49 in the 1894 collection of 49 Deutsche Volkslieder (WoO 33). Note that Brahms composed the slow movement of op. 1 in April 1852, so it predates the other three movements in the sonata (which date from spring 1853) as well as the entire op. 2 sonata (November 1852). Among Brahms's extant instrumental works, it postdates only the op. 4 Scherzo (from August 1851); see Bozarth, ibid., 349.

2. Another interpretation is available, one in which the moon correlates with the woman herself and thus objectifies the (now more distant) narrator's hopes and fears. Such a reading draws on a cultural tradition of correlating the opposition sun-moon with male-female or husband-wife—where the light of the feminine moon depends for its existence on, and is weaker than, the light of its marital partner, the masculine sun. For a discussion, see Wunder, *He Is the Sun, She Is the Moon*, esp. 202–8.

3. Genette, *Narrative Discourse*, 29–32, 212–62. See also the summary of this issue in Culler, foreword to Genette, *Narrative Discourse*, 10. Parmer also notes this feature of the poem in "Brahms, Song Quotation, and Secret Programs," 179.

4. For more on this distinction between different types and positions of narrative agents, see Chatman, *Coming to Terms*, esp. 139–60.

5. Genette, *Narrative Discourse*, 29–32 (esp. 31–32) and 161–211; see 189–94 for "focalization" (*focalization*). See also the commentary in Culler, foreword to *Narrative Discourse*, by Gérard

Genette, 10. "Filtered" is Seymour Chatman's term; see *Coming to Terms*, 144. Chatman (ibid., 139–60) further develops the concept of "point of view."

6. Parmer ("Brahms, Song Quotation, and Secret Programs," 179) notes that the "outward and upward view" of the first two stanzas is redirected by the fourth stanza "down into the house from which the lyric subject gazes," revealing "the central poetic image, two faithful lovers."

7. For a critique of analytical approaches that make direct correlations among events in the poetry and the music—as in Bozarth's reading ("Brahms's *Lieder ohne Worte*") and, to some extent, my own—and for an alternative analysis of the movement that concentrates on Brahms's composing out of a synthesis between the monophonic opening melody in mm. 1–2 and the accompanied countermelody in mm. 3–4, see Parmer, "Brahms, Song Quotation, and Secret Programs," 178–81.

8. Bozarth, "Brahms's *Lieder ohne Worte*," 348: "Brahms's attribution of the poem to the tradition of the Minnesingers [made in a note that appears on the score, "Nach einem altdeutschen Minneliede"] was purely the product of the young composer's imagination, as is the *Barform* structure of his theme."

9. Indexical signs depend for their significative value on an "association by contiguity, not association by resemblance or intellectual operations"; *iconic signs* depend on the semiotic principle that "anything is fit to be a *substitute* for anything that it is like." See Monelle, "Music and the Peircean Trichotomies," 101–2; and Monelle, *The Sense of Music*, esp. 14–19.

10. Dickensheets ("The Topical Vocabulary of the Nineteenth Century," 109) correlates similar pulsating triplet accompaniment figures with "the pounding heartbeats of barely suppressed passion." According to Dickensheets, the heartbeat is a common token within various nineteenth-century styles, topics, and musical dialects.

11. On Brahms's use of the Neapolitan region, or flat-side key areas in general, to house disturbances or various other moments of contemplation or reflection (Bozarth: "psychological states"), see Bozarth, "Brahms's *Lieder ohne Worte*," 353. On the use of what can be thought of as a ♭VI–♭II–♯IV/♭V complex, rather than simply a preference for the Neapolitan alone, see Smith, "Brahms and the Neapolitan Complex." See also Webster, "Schubert's Sonata Form and Brahms's First Maturity"; Webster, "Schubert's Sonata Form and Brahms's First Maturity (II)"; and Wintle, "The 'Sceptered Pall': Brahms's Progressive Harmony."

12. A *prototype* is the unit of music subject to transformation; see Rothstein, *Phrase Rhythm in Tonal Music*, 64.

13. Note that strictly speaking, in literary narratives diegetic story time cannot *slow down* per se; scenes and dialogues do not normally unfold in slow motion. Such effects are obviously more possible in film and music. In literature, decelerations are normally produced by the insertion of extranarrative elements—extended descriptive pauses; commentarial asides; short-lived, memory-elicited analepses; or others. See Genette, *Narrative Discourse*, 95.

14. The concept of the implied reader is related to that of the implied author. The implied reader is not the actual flesh-and-blood reader of a text but rather the reader that the implied author asks the actual readers to become when they read; the implied reader is the "relatively stable audience postulated by the implied author" and thus the reader for whom that implied author writes, with all the knowledge and competencies such an assumption entails (Booth, *The Rhetoric of Fiction*, 420). The most informed, text-adequate readings are those in which the actual reader becomes—shares the same knowledge and the same values as—the implied reader that the implied author sought to create; see Booth, ibid., 417–25. In reality, it is hard not to recognize that the implied reader is more closely tied than may be apparent (in Booth's formulations of the concept) to the actual reader, who comes to a text with certain preconceived and preformed values and priorities—values and priorities that the text's actual author may anticipate, of course. These nuances have not escaped Booth's notice: for more on the creative role of actual readers in reading a text, see Booth's afterword to the second edition of *The Rhetoric of Fiction* (esp. 422–25, including 422n11); see also Booth's comments in Iser, "Interview."

15. Genette, *Narrative Discourse*, 87–88.

16. Hepokoski and Darcy (*Elements of Sonata Theory*, 150–63) couch their discussion (of the problem of where to locate a sonata's EEC in cases in which an S-theme produces more than one PAC) in temporal terms that I find highly suggestive. They write that the effect of immediately repeating a cadence or an entire theme following an apparent EEC can be that of "undoing the closure provided by the preceding cadence in order to resituate it a few measures later with the next PAC. Metaphorically, such a situation is like that of closing a door behind one (the first PAC), then reopening it and walking through it a second time (with the second 'door-closing' PAC serving as the EEC)" (150); the effect can be one in which a sonata momentarily "goes back in time" or "turns back [its] sonata clock" in order to "re-experience the same thing in perhaps a different way (and yet with the awareness that one has done it before)" (ibid.); "compositional time, or the impression of an elastic and manipulable time elaborated aesthetically in the process of the work's unfolding, can exist in a provocative interplay with neutral, nonrepeatable, and external clock time, which keeps ticking onward regardless of what happens inside a composition" (ibid.). See also Schmalfeldt's ("Cadential Processes") "one more time" technique, in which certain harmonic progressions signal an imminent cadence, then jettison that cadence, "back up," and "try again."

17. Kinderman, *Beethoven*, 240.

18. What "might have been" is Leonard B. Meyer's phrase. See Meyer, *Explaining Music*, 111–13; see also Meyer, "A Pride of Prejudices; or, Delight in Diversity," 274–76.

19. Berger, in *Bach's Cycle, Mozart's Arrow*, has described similar parenthetical interpolations in music of late Beethoven in similar terms: inside the interpolations, "the normal laws governing musical time and space, the sense of directed motion and the concomitant sense of change and time passing, are suspended. . . . [This] alternative world is not one of action and change but of contemplation of the eternal and timeless" (330).

20. Genette, *Narrative Discourse*, 95. In a pause, NT (narrative time) = n, ST (story time) = 0; in a *scene* (*scène*), NT = ST in a *summary* (*sommaire*), NT < ST; and in an *ellipsis* (*ellipse*), NT = 0, ST = n. Genette does not include the form of the equation that describes story time as proceeding more slowly than narrative time, which he regards as impossible in literary narratives.

21. For *apotheosis*, see Cone, *Musical Form and Musical Performance*, 84. See also Klein, "Chopin's Fourth Ballade as Musical Narrative," 30–35.

22. An expanded cadential progression (ECP) is "an expansion of the cadential progression to the extent of supporting a complete phrase (of at least four measures) or group of phrases" (Caplin, *Classical Form*, 254). See also Caplin, "The 'Expanded Cadential Progression.'"

23. I use the term *failure* throughout in the sense in which it appears in Sonata Theory, referring to the staged inability—staged by the implied composer—of a musical structure to accomplish a task expected or demanded of it—by the implied listener—within the context of norms operative at a given moment and in a given genre. To describe an event, such as a cadence, an exposition, or an entire sonata, as having failed invokes no value judgments and implies no negatively charged opinions with regard to the music, the composer, or the composer's ability to compose tonal music. See Hepokoski and Darcy, *Elements of Sonata Theory*, 614–21. See also Monahan, "Success and Failure in Mahler's Sonata Recapitulations."

24. Bozarth describes the last variation as one in which the "true hearts are united in free counterpoint" and the coda as "a duet in strict imitation" between the baritone (the poet) and soprano (his beloved). See Bozarth, "Brahms's *Lieder ohne Worte*," 352. Parmer ("Brahms, Song Quotation, and Secret Programs," 180–81) also hears the coda as signifying the lovers' unification.

25. On the documentary evidence connecting the movement and the poem—a connection which in this case is not explicit because of the omission of the text and any references to it in the score itself (unlike in op. 1)—see Bozarth, "Brahms's *Lieder ohne Worte*," 353–58. See also Bozarth, "Brahms's Lieder Inventory of 1859–60," 111; and Kalbeck, *Johannes Brahms*, I:212.

26. For the strict, Classical definition of the *sentence* (originating in Schoenberg and Erwin Ratz), see Caplin, *Classical Form*, 35–48. For an expanded view of sentences in the nineteenth century, in which presentation modules are not necessarily tonic prolongational (as Classical presentations are normally strictly defined) and continuation modules may not be as closely related to their presentations as are most normative Classical continuations, see Vande Moortele, "Sentences, Sentence Chains, and Sentence Replication"; BaileyShea, "Wagner's Loosely Knit Sentences and the Drama of Musical Form"; BaileyShea, "The Wagnerian *Satz*: The Rhetoric of the Sentence in Wagner's Post-Lohengrin Operas"; and BaileyShea, "Beyond the Beethoven Model: Sentence Types and Limits." Hepokoski and Darcy describe the sentence gesturally, as an anapestic figure comprising "an initial double- (or triple-) impulse that proceeds to 'take off' into a longer or more conclusive idea: two preliminary bounces on the diving-board, followed by a third that precipitates the actual dive" (*Elements of Sonata Theory*, 84n14, 106, and 106n8).

27. For *basic idea*, see Caplin, *Classical Form*, 37–40.

28. On the *period*, see Caplin, ibid., 49–58. See also Vande Moortele, "Sentences, Sentence Chains, and Sentence Replication," 131.

29. Bozarth, "Brahms's *Lieder ohne Worte*," 356.

30. Rothstein, *Phrase Rhythm in Tonal Music*, 93–94.

31. Vande Moortele, "Sentences, Sentence Chains, and Sentence Replication," esp. 145–48. Related is the procedure known as the *Satzkette* ("sentence chain")—chains of modules each with a fully or partially articulated sentential impulse of their own—first mentioned by Schoenberg and recently elaborated in BaileyShea, "The Wagnerian *Satz*," 190; and in Vande Moortele, ibid., 140–44.

32. See Bozarth, "Brahms's *Lieder ohne Worte*," 357, on the "disconsolate sounding $G\flat$–$F\sharp$ echoes in the cadential extension, bars 44–5."

4 Music without Text: Forms of Atemporality

Rhetorical strategies in non-text-based Romantic music can be understood as analogous to the strategies that appear in the text-based slow movements by Brahms. Expressive meaning in such music may thus be interpreted in analogous ways. This chapter draws on the piano sonatas of Schumann, Brahms, and Chopin to examine situations that may be interpreted in terms of what I have defined as durational atemporality, ruptured atemporality, and conflations of these two atemporality types.

§1. Durational Atemporality: Schumann op. 11/i and Brahms op. 1/i

The first movement of Schumann's Piano Sonata in F♯ minor, op. 1, like many Romantic-era sonatas (especially those in the minor mode), maps onto a pastoral narrative and the characteristic oppositions therein, including imperfect reality versus idealized unreality, present versus past, and retreat versus return. In such movements, P typically can be understood as signifying a present, imperfect reality, while S can be understood as signifying the image of Arcadia—the lost, unreal, idealized place or time (usually construed as in the past) that provides a refuge for escape. In this movement specifically, an agitated, unsettled, minor-mode P (mm. 53–94, followed by TR, mm. 95–145) poses an opposition to a lyrical, graceful, elegant, relative-major S (mm. 146–68, followed by C, mm. 168–75). This S, part of which is shown in example 4.1, invokes a Classical, Mozartean singing style and is probably best thought of as a relative of the very common Romantic-era S-type known as the *Gesangsthema*—the expansive, *cantabile*, *legato* S-theme that offers maximal contrast with P and that can be regarded as a first-level default option for S-themes in Romantic sonata movements.[1] It comprises two sentences, the first an antecedent and the second a consequent within a larger, compound period. The antecedent includes a presentation with a twice-stated two-bar basic idea (m. 146–47 and 148–49) and a four-bar continuation with an undercut cadence; the ominous, low-register rumbling of the initiatory idea from P in m. 149 (compare mm. 53–54) and the undercut cadence in m. 153 (the G♮ in the right hand effects a deflection toward the subdominant D major via its own dominant seventh) may be the first signs that all is not well. The consequent produces a III:PAC (EEC in this sonata's exposition) at m. 168.

The consequent module is the key to understanding this theme's characteristically Romantic aesthetic. It also provides a good opportunity to consider how

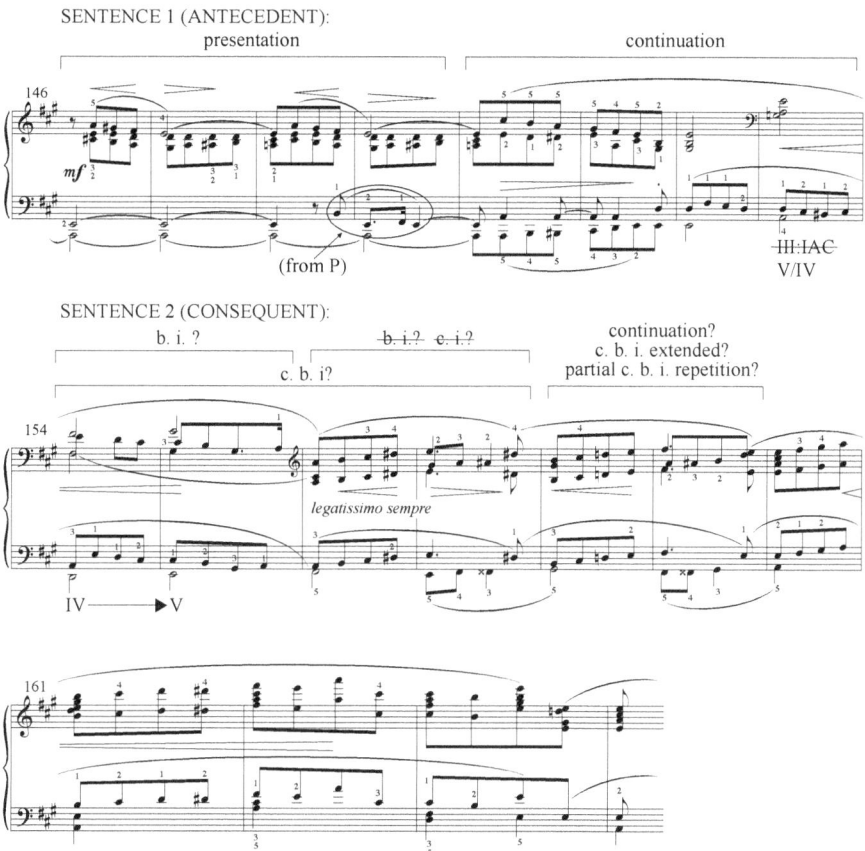

Example 4.1. Schumann, Piano Sonata in F♯ minor, op. 11, i, S (proposed analysis).

an idiosyncratic phrase-rhythmic detail explainable within current understandings of phrase- and sonata-structural syntax may nevertheless be folded into the rubric of durational atemporality. The consequent opens with what appears to be a two-bar basic idea in mm. 154–55 ("b. i.?" in example 4.1)—an idea almost parallel to, but still not exactly the same as, the basic idea from the antecedent. That is, the descending four eighths figure in mm. 154–55 is clearly related to, but does not repeat exactly, the descending four eighths of the initial basic idea, mm. 146–47. This is the beginning of a series of complications. First, the consequent opens at m. 154 not on the tonic, as might have been expected, but rather on the subdominant (following from the V7/IV in m. 153, as mentioned); m. 155 then moves to the dominant. This harmonic motion—essentially an auxiliary cadence that opens the consequent—creates an expressive effect in which mm. 154–55 can be heard as trying to produce some kind of pseudocadence, perhaps to compensate for the missed authentic cadence at m. 153 or perhaps to try to locate a tonic that has been temporarily lost or misplaced. Second, whereas the expectations associated with normative sentence rhetoric would lead the implied listener to anticipate some form of repetition of the new basic idea in mm. 156–57, at m. 156 Schumann instead introduces a new idea that contrasts in significant ways with (even while it still may be heard as deriving from) the foregoing music: an ascending gesture now inverts—as if rejecting, via an expressive reversal—the descending basic-idea figure from mm. 154–55 (and, for that matter, also the original basic idea, from mm. 146–47). Third, this last gesture in particular throws the overall phrase-organizational strategy into question: should the implied listener assume that mm. 156–57 comprise a contrasting idea ("c. i.?" in example 4.1) that at once replaces the expected basic-idea repetition and converts the theme's consequent structure, midstream, from that of a sentence to a period? If so, mm. 154–57 would have to be heard retrospectively as a small antecedent module (basic idea + contrasting idea), or perhaps (once m. 157 fails to produce a cadence) a form of Caplin's *compound basic idea*—a module that looks like an antecedent in that it includes a basic idea and a contrasting idea, but one that does not terminate with the cadence normatively required at the end of an antecedent.[2] And fourth, what follows in mm. 158–59 adds to, rather than clarifies, the confusion: these two bars obviously repeat the contrasting idea from mm. 156–57. Should this be considered an extension of the contrasting idea, such that the compound basic idea now occupies six bars (mm. 154–59) instead of four (mm. 154–57)? Or should m. 158 be understood as initiating a sentential continuation, such that the whole module (starting at m. 154) engages with Caplin's "hybrid 3" option, *compound basic idea + continuation*?[3] Or—even more complex—should the implied listener assume that mm. 154–57 constitute a sentential basic idea of which m. 158 was supposed to initiate a repetition (such that mm. 154–61 hypothetically would have produced a sentential presentation, with two four-bar compound basic ideas), but that instead the first two bars of the repetition (the repetition of mm. 154–55) have been elliptically omitted?

Any of these options may serve as adequate explanations; clearly, the theme's local-level organization is ambiguous and extremely complex. I would argue that the ambiguity is best accounted for, structurally and expressively, by allowing for a kind of temporal layering within the theme's implied narrative. That is, as shown in example 4.2, m. 156 is best regarded as initiating a new sentence, in which mm. 156–57 and 158–59 comprise a double statement of a new basic idea and thus mm. 156–59 as a whole comprise a new presentation module. Such a reading is fortified by the fact that the basic-idea repetition in mm. 158–59 engages with one of the normative repetition options within Classical sentence rhetoric—Caplin's *sequential repetition* option[4]—and that m. 160 engages with normative continuation rhetoric, spinning out the basic idea in the same manner as was heard just moments before (in which mm. 160–61, like mm. 150–51, extend an initiatory motive into a longer scalar figure). And such a reading leads to the conclusion, perhaps retrospectively, that mm. 154–55 are the exceptional measures: they may be heard as producing a momentary tarrying or hesitation in the theme, briefly derailing its normative, generically obligatory, forward-vectored motion toward a cadence. Analogous to the untexted measures in the two Brahms slow movements, these measures effect a shift in level of discourse: mimesis shifts to diegesis, the discourse of the narrative is made apparent, and the voice of the narrating agent is suddenly audible. In this sense, they produce what we can understand as another musical analog for an anisochrony—a durational atemporality in which the consequent module steps away from the theme's first-narrative, temporal level and into an atemporal stream. Measures 154–55 thus delay by two bars the onset of the sentential consequent that was expected at m. 154, just as, for instance, m. 29 in Brahms's op. 1/ii delays by one measure the onset of the expected module 1^b. The narrator slips from telling the story into exploring his own consciousness; the agent pauses to contemplate, reflect, ponder, or reminisce, in what may be a brief spell of absent-mindedness or a quick daydream. Perhaps in this instance, in light of the early signs of unrest in the antecedent (mm. 146–53), we should hear the narrator pausing to wonder about or comment on "what might have been," had the story unfolded differently; maybe we can hear the narrator as having succumbed to a momentary lapse in confidence, prompted by doubts about the S-theme's own viability or about the possibility of a satisfactory EEC (realizing the Arcadian dream). Such doubts could be understood as triggered by the cadence-gone-awry in m. 153 and by the attendant failure of m. 154 to sustain normative sentential consequent rhetoric.

All of this can be regarded, moreover, as expressively motivating what happens in the theme's remaining measures: the new basic idea proposed at m. 156—the narrator's proposed replacement for the original basic idea from m. 146—reaches upward, striving hopefully for a cadence that is suddenly in sight; a continuation module launches in m. 160 and leads confidently (note the *crescendo*) toward that cadence; and the cadence itself is accentuated by a classic instance of Schmalfeldt's "one more time" ("OMT" in example 4.2), in which an evasion of melodic closure at m. 164 b. 1 triggers a resetting of the clock and an emphatic repetition of the entire continuation (mm. 164–68 = 160–64). The narrator thus closes insistently, reassuring the implied listener—or perhaps reassuring himself, in the face of his own self-doubt—of the reality, even if fleeting, of the imagined Arcadian ideal.

* * *

A similar but more complex example of durational atemporality in an untexted movement appears in the S-theme from the first movement of Brahms's Piano Sonata in C major, op. 1. The procedures here compare especially well with those in mm. 9–18 of Brahms's op. 2/ii, as discussed in chapter 3. There, an unsounding referential prototype duration was expanded in length; the expansion was heard as producing an anisochronous effect, slowing the referential narrative rhythm and thus revealing aspects of the narrative discourse. Here, something similar happens, but to make sense of it, some additional sonata-structural context is needed. As shown in example 4.3, the exposition's TR launches in m. 17 and modulates from C major to the mediant E minor, arriving in m. 36 on a iii:HC MC. But the sonata

86 | *Sonata Fragments*

Example 4.2. Schumann, Piano Sonata in F♯ minor, op. 11, i, S (revised analysis).

refuses to accept this MC in a straightforward, uncritical fashion. Instead, it problematizes the MC in the three bars of caesura-fill (CF, mm. 36–38), which in effect delay the onset of S by questioning the foregoing half cadence. The bass shifts up from the B in m. 36 to an upper-neighbor C in m. 37, which supports an A-minor triad—presumably iv6 in E minor; in m. 38, the bass returns to the MC's original B and the harmony returns to the dominant, in an apparent effort to dismiss the question just posed. But then, m. 39—a moment that rhetorically signals the downbeat of S-space (*a tempo, dolce, con espressione*) and thus one at which we might reasonably expect confirmation of the E-minor tonality proposed by the MC—returns, very surprisingly, to the quizzical, first-inversion A-minor triad sounded for a tantalizingly brief moment in the CF, in m. 37. Thus, rather than opening confidently on a root-position tonic in the expected key, S instead equivocates, opening on an embellishing harmony that was staged moments before as the musical equivalent of a question mark. S thus refuses to accept—or perhaps blatantly rebuffs—the proposed key of E minor. This S-opening must be regarded, in context, as highly unusual, expressively marked, and troubled; it invites such readings, moreover, regardless of whether one chooses to privilege one or another of the two keys in question—A minor or E minor—as "the" key of the S-theme.[5] And the signified disturbance is not entirely unmotivated. It may have been foreshadowed in the TR, which encountered a crisis on its way to the MC: by m. 25, it had established E minor as the tonality of choice; around mm. 29–30, it appeared to rethink this move by shifting to a more hopeful E major; and, finally, by the time it reached the dominant-lock, in m. 34, it had collapsed back into the more negative E minor. This indecision may prefigure—in the sense of the gateway strategy discussed earlier, in connection with mm. 50–55 in Brahms's op. 2/ii—the problematizing of the S-theme-to-come. In light of it, perhaps the equivocal S-opening at m. 39 may be understood as part of an ongoing tonal duel—one in which if we cannot have E major, then we cannot have E at all, major or minor; or, in light of the S-theme's attempted cadence in A minor later, at m. 75, perhaps we should read the S-opening retrospectively, as a gesture that does not so much question an existing tonic but rather one that recommends a new one—a replacement (A), perhaps, for a tonic (E) that was proposed earlier in various guises (major and minor) but was eventually, for one reason or another, deemed unsatisfactory.

The S-theme that follows proceeds to sink so deeply into an atemporal fog that it becomes the musical embodiment of the indecision to which the TR alludes. In fact, it waffles between A minor and E minor no fewer than three times before finally concluding not with an unambiguous cadence in one or the other of those keys but rather with one of the most indecisive musical gestures imaginable: the highly ambivalent cadence attempt at m. 51 (on which more in section 3). Brahms formats the opening four bars of S (mm. 39–42) as an antecedent, with a two-bar basic idea (mm. 39–40) followed by a two-bar contrasting idea (mm. 41–42). These measures articulate a cadential progression toward a weak IAC in A minor (that is, a vi:IAC) in m. 42, and thus for the moment S appears to accept the tonal implications of the first-inversion A-minor triad in m. 39 (apparently rejecting for now the possibility that the chord might be the opening gambit in an off-tonic S-opening, on the subdominant in E minor). What follows appears to confirm this decision, in the sense that the first bar (m. 43) of the ensuing consequent module moves, finally, onto a confident, root-position A-minor triad—complete with an authoritative, low-register sounding of the chord root. But at this same moment, S begins to

Example 4.3. Brahms, Piano Sonata in C major, op. 1, i, TR and opening of S.

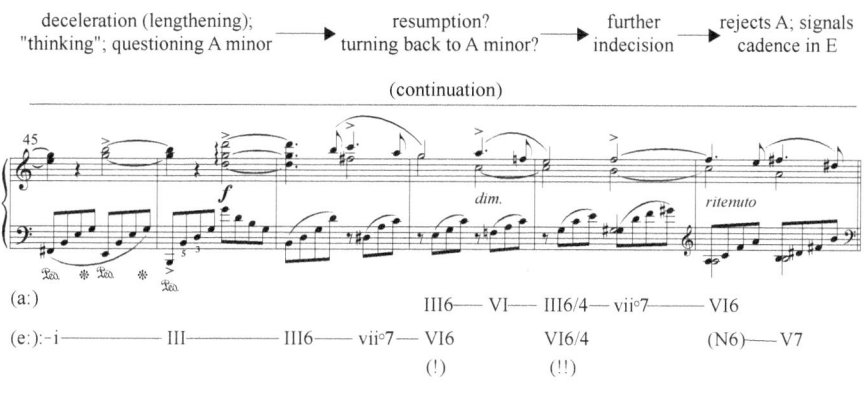

Example 4.3. (*Continued*)

go awry in other ways. Measures 43–44 introduce an idea obviously based on, but still not the same as, the original basic idea (compare m. 39–40), and the theme seems to proceed not with the consequent rhetoric that the implied listener expects (in the wake of the foregoing antecedent) but with what appears to be sentential continuation rhetoric instead. This is an important feature: the theme seems to have abruptly abandoned its original proposed period design to embrace Caplin's "hybrid 1" category, *antecedent + continuation*.[6] The move should be regarded as highly expressively charged, rather than as a maneuver that can easily be rationalized, or even dismissed, by invoking precedents for hybrid themes in the Classical and Romantic repertoire. In fact, in the present context—in the wake of the ambiguity surrounding the TR, MC, and S-opening—it invites an interpretation of some sort of expressive reversal or rhetorical breakdown, one that may be understood as part of an emerging shift in level of discourse in which the narrator intervenes in the story in response to a crisis.

Numerous features of the ensuing music reinforce such a reading. Measure 44 seems to completely forgo any motivic or harmonic connection to the original basic idea: in effect, it comprises a musical non sequitur, in which a puzzled rest appears in the right hand on b. 2 and the bass steps downward, in equally puzzled fashion, to G, in support of a C-major triad in $^6_4$ position. This harmonic motion is far from expressively neutral: the unexpected rearing up of C major constitutes a reappearance within the S-theme of the sonata's home tonic, the shadow of which still looms ominously over the narrative; the C-major triad is also one of the possible diatonic mediators between A minor and E minor, the two keys that were in question earlier. It functions here in just such a fashion—as a pivot around which S makes a turn backward, reverting from the A minor on which it had apparently settled by m. 43 to the E minor promised earlier, at the MC in m. 36. Measure 45 then veers onto an E-minor triad (see b. 3; the F♯ in the bass on the downbeat is a dissonant passing tone), rejecting A minor even more decisively. And in mm. 45–46 the right-hand arpeggiation reaches upward, through an E-minor triad (E to G in m. 44, continuing with G to B in m. 45) and then on to D—where the latter is the last step in a G-major triad that emerges in m. 46, functioning as III in E minor.

Measures 44–46 thus seem to be striving for an E minor that was thought to be lost just moments earlier. They also appear to be staged so as to imply that a resumption of tonal and rhetorical clarity may be close at hand; m. 47 suggests something similar in that it returns to a dotted-rhythmic figure characteristic of initial basic idea, from m. 39. Perhaps the narrator will continue with the story, in E minor, following a momentary hesitation, reconsideration, or temporary retreat into absent-mindedness—something like what happened in mm. 154–55 in Schumann's op. 11/i. But this is not to be, and the entire theme quickly becomes mired in confused indecision. First a dominant-functioning vii°7 in E minor at m. 47 b. 3 fails to resolve normatively at m. 48 b. 1: all the voices in the vii°7 move as expected except for the seventh (C), which sustains into m. 48 as a suspension and produces a C-major triad at m. 48 b. 1. Thus, C major rears up once again (!). The suspended C itself carries a markedly elevated significative value: the suspension is obligated to resolve via descending half step to B (in fact, the C-major triad at m. 48 b. 1 may be understood as a tonic triad in E minor, embellished with a 6-5 suspension), but that resolution never occurs. The C's descent is blocked, in effect, by a stepwise ascent in the bass: E at m. 48 b. 1 ascends to F♮ on b. 3 in the same measure. The narrator thus resists the move to E minor; the bass pushes back against the descending C just as one might push back against a sagging ceiling in a last-ditch effort to prevent its collapse. The F♮ in the bass, furthermore, signals another tonal about-face, back to A minor (!!) in that one would expect the F to step down to E (as $\hat{6}$ to $\hat{5}$ in A minor) and proceed to a cadence. But instead, the F moves *upward*, to G (m. 49 b. 1), which supports yet another C-major triad (!!!) that functions as another pivot. From here, the theme again has two options: either proceed in A minor or turn back to E. It chooses the former, with G ascending to G♯ at m. 49 b. 3 in support of a vii°7 in A minor. But, in a conspicuous, startling replay of the nonresolving rejection gesture from mm. 47–48, all the voices in this vii°7 proceed as expected except the seventh (this time F), which sustains as a suspension from m. 49 into m. 50. This time, the suspension not only fails to resolve downward, as the C failed to do so before, but it immediately—indeed, shockingly—reneges, stepping *up* by half step to F♯ at m. 50 b. 3. This move, together with the simultaneous step up in the bass from A to B and the dominant-seventh chord that results, explicitly signals an imminent cadence in E minor. The lights have come on, the narrator is apparently satisfied, and the story is back on track. S has finally found a way to proceed in the key, E minor, that was promised at the outset by the MC.

All of these events in this extraordinarily complex continuation module can be heard as having the collective expressive effect of slowing the referential narrative rhythm—of suspending or delaying the theme's forward-vectored motion by rhetorically deflecting it away from what should have been (indeed, what at m. 43 we still have no reason to believe will not be) a structurally and expressively unproblematic four-bar continuation. This is an instance of durational atemporality: we begin to experience the story not at the pace of its actual events but rather at a pace filtered through the consciousness of a subjective agent— one who experiences and expresses independently from the pace of the story itself (that is, independently from the pace of the thematic prototype). As mentioned, the situation parallels very closely that of mm. 9–18 in Brahms's op. 2/ii: in both examples, a unit that the implied listener expects to be four bars long (the continuation module at m. 13 in op. 2/ii; the consequent at m. 43 in op. 1/i) becomes lengthened as a result of a series of digressions away from the first-narrative trajectory. Either situation can be rationalized as a large phrase expansion that may not be wholly unexpected in music of Brahms, in which these kinds of fluid, dynamically shifting phrase structures are hallmark features; it certainly is not uncommon in music analysis, moreover, to think of longer phrase units in Classical-Romantic instrumental music as expansions of underlying, unsounding four-bar prototypes. But the important point is that these gestures can also be understood as carrying heightened expressive significance within a Romantic aesthetic environment that relies on a fragmented sense of narrative temporality to create novelistic effects. That is to say, they can be interpreted as discursive shifts that signal not logical continuations of an ongoing story or logical extensions of an ongoing phrase but rather forms of discontinuities—deflections away from the narrative's expected path and into an atemporal stream in which we experience the story not mimetically but rather diegetically, focalized through a subjective agential presence.

§2. Ruptured Atemporality: Chopin op. 58/i and Schumann op. 11/i

Similar expressive concerns emerge in situations that engage with forms of ruptured atemporality. Example 4.4 provides an annotated interpretation of the passage shown in example o.1—the opening of the first movement of Chopin's Piano Sonata in B minor, op. 58.[7] As mentioned, a sentential P yields to a TR—of the type known in Sonata Theory as a *dissolving continuation* (opening here on the subdominant E minor)[8]—in m. 9, which itself produces first a dissolution beginning around m. 13, then a dominant-lock in B minor (m. 14 b. 3), a chromatic disturbance (mm. 17–18), and, perhaps most significantly, a fully diminished-seventh chord (m. 19 b. 1) that brusquely denies the promised resolution of the dominant seventh in G minor from m. 18 b. 4, even while it ostensibly supports the resolution of F♯ to G in the upper voice).

Example 4.4. Chopin, Piano Sonata in B minor, op. 58, i, P and TR.

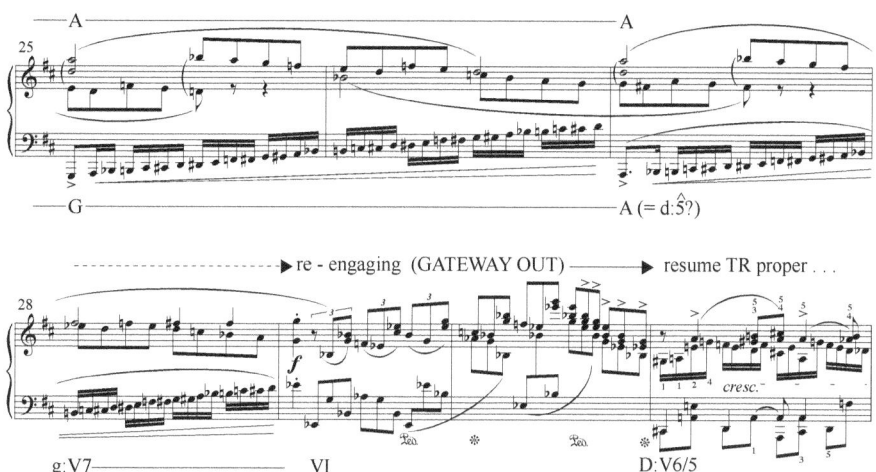

Example 4.4. (*Continued*)

The passage is complex and invokes the presence of multiple temporal streams in its discourse. Observe that the dominant-lock that begins at m. 14 forecasts an impending MC, but in fact, the MC does not materialize until much later—not until m. 39 (not shown in example 4.4). When the MC does arrive, it is not the expected i:HC MC predicted by the F♯ pedal from m. 14, but instead a first-level default III:HC MC. The chromatic shift in mm. 17–18, furthermore, is expressively marked. Measure 17 b. 1 reinterprets the dominant seventh in B minor from m. 16 b. 4 as a German augmented-sixth chord and proceeds onto a $^6_4$ chord—one probably best understood as an *arrival* $^6_4$—in B♭ major, locally one of the most distant possible keys. It leaves the foregoing dominant seventh from mm. 14–16 essentially hanging in midair: A♯ becomes B♭ in the upper voice, and the bass F♯ moves downward by half step to F♮. The bass F♮ in m. 17, moreover, sounds a full two octaves higher than the F♯ in m. 16, as if it cannot be thought of as following directly from the F♯ in a normative voice-leading sense. In fact, Chopin never even respells the F♯ as a G♭ before making the enharmonic reinterpretation, as if signaling (silently, in the notation) that the two pitches should not be thought of as too closely linked. Thus, the dominant-seventh chord, the F♯, and even the TR itself can all be understood as having been cast aside in favor of new music that seemingly comes out of nowhere. Indeed, mm. 17–18 are sharply differentiated from what comes before with regard to tonality (the distant B♭ major, as mentioned, which itself proves unstable and points toward its own relative, G minor, via a dominant-seventh chord at m. 18 b. 4), rhythm (mm. 17–18 introduce a new, contrasting triplet motive), and texture (which becomes loosely imitative here for the first time in the movement).

If mm. 17–18 seem to introduce into the movement a problematic discontinuity, this should be regarded as precisely the expressive aim. And again, as in the opening of the S-theme in Brahms's op. 1/i, the disturbance is not entirely unmotivated: the i:HC MC that appeared to be forthcoming in mm. 14–16—which would have been the terminal cadence in a nonmodulating TR—is one of the lower-level default MC-options in minor-mode sonatas, at least in the Classical repertoire, in which it is often staged as a compositional "problem" in need of emendation.[10] This is consistent with what happens here, in which mm. 17–18 can be regarded as problematizing the F♯ dominant-lock and questioning the structural viability of the proposed TR-trajectory. But even though this may be a fundamentally Classical procedure, the musical rhetoric proves decidedly Romantic, as becomes clear especially at m. 19 b. 1: here, a radical rhetorical gesture introduces into the TR a more severe, even more expressively marked discontinuity than had been heard before, at the enharmonic shift. A fully diminished-seventh chord brusquely denies the promised resolution of the dominant seventh in G minor from m. 18 b. 4, even while it ostensibly supports the resolution of F♯ to G in the upper voice.

And, if mm. 17–18 comprise an initial tremor, m. 19 signifies a veritable earthquake. The expressive effect of the fully diminished seventh is so strong that it can be thought of as opening up a fissure in the TR-space—a hole, literally, into which Chopin inserts, in mm. 19–28, an exceedingly complex ten-bar block of music that can be understood as disengaging from the foregoing eighteen bars and, in a larger sense, from the sonata as a whole.[11] The music in these ten bars signifies its distance from the music around it largely by cueing various forms of temporal disorientation: even as early as mm. 17–18, for example, there appears an anapestic, Beethovenian "fate" figure (˘˘˘/, notated ♪♪♪ | ♩) derived from the movement's first bar—as if the TR begins to look back to the P at this point, perhaps as part of an initial effort to redirect itself away from the impending i:HC MC. But mm. 19–20 promptly turn around and look the other way, abandoning the fate figure in favor of a considerably higher degree of rhythmic fragmentation; observe the rests, for example, in the formerly active bass voice. An inverted, unresolved dominant-seventh chord follows at m. 20 b. 1: this chord looks forward, as mentioned, toward E♭, a tonal center that never fully materializes. Measures 23–27 also look forward, via the arrival in m. 27 on A in the bass, toward D minor (or perhaps D major)—a fleeting glance, perhaps, at what will become the sonata's second key. But m. 28 should be understood as turning around again: its F♯–E♭ dyad on the downbeat, its upward-leading F♯ in the upper voice on bb. 3–4, and its downward-leading C♮ in the inner voice on the second eighth of b. 3 all imply dominant function in G minor. Indeed, this measure probably resurrects the V7 in G minor from m. 18 b. 4 that had been abruptly discarded at m. 19. Other details in this music, especially in mm. 23–28, may not be overtly forward- or backward-looking, but they also underscore the confusion. Specifically, neither the impressionistic, chromatic, left-hand scalar activity nor the structural rising line in the bass (see the F–G–A motion on the downbeats of mm. 23, 25, and 27, respectively) succeed in producing directed voice-leading motion in any conventional sense: the two imitative upper voices, rather than producing a sequence as might have been expected, instead become stuck on A; and in the bass the pitch content in the rising chromatic lines remains completely unchanged (except for the notes on the downbeats) within each two-bar group.

Amid the swirling confusion, m. 29 initiates an exit strategy; the TR begins to regain its footing. First, m. 29 signals a disengagement from what comes before it, very much like the way in which m. 19 signaled a disengagement from m. 18: the E♭ in the bass at m. 29 b. 1 interrupts with a disjunctive tritone leap the structural bass line F-G-A active in mm. 23–27—which the implied listener might have assumed was aiming at B♭, if not, as mentioned, foreshadowing D major via its arrival on the dominant-functioning A. Second, m. 29 sounds as if it resumes the TR-trajectory that had been cast aside earlier. Its E♭-major triad deceptively resolves (as V7-♭VI in G minor) the implied dominant from m. 28; because m. 28 had resurrected the harmony of m. 18, m. 29 can be heard as proposing the very resolution that the diminished seventh in m. 19 had pushed aside. The rhythmic reversion in m. 29 to triplets, last heard in mm. 17–18, also emphasizes this connection. Third, starting from m. 29 the TR proceeds again in a highly normative fashion: the key of D major arrives by m. 31; a dominant-lock in that key emerges at m. 33—where, incidentally, the V♭9 subsumes the fully diminished seventh from m. 19 (C♯–E–G–B♭); and the music mounts an aggressive drive toward the MC, which arrives in m. 39. Two bars of caesura-fill (CF) in mm. 39–40 give way, finally, to the sonata's S-theme—a typically Chopinesque nocturne in the relative major (D major) that should be regarded as this movement's musical image of the longed-for Arcadian paradise.

While the complexity of this TR might not be wholly unexpected in a sonata written in 1844, and while in purely syntactical, formalistic terms some of its complexities may be explainable within existing analytical methodologies, it can also be understood as comprising a series of rhetorical gestures all of which carry considerably heightened expressive values when viewed in terms of signified temporality and the musical narrative it engenders. The most important of these, of course, is the fully diminished-seventh chord at m. 19—which, as mentioned, can be regarded as an extreme gesture of denial that produces an acute, rhetorically emphasized discontinuity. This diminished seventh, together with the music that follows it, can thus be thought of not so much as logically continuing from the music that precedes it but rather as deflecting away from that music—as turning away, that is, from the normative, forward-vectored sonata-in-progress, like a sudden, abrupt about-face. If a text were present, as in the Brahms slow movements, then m. 19 is where the untexted music would begin. As such, the diminished seventh initiates a shift in level of discourse: mimesis shifts to diegesis, and we shift from the first narrative into a parallel, atemporal stream. The situation is analogous to that of Brahms's op. 1/ii, mm. 47–49 and 51–53. There, expressively charged, interruptive silences gave way to a series of upper-register flourishes staged as separate and independent from the surrounding music. The silences were understood as producing ruptures, or fractures, and the flourishes were understood as short, parenthetical interpolations that were inserted into those fractures and that suspended the movement's forward-looking, linear teleology. Here in the Chopin, the compositional details may be different and obviously there is no parallel text, but the temporal meaning can nevertheless be understood similarly: the diminished seventh in m. 19 ruptures the musical fabric just as did Brahms's rests; mm. 19–28 comprise an interpolated, diegetic excursus, away from the first narrative and outside the form proper, just as did Brahms's flourishes. In both examples, the ruptures and subsequent interpolations forcibly pull apart an underlying formal structure that continues to unfold in their wake: in the Brahms, mm. 50 and 54 continued from where mm. 47 and 51 broke off, whereas in the Chopin m. 29 resumes as if following directly from m. 18. Aspects of deep-level metric structure in the Chopin underscore this point: that is, mm. 19–28, plus the two-bar prolongation of the E♭-major triad in mm. 29–30, mask an underlying, normative four-bar phrase—a metric unit that is ubiquitous in Chopin's style and, indeed, in Romantic music in general.[12] Example 4.5a shows this normative phrase (the revelation of which requires only the removal of material and almost no recomposition whatsoever), interpreting the B♭-major triad in m. 17 and the E♭-major triad in m. 29 as ♭VI and ♭II, respectively, in the eventual key of D major. Example 4.5b reinserts the two-bar prolongation of the Neapolitan, E♭. And example 4.5c reinserts the interpolation and shows, for context, the metric structure of the exposition through the onset of S at m. 41. The entire exposition, as shown, comprises seven four-bar phrases, the fifth of which is expanded twice—first by the interpolation, then by the prolonged E♭-major triad.

This entire sequence of events invites an interpretation in which we hear, first, a crisis, signified by the nonmodulating TR proposed in mm. 13–16; second, a momentary hesitation (gateway, mm. 17–18) on the part of a suddenly apparent subjective agent—the revealed narrator-as-protagonist—who is apparently wondering about what to do; third, that narrator's own, personal response to the crisis (interpolation, mm. 19–28)—a response in which he completely loses his requisite objectivity and distance, steps into the story to intervene, and offers, with a certain incoherent urgency, a warning that the story's chosen path needs to be reconsidered; and fourth, a continuation of the story from exactly the point at which it left off (gateway, mm. 29–30, followed by full resumption, mm. 31ff.), with whatever warning the narrator has proffered now duly noted. The interpolated, atemporal pause comprises a musical analog to what Genette would describe either as an anachrony—an analepsis (perhaps triggered by some kind of memory) or a prolepsis (perhaps triggered by the crisis encountered moments before)—or a pure achrony, with no clear or specific temporal relationship to the surrounding music.

* * *

Almost exactly the same series of expressive events occurs in the first movement of Schumann's Piano Sonata in F♯ minor, op. 11. The example differs only with regard to local, surface-level compositional details. The movement includes a fifty-two-bar slow introduction followed by a P-theme that launches in m. 53. P comprises two structurally identical statements of a twenty-bar sentence, where each sentence comprises, in turn, an eight-bar presentation (with two four-bar basic ideas, at mm.

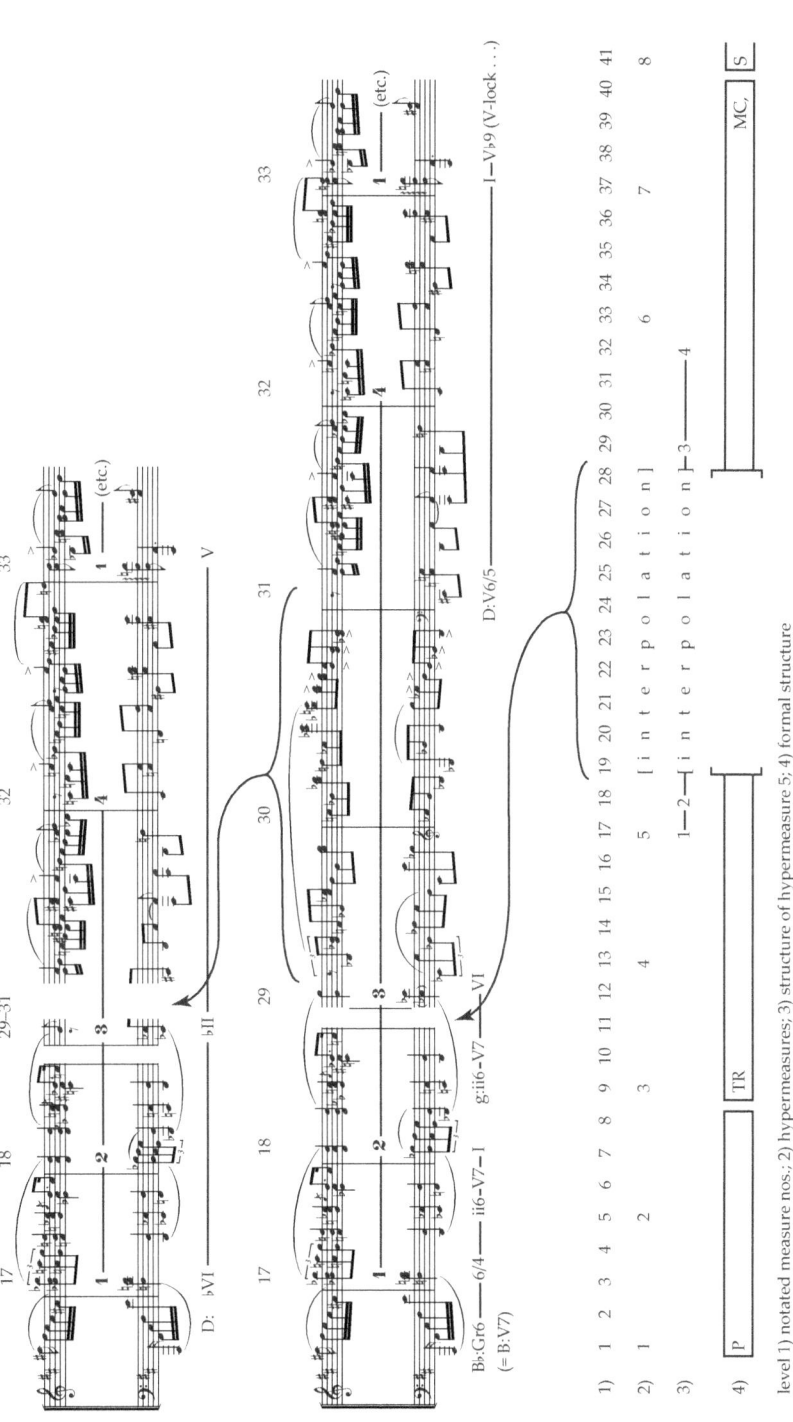

Example 4.5. Chopin, Piano Sonata in B minor, op. 58. Metric structure in the TR.

55 and 59 and again at mm. 75 and 79) and an expanded, twelve-bar continuation (beginning at mm. 63 and 83). Each sentence, furthermore, composes out a i-ii($\sharp$5)-iv-V harmonic cycle in the tonic F$\sharp$ minor: each opens on the tonic (at the initial basic-idea statement, mm. 55 and 75), proceeds to the minor supertonic (a G$\sharp$ minor triad, at the basic-idea repetition, mm. 59 and 79) and then to the subdominant (beginning of the continuation, mm. 63 and 83), and ends on the dominant (toward the end of the continuation, at mm. 69 and 89). TR, shown in full in example 4.6, commences at m. 95; the *fortissimo* dynamic level and the expanded texture here both contribute to the sense of energy gain characteristic of TRs in general, in both the Classical and Romantic repertoire. This is another dissolving-restatement TR-type, very much like the TR in Chopin's op. 58. Schumann's is somewhat more complex in that it is longer and it involves the strategy known as sentence replication (mentioned earlier, in chapter 3, section 2): the two P-theme sentences at mm. 55 and 75 can be understood on a higher structural level as two long basic ideas, such that P as a whole functions as the presentation in a long sentence the (dissolving) continuation of which launches at m. 95. The dissolution itself begins relatively quickly: at m. 99—the minor-supertonic portion of the i-ii-iv-V cycle—what should have been the second basic-idea statement is spun out into a new idea of its own and triggers what appears to be an entirely new sentence, tonicizing G$\sharp$ minor. This eight-bar sentence (presentation, mm. 99–102; continuation, mm. 103–106) essentially overwrites the four-bar basic-idea statement that was expected in its place, hypothetically in mm. 99–102.

This constitutes a disturbance in the narrative. It produces a sense of disruption in what had been, up until this point, a comfortable, even Classical, TR-trajectory. The sonata seems to have become stuck on G$\sharp$ minor, on the supertonic step of the governing harmonic cycle; it seems to have taken an unexpected wrong turn, as it were, momentarily losing its sense of direction. The implied listener wonders where it all might lead. None of this is necessarily unusual: one may well hear the detour as part of the TR-dissolution, in which it would be expected to produce, eventually, an MC, and perhaps even a modulation to the relative major or the minor dominant. But into this context enters m. 106 and its arrival on a B-major triad, complete with a fermata—a quizzical gesture indeed, as if the sonata suddenly finds itself in an unexpected spot and wonders aloud how it got there and how it might get out. The fact of the harmonic arrival itself—staged as a half cadence and as such apparently a proposal for the MC—is not, furthermore the most surprising feature here: the real surprise is the tonality, where, if this is an MC, it is a VII:HC MC that presumably paves the way for a tonally deformational S-theme in the key of the subtonic. But perhaps the event is not an MC at all; perhaps it signals a forthcoming continuation of the TR itself, from the (now major) subdominant portion of the i-ii-iv-V cycle following an eight-bar stall on the cycle's supertonic step.

Either way, the event in m. 106 is a curious one. What follows clarifies its function and suggests that it should be understood within a reading that accounts for multiple signified temporal levels in the narrative. As shown in example 4.6, the disturbance in mm. 99–106 can be construed as a gateway that prefigures a forthcoming rupture; these measures constitute a composed-out crisis point in the story, one dire enough to prompt the narrating agent to forgo his distance and intervene directly. Their narrative function can thus be thought of as analogous to that

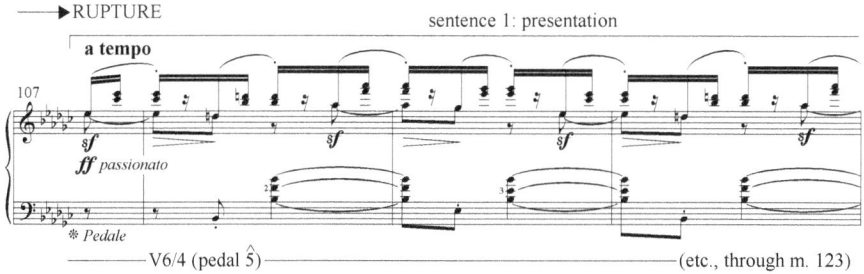

Example 4.6. Schumann, Piano Sonata in F♯ minor, op. 11, i, end of P and TR.

100 | *Sonata Fragments*

Example 4.6. (*Continued*)

Music without Text | 101

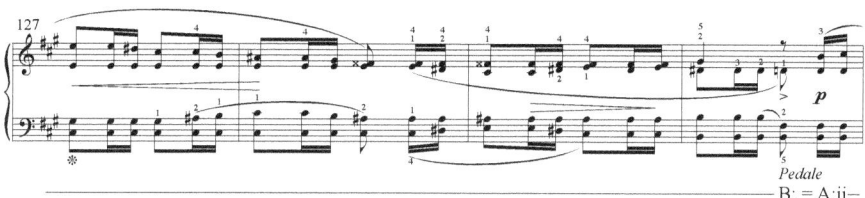

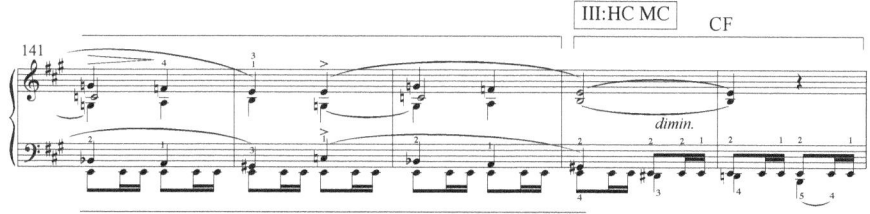

Example 4.6. (*Continued*)

of mm. 17–18 in Chopin's op. 58: a small tremor that foreshadows an impending earthquake. Schumann's earthquake—the rupture itself, or the moment of the most extreme discontinuity—occurs at m. 107. Here, the momentary silence that follows the fermata in m. 106—analogous to Brahms's thirty-second rests in op. 1/ii, mm. 47 and 51—yields to a tonal non sequitur analogous to Chopin's interruptive fully diminished-seventh chord: the B-major triad from m. 106 becomes ♭VI (= C♭) in the key of E♭ minor—a key even more tonally deformational than the subtonic E major one might have thought was coming instead—and proceeds into two identical statements of an eight-bar sentence in that key, in mm. 107–14 and 115–22. These two sentences are staged explicitly as "not-the-S-theme," so distant is their rhetoric from what one would expect from a nineteenth-century Arcadian S; instead, they constitute an interpolated interjection, analogous to mm. 19–28 in the Chopin. They signify a retreat from present, temporal reality into a composed-out moment of atemporal fantasy that exists purely in the mind of the narrator—a subjective presence staged in the music as having intruded upon the story to comment, reminisce, reflect, or (especially in this case) aggressively cajole the sonata into reconsidering its chosen trajectory. At least three immanent features of this music work to signify such meanings: all sixteen bars are delivered *passionato*, at a *fortissimo* dynamic level, as if frantically shouting; all are sounded over a destabilizing, tonally vertiginous dominant pedal rather than a root-position tonic; and the tonality—E♭ minor—is heavily marked. With regard to the latter, the critical point to bear in mind is that even in the nineteenth-century sonata, the deployment of, or even a proposal for, an S-theme, or any portion thereof, in a key other than the Classical norms of major dominant (in a major-mode sonata), or relative major or minor dominant (in a minor-mode sonata), must be regarded as an expressively charged situation—a staged transgression in which the sonata wanders into forbidden, impossible territory. Here, in the middle of an exposition in F♯ minor, E♭ minor signifies just such an impossibility: it is simply not viable as the sonata's second key; it is so far away from acceptable norms that it should be regarded as simply inconceivable as the key of the S, let alone the key of the EEC.[13] Thus, the B-major arrival, the fermata and the subsequent gap, and the non sequitur that follows should all be regarded as producing a shift in level of discourse, and mm. 107–22 as an interpolated, diegetic peroration of the narrator.

Schumann's exit strategy—the gateway out, the righting of the ship—begins at m. 123: the *fortissimo* collapses to a contemplative (or perhaps a searching, or an uncertain) *piano*, and renewed concern with a motive derived from the original basic idea (compare m. 123 with mm. 55, 75, and 95) signals reengagement with the events of the deferred TR. In this sense, m. 123 is analogous to Chopin's m. 29, although Schumann's gateway ultimately proves longer and more complex than Chopin's. Schumann essentially stages a protracted search for the correct pathway back into the story's first-narrative stream: a sequential descent through a whole-tone segment in the bass (E♭ in m. 123, C♯ in 127, B in m. 131) leads to a tonicized B minor (m. 131); B minor, in turn, as subdominant in the original F♯ minor, signals a resumption, from the subdominant step, of the i-ii-iv-V cycle that began back in m. 95, stalled at m. 99, and broke off altogether at m. 107. In fact, m. 131 even appears to signify an epiphany, where the expressive, satisfied *poco ritenuto* in mm. 132–33 connotes a sense of "finally, back to where we need to be," or perhaps "finally, the way forward is clear."[14] B minor functions, furthermore, as supertonic in A major, and it provides a pivot onto the dominant in that key at m. 134; m. 135 then fully resumes the TR proper. In the same way that Chopin's mm. 33ff. led unproblematically to a first-level default MC, the eight-bar sentence that follows here (mm. 135–42) likewise produces a dominant-lock in A major at m. 140, a III:HC MC at 144, two bars of CF in 144–45, and S at 146 (shown in examples 4.1 and 4.2).

Thus, the narrative trajectory of the first half of the Chopin and Schumann expositions proves nearly identical: each comprises a P, followed by a TR-initiation, a TR-crisis, an atemporal interpolation with a gateway in and a gateway out, and finally a full resumption of the TR and, with it, the first-narrative proper. Other than surface-level details, the only real difference in the Schumann is the length of the gateway passages and the extent to which they are developed: Schumann's occupy eight and thirteen bars, respectively, and they comprise fully formed sentences (one in the first gateway, two in the second). Chopin's two-bar gateways are shorter, more concise, and more efficient. The result is that in the Schumann the entry into, and the exit from, the atemporal stream is not as cleanly articulated as in the Chopin, and it would be more difficult to remove Schumann's interpolation and stitch back together the music that remains behind, in the manner of example 4.5.

§3. Conflated Atemporality Types: Brahms op. 5/v, Schumann op. 11/iv, and Brahms op. 1/i

Some situations in the Romantic sonata repertoire may be understood as conflating the two atemporality types, durational and ruptured, as happens in Brahms's op. 2/ii, mm. 2 and 4: a durational expansion allows for a rupture on top of it; an anisochronous expansion or lengthening of the temporal flow in one voice opens up space for a separate shift in level of discourse in another. Often, as in the Brahms, the strategy involves a pedal tone in one voice (usually the bass), where the pedal may emerge out of some salient feature of the first-narrative music—perhaps a single note, itself expressively marked; the pedal is then accompanied by a discontinuity in some other voice or voices, usually above the bass.

A good introductory example occurs in the very interesting rondo finale (the fifth movement) of Brahms's Piano Sonata in F minor, op. 5. Some context will help illuminate the example. The movement opens with a curiously tentative rondo theme that seems to be slow to get fully under way, as if unable to harness the energy latent in the first four measures' rolling, $^6_8$, syncopated, dotted-rhythmic figures. Measures 1–2 open confidently enough, with a *mezzo forte* basic idea, but the music stalls at, for example, m. 3 (the beginning of a response gesture, sounded at a reticent *pianissimo*), mm. 5–6 (an apparent attempt at continuing the basic idea, but still *pianissimo*, with a halting *decrescendo* and an equally hesitant *ritardando* that wonders aloud about how to proceed), and mm. 9–10 (which resemble mm. 5–6). Momentum finally seems to coalesce at m. 15, where there appears, finally, a more complete, more confident version of the rondo theme.

At a local level, the entire fifteen-bar opening can be interpreted as engaged in a provocative dialogue with various forms of atemporality, both the durational and the rupture types. The rondo theme also contains a particularly salient feature that proves central in an interpretation of what happens later in the movement: the theme hinges on a rocking motion in F minor, from tonic to subdominant and back to tonic again, as in mm. 1–2. The central role in this gesture of the subdominant B♭ minor may signify a backward glance at the sonata's fourth movement—a slow intermezzo opening in B♭ minor which comprises its own look backward (a "Rückblick," as Brahms titled the movement) to the sonata's actual slow movement, movement 2; as such, the finale's rondo theme may be an attempt to come to terms with events that transpired earlier in the sonata. All three of the theme's opening harmonies, furthermore, appear in root position, such that the bass moves $\hat{1}$–$\hat{4}$–$\hat{1}$ and provides contrapuntal support for a melody that articulates upper-neighbor motion, C–D♭–C. This melodic figure is especially critical, and various forms or fragments of the gesture are composed out over the next fifteen bars: it appears, for example, as D♭–C in mm. 3–4, A♭–G in mm. 7–8, and C–D♭–C in mm. 11–16. The last of these is heavily embellished and drawn out over six bars of music, such that its completion at m. 15 provides some of the impetus for the energy gain distinctly audible in that measure, propelling the movement into its first rondo refrain.

Formally, the entire movement is fundamentally in dialogue with the five-part rondo (ABACA) at its largest structural level: refrain 1 (module A) opens at m. 1; episode 1 (B) appears—with its singing-style, F-major "F-A-E" theme—at m. 39; refrain 2 (A) tries unsuccessfully to start at m. 71 before successfully launching at m. 104; episode 2 (C)—a transcendent, D♭-major hymn-topic theme that tries to regain the paradise that slipped away in the central refrain—ensues at m. 140; and the final refrain 3 (A) tries to emerge at m. 195, battles with C-episode material in mm. 197–215, and tries again at m. 216 before being overwritten completely by a celebratory, salvational F-major coda at m. 249, complete with a mensural canon on a motive from the C-episode's hymn that rescues the movement from F-minor disaster. Refrains 2 and 3 both encounter difficulty in getting under way, much like the movement's fitful opening. Refrains 1 and 2, moreover, once under way, manage to continue all the way to a cadence—a i:PAC in both instances, at, respectively, mm. 33 and 134. Each is then followed by short transition-link (mm. 33–38 and 134–39) that bridges these modules to their subsequent contrasting episodes, at mm. 39 (B) and 140 (C).

Episode B is of central interest for the conflated atemporality types. As shown in example 4.7, it breaks down around mm. 64–65, failing to produce a cadence of its own. The breakdown is one in which the brightened, positively inflected world of F major gives way to an ominously darkened F minor via the introduction of an A♭ in the left hand at the end of m. 64. The music that follows then toys briefly with the idea of somehow integrating or recontextualizing this expressively problematized A♭: mm. 66–69 tonicize the relative A♭ major, as if trying to recapture the major mode that was lost just moments before, but tonic F minor eventually returns via its own dominant at m. 70.

At this point, the home key having reappeared, the implied listener might reasonably expect a launch of the central refrain. And, in fact, there does appear to be a nod in this direction: cascading sixteenths in m. 71 crash onto what could be the

Example 4.7. Brahms, Piano Sonata in F minor, op. 5, v. End of episode 2 (B) and beginning of refrain 2 (central A).

106 | Sonata Fragments

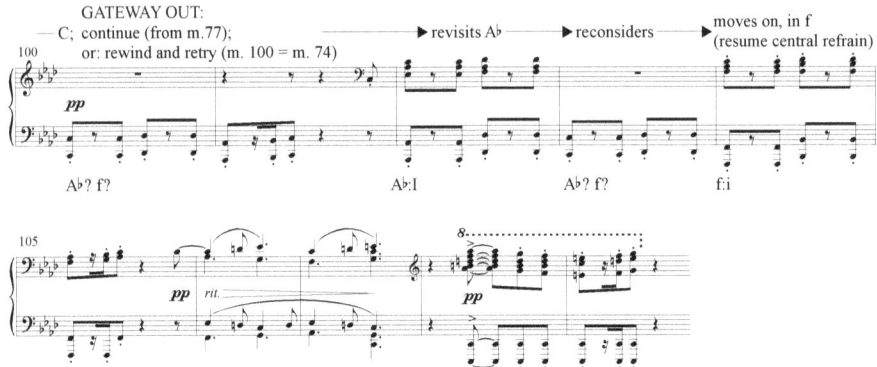

Example 4.7. (*Continued*)

theme's downbeat at m. 72, with the C-D♭ neighbor figure now in the bass instead of the upper voices. But this moment turns out to be only a false start, with the harmonic function in m. 72 (still dominant in F minor) undermining the theme's security; it gets no further than its first utterance of the upper-neighbor D♭, at m. 72 b. 2. An immediate, second attempt at the same cascading sixteenths ("trying again," m. 73, = m. 71) produces the same neighbor-note figure in the bass (m. 74, = m. 72), which this time manages to continue past its first D♭—as if perhaps this measure (m. 74), or maybe the next (m. 75), might produce a successful rondo-theme launch. But m. 75, surprisingly, reharmonizes the C-D♭ figure in the key of A♭ major, as if looking backward to what happened in mm. 66–69. Once again, the A♭ tonicization suggests a staged compositional problem: the first-default tonal level for the rondo theme is the tonic, F minor, not the relative major. Measures 75–77 proceed by considering the possibility that C-D♭ might be $\hat{3}$–$\hat{4}$ in A♭ major instead of $\hat{5}$–$\hat{6}$ in F minor—another "right mode, wrong key" gesture, perhaps, that again tries to stave off for just a moment the impending F-minor doom. A wrong-key statement of the theme then gets fully under way at m. 75, but derails after one measure: the upper voices drop out in m. 76 even as the bass continues to oscillate, futilely, between C and D♭—wondering aloud, perhaps, about its own tonal viability and about where it might go from here.

One more attempt to launch the rondo theme in A♭ major occurs at m. 77. At this point, the failure, or the inability, to correct the staged problem triggers a striking, rhetorically charged event for which the tonal disturbance in mm. 75–77 retrospectively functions as a gateway passage. That is, at the last eighth note in m. 77, in the left hand, the upper-neighbor D♭—one of the theme's most salient features—is struck and sustained, like a tolling bell. It then becomes frozen in place, refusing to relent and give way to the rest of the refrain. Thus, what should have been a single moment in linearly directed time—a single beat, a single upper neighbor—becomes captured, immobilized, and projected spatially into the distance, seemingly for as far as one can see: the D♭ sustains for a full twenty-two measures, from

m. 78 through m. 99. Within this spatial world, there appears in the upper voices—tripping lightly along the walkway laid down before it, plank by plank—an ethereal, otherworldly reminiscence delivered by the narrating agent, who sacrifices his objectivity and intervenes diegetically in order to stem the crisis.[15] Temporally, the situation is a larger, exploded version of what happened at the beginning of the slow movement of Brahms's op. 2: this is another durational expansion with a rupture on top, another anisochrony that opens up room for a fracture and a discursive shift. In op. 2/ii, m. 2 captured and extended in time as a pedal tone the last note of m. 1 (A♯), just as m. 4 did the same thing with the last note of m. 3 (B); the pedals, in turn, provided room for ruptures in the upper voices above. In exactly the same way, here in op. 5 mm. 78–99 capture and extend in time as a pedal the last note from m. 77. The upper voices simultaneously rupture and disengage from the first narrative, and the form comes apart. The disengagement is signified specifically in the marked discontinuities in register (the upper voices shift up by two full octaves at the last eighth note in m. 77) and dynamic level (m. 78 embarks on a whispering *pianissimo*, then fades away into the distance beginning around the *dim. ma in tempo* marking in m. 90). The harmonic language in the interpolated excursus, in turn, explicitly connotes the narrator's objective distance and intense introspection. Measure 77 opens in D♭ major, for example, but mm. 83–89 reinterpret the D♭ as C♯ (see especially the A7 chord in mm. 83–84), as if wondering how the D♭ might be dispensed with or absorbed into the tonal structure—openly asking, perhaps, "if not $\hat{1}$ in D♭ major, $\hat{6}$ in F minor, or $\hat{4}$ in A♭ major, then what?" The entire interpolation thus constitutes one large, angst-ridden reconsideration of the D♭—or, perhaps better, it comprises one long, final look backward at a D♭-major Arcadia that had been a central focus of the narrative in this sonata's first and second movements (see m. 91 in movement 1; see m. 37 and the apotheosis at m. 144 in movement 2).[16]

By about m. 96, the consternation appears to have passed and the narrator seems to find peace by accepting that the D♭-major paradise will remain permanently out of reach. The music signifies as much by accepting D♭ as $\hat{6}$ in F minor. The upper voices settle on F-A♭ dyads in mm. 96–99; these obviously constitute the upper third and fifth of a D♭-major triad, but they also make possible a simple, direct shift to F minor via the yielding of D♭ down by half step—which occurs, finally, in m. 100. This move completes the C–D♭–C motive that was begun all the way back at m. 77, and thus temporally it also signals the beginning of the gateway out of the interpolated stream; the rondo theme's initiatory gesture reappears immediately in mm. 100–1. One more fleeting glance backward at A♭ major in mm. 102–3 (as if bidding A♭ a final farewell) yields to a full resumption of the central refrain, and with it the first narrative, at m. 104 (mm. 104–5 ≈ mm. 1–4, m. 106 ≈ m. 5, m. 107 = m. 6, etc.). Measure 100 thus resumes a formal process that was begun at the pickup to m. 72 but suspended at m. 78, such that, as shown in example 4.8, mm. 77–100 comprise a total of five iterations of the C–D♭–C motive, the last of which proceeds successfully into the rondo refrain itself. Measure 100 might also be heard as a resetting of the clock, in effect backing up to m. 74 and rewriting the narrative from that point forward—proposing, in effect, a more satisfactory version of the story, delivered with a newfound confidence apparently obtained while sequestered in the atemporal stream of mm. 78–99.

The interpolated mm. 78–99 can thus be thought of as another form of what Genette would describe structurally as a pause: story time stands still while narrative time continues to flow. The particular sequence of events in this example, moreover, also provides an especially compelling musical analog for one of Bakhtin's chronotopes—specifically, the road chronotope, a metaphor for a narrative that moves forward in time along a temporally vectored "road," but occasionally pauses, momentarily, in order to allow for the unfolding of a spatially conceived episode. Here, the normative rondo form stands in for the main road; a single note—the D♭ at mm. 77–78—represents a station along that road at which the story temporarily comes to a stop. Within the interpolated episode, forward mimetic motion momentarily ceases, and we follow the narrator outside the first narrative into a contemplative respite, a meditative trance, or some other diegetic stream of events or stream of consciousness. Eventually, the first-narrative gears reengage and we step back onto the road: m. 100 continues with the story from where m. 77 left off.

* * *

The second example, very similar in its large outlines, comes from the exposition of the fourth and final movement of Schumann's Piano Sonata in F♯ minor, op. 11. Typical of Schumann, this is a sonata movement in an exceptionally rich and complex dialogue with Classical conventions. A P in m. 1 (formatted as an aaba song form) proceeds to an independently thematized TR at m. 17, which goes tonally awry around m. 20 and produces an MC in m. 24 on the dominant in the "impossible" key of E♭ major (a look backward, perhaps, at the interpolated E♭-minor peroration in the first movement, discussed in section 1). There follows at m. 25 what should probably be understood as a contemplative, meditative, TR-based module in dialogue with the S⁰ concept (that is, a preliminary or preparatory module that precedes or somehow sets up the S-theme proper),[17] over the dominant in E♭, followed by a proposal for an S¹ in m. 33, now on the tonic in E♭. This tonally transgressive S

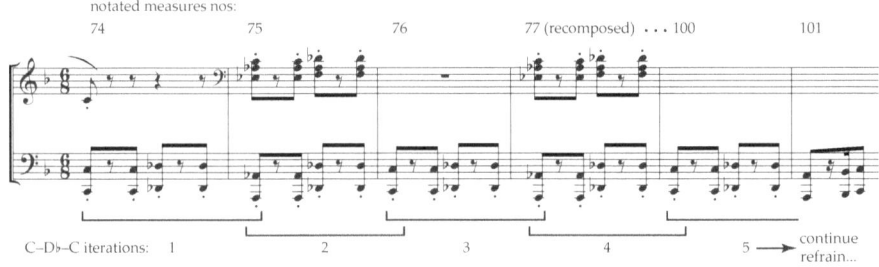

Example 4.8. Brahms, Piano Sonata in F minor, op. 5, v. Recomposed opening of refrain 2 (central A).

breaks down around m. 37 and gets abruptly discarded in m. 38, at which point the sonata resets the clock and makes a second attempt at an exposition-gone-wrong: we revert first to the S^0 at m. 39 (= m. 25), then all the way back to the P at m. 50 (= m. 1). This latter move initiates a rotational restart: TR appears again in m. 66 (= m. 17) and produces another MC at m. 73 b. 1 (= m. 24)—this time, a normative III:HC MC, after which a new, lyrical, A-major S-theme dives in excitedly on the very next beat, m. 73 b. 2.

This S is shown in example 4.9. Schumann formats it as a sentence comprising a presentation with two compound basic ideas (mm. 73–76 and 77–80, the second a fifth higher than the first) and a short continuation in mm. 81–85. The continuation sequentially treats a fragment of the original basic idea, where the descending thirds gestures beginning at the left-hand pickup to m. 81 (G–$F_\sharp$–E in mm. 80–81, G–$F_\sharp$–$E_\sharp$ in mm. 81–82, A–$G_\sharp$–$F_\sharp$ in mm. 82–83) derive directly from the basic idea's characteristic descending-third motive in mm. 74–75. But trouble lurks beneath what so far appears to be a contented, unproblematic surface. As suggested in example 4.9, m. 84 b. 1 introduces a disturbance: at the very moment the implied listener expects (because of the rising sequence in mm. 80–83) an F_x, an $F_\sharp$ appears instead, essentially repeating the $F_\sharp$ from m. 83 and canceling its obligatory upward resolution. This can be heard as signifying a stagnation, in which normative forward progress through the continuation module momentarily stalls. The $F_\sharp$ in m. 84, confused and disoriented, proceeds by resolving downward, not upward, back to the $E_\sharp$ from two bars earlier (from m. 82). This is an ominous event. It produces a rhetorical "backing up"—a miniature version of the resetting-the-clock gestures heard earlier in the exposition—in which the continuation reverts to the contrasting-idea portion of the presentation's compound basic idea; that is, mm. 84–85 repeat a motive heard earlier, in mm. 75–76 and 79–80. And it prompts the S-theme to immediately accept the tonal implications of the $E_\sharp$: m. 85 is staged as a half cadence in none other than the key of $F_\sharp$ minor—the movement's home key (!).

This is a staged crisis, in which the S-theme has proven itself incapable of holding on to the brightened, positive, Arcadia world of A major and has been overwhelmed by the force of present, tonic-minor reality. The crisis triggers the striking rhetorical move that follows, immediately after the half cadence: at this point, what appears to have been a sentential antecedent (with a terminal half cadence) in mm. 73–85 yields not to the expected sentential consequent but instead to an entirely new period, emerging as if from out of nowhere, with its own sentential antecedent in mm. 86–93 and its own consequent (also sentential) at m. 94.[18] This new music immanently signifies its own distance from what precedes it: the material at m. 86 is more closely related to the contemplative S^0-idea from m. 25 than to the foregoing antecedent; it suppresses, rather than engages directly with, Schumann's typically lyrical, singing-style S-rhetoric; and the *pianissimo* marking (even softer than the foregoing S-antecedent) signifies "from a distance," while the *marcato un poco* (which contrasts with, for example, the *sempre legato e molto espressivo* at m. 77) similarly signifies "in a different voice."

110 | Sonata Fragments

Example 4.9. Schumann, Piano Sonata in F♯ minor, op. 11, iv, S.

Example 4.9. (*Continued*)

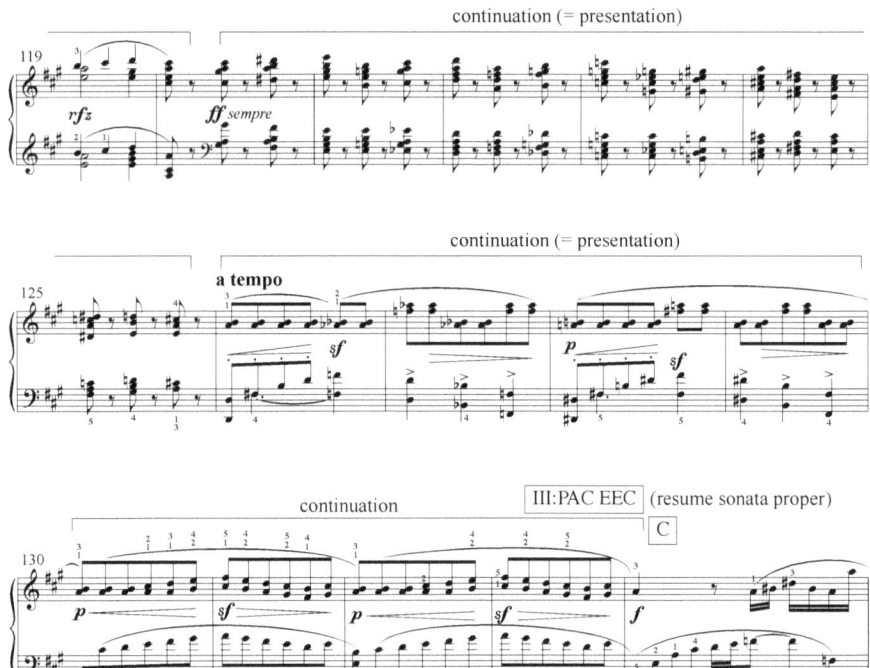

Example 4.9. (*Continued*)

As such, m. 86 connotes a sharp discontinuity—an interruption of, rather than a logical continuation of, the S-theme itself. The camera cuts abruptly to a new shot; what was expected is pushed aside or overwritten by what is made audible. The rhetoric is that of fragmented temporality, and the strategy is the same as in Brahms's op. 5 finale: here again, a single moment in time—a single problematized or rhetorically charged note, this time the C♯ from the half cadence in m. 85—is seized and projected spatially into the distance as a pedal point, this time persisting for the next twelve bars (mm. 86–97). Over this pedal the upper voices rupture, the level of discourse shifts, and the form comes apart; into the spatial world opened up by the durational expansion there steps the narrating agent, intruding diegetically on the story-in-crisis with another atemporal, commentarial excursus. In retrospect, the disturbances in mm. 84–85 comprise a gateway passage that prefigures the rupture and the onset of a large interpolated module, one that can be construed specifically as a musical analepsis—a reminiscent, longing, angst-ridden look backward in time: the syncopated sixteenths in m. 86 (literally backward-looking, as mentioned, in that they summon up the material from m. 25) constitute a musical icon for the narrator's own heartbeat—a musical image of the narrator's inner pulse, as it were, throbbing with sorrow and regret, unable to maintain his objectivity and detachment from the story; and the lamenting, *pianto* appoggiaturas sounding in both the right and left hands comprise painfully wishful, "all is lost" gestures—yearning, heart-rending reflections on "what might have been" had the S not failed to hold on to the idealized, Arcadian A major.

What follows at once composes out the narrator's reminiscent longing and stages a recovery operation in which the music gradually reenters the temporal, first-narrative stream. As shown in example 4.9, m. 94 initiates a lengthy, discursive, typically Schumannian sentence chain (*Satzkette*): a presentation module in mm. 94–97 yields to a continuation at m. 98; mm. 98–101 are then reinterpreted as a presentation for the continuation at m. 102; and so on until the terminal cadence in m. 134.[19] Measure 98 specifically can be regarded as the beginning of the gateway out of the interpolation—where this gateway composes out the narrator's gradual awakening to the possibility that S-viability might be close at hand. The reminiscent, lamenting gestures from before are now abandoned, replaced by a modulatory fifths cycle that arrives at m. 105 on a V7/V and, at m. 106, a lengthy, elaborated dominant-lock, all in the newly recovered key of A major. The narrator gradually gains confidence and conviction, with an *accelerando* (m. 110) and a *crescendo* (m. 112) both contributing to an aggressive drive to the downbeat of m. 114. The pickup to m. 115 musically realizes the narrator's full awakening: the moment is a staged epiphany—a vigorous outburst, *brillante e veloce*, with repeated *sforzandos* that culminate in a *fortissimo* at m. 120. A solution to the crisis is imminent: one final sentence (presentation in mm. 126–29, continuation at m. 130) leads, at m. 135, to a long-awaited PAC in A major—EEC in what was, looking back, a long, tortured sonata exposition.

Schumann's treatment of the multiple temporal streams in this passage diverges in interesting ways from that of earlier examples. The differences can be thought of in terms of the scenarios depicted in figure 4.1. The TR-interpolations in Chopin's op. 58/i and Schumann's op. 11/i, as well as the interpolation near the beginning of the central refrain in Brahms's op. 5/v, behave according to the model in figure 4.1a, whereas the S-interpolation here in Schumann's op. 11/iv (along with the interpolation at the end of the S-theme in Brahms's op. 1/i, on which more presently) behaves according to the model in figure 4.1b. In figure 4.1a, a rupture (perhaps sounded over a durational expansion, and perhaps entered into and exited from via a gateway passage) initiates an interpolated block of music that interrupts and momentarily suspends the first narrative. Points A^1 and A^2 together represent the "present moment"—the moment at which the first narrative is interrupted and pushed apart to make room for the interpolation. Point A^1 specifically is the moment of interruption, while point A^2 is the moment of resumption—the moment at which the story continues from where it left off, such that, in terms of story time, $A^1 = A^2$. The interpolated material can thus be more or less neatly removed and the material that remains stitched back together, without disturbing the larger outlines of the narrative form as a whole. In figure 4.1b, on the other hand, the interpolated stream interrupts the first narrative, as in 4.1a, but then it proceeds as if overwriting (rather than simply suspending) the temporal material that would otherwise have been present in this space. When the first narrative continues at, say, some point B further along the way, that moment is later in time than point A^1/A^2, such that the story does not simply continue from the moment at which it was interrupted but from some other moment further along. The result is that some part of the first narrative goes permanently missing and never appears on the surface of the story. The practical result here in Schumann's op. 11/iv, for example, is that the consequent module that "belongs" with the antecedent in mm. 73–85 is never actually heard; the atemporal interpolation rejoins the temporal stream at the moment of the EEC, which is presumably at the end of (or at some point after) the hypothetical missing consequent. Both of the situations described in figure 4.1 can be productively defined in terms of two of Genette's categories of anachronies: scenarios adhering to figure 4.1a comprise musical analogs for *external* (*externe*) anachronies—those "whose entire extent remains external to the extent of the first narrative"; situations adhering to figure 4.1b comprise musical analogs for *internal* (*interne*) anachronies—specifically an *internal analepsis*, in Schumann's op. 11/iv— anachronies that extend past the point in time at which the first narrative was originally interrupted.[20]

* * *

The last example comes from the S-space of the first movement of Brahms's Piano Sonata in C major, op. 1, the opening module of which I discussed above, in section 1; figure 4.2 provides a complete formal diagram of the movement. As mentioned, in m. 50 the S-theme finally points, via a dominant seventh, toward a cadence in E minor, the very key that had been proposed by the TR and the MC but then questioned (at the MC itself, mm. 36–38), rejected (at the S-downbeat, m. 39), and taken up again and debated extensively (in the wandering, vacillating, anisochronous S-continuation, mm. 43–50). Thus, at first m. 50 appears to comprise the final, decisive move in a troubled S-theme; cadential closure seems imminent. However, as shown in example 4.10, any will to move forward in E minor that may be suddenly audible at this moment—any conviction to produce a cadence in that key— quickly proves fleeting: the dominant-seventh chord resolves, at m. 51, not onto the expected tonic triad in E minor but instead onto an A-minor triad with the fifth, E, in the bass. This moment has baffled a number of commentators, for good reason: the harmonic and formal functions articulated at m. 51 are ambiguous at best and invite multiple readings. Some have chosen to simply read the event as initiating a new S-theme (or a new component thereof) in its own right; others have chosen to hear m. 51 as a "half cadence" and the elided downbeat of a consequent module, one that follows directly from the antecedent in mm. 39–50 (this option requires insisting—problematically, as mentioned earlier—that the S-theme is in the key of A minor).[21] Alternatively, perhaps m. 51 should be understood as manifesting in miniature a Brahmsian procedure that Peter Smith describes as *dimensional counterpoint*, in which aspects of form, harmony, and voice-leading structure may be misaligned.[22] That is, the chord may be an embellished tonic triad in E minor the

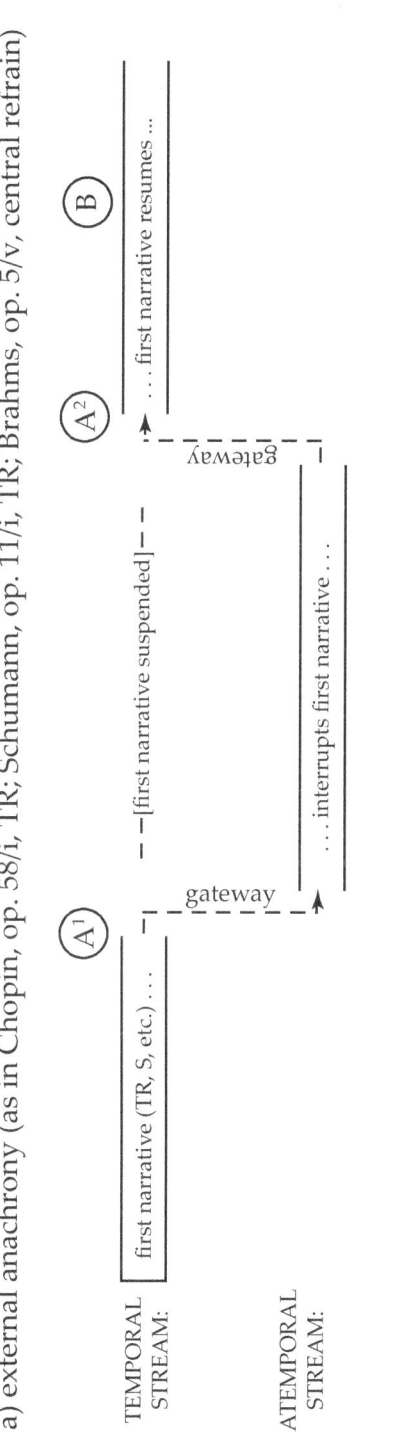
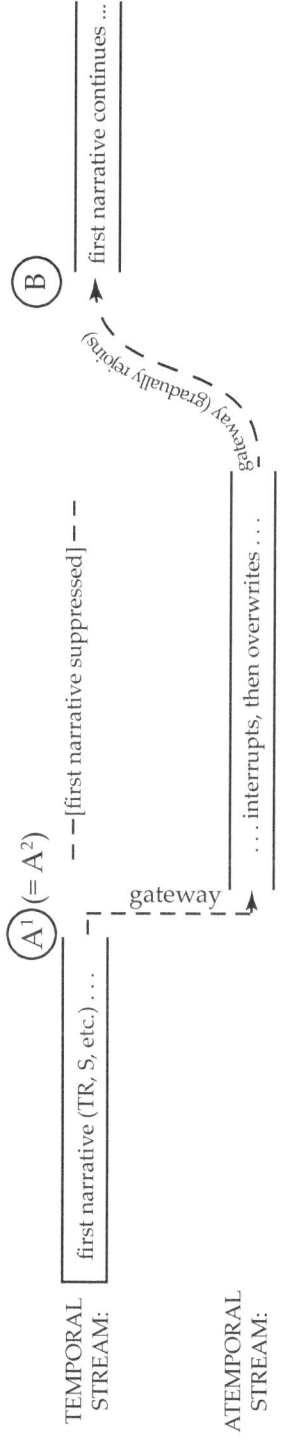

Figure 4.1. Internal and external anachronies.

third and fifth of which arrive late due to the presence of two appoggiaturas, A and C, that eventually resolve onto G♯ and B (at m. 54, repeated in m. 58) in what amounts to a composed-out $^6_4$-$^5_3$ appoggiatura figure. Perhaps in this sense mm. 51–54 would be understood as composing out the cadence that was forecast in m. 50—a cadence on E, now E major instead of E minor (where the G♯ in m. 54 is a Picardy third, and the $^6_4$ chord itself, from m. 51, may harken back to the blocked resolutions of the dominant-functioning seventh chords heard just moments before, in m. 47–48 and 49–50). Still another alternative is to think of m. 51 as a locally stable harmony—one of Hatten's arrival $^6_4$ chords that substitutes or stands in for the E-minor triad that was expected in its place.[23]

In my view, the "half cadence" reading comes closest to explaining the situation. But the event is more complex than such a formalistic reading might suggest, and in fact, the conditions here are best understood as invoking a fragmented, multivalent treatment of temporal space. As in other similar, expressively charged contexts, the fact that the chord in m. 51 rejects an anticipated cadence by forcibly denying an anticipated resolution onto an already highly problematized tonic E minor suggests that it should be regarded as a rhetorical gesture that carries with it significantly heightened expressive meaning. In fact, it can be regarded as the

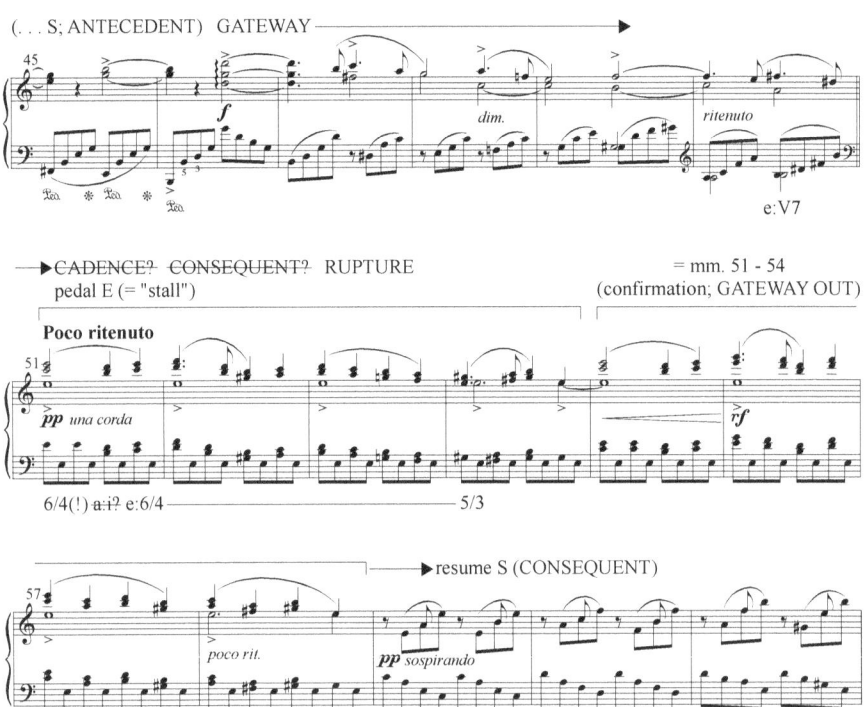

Example 4.10. Brahms, Piano Sonata in C major, op. 1, i, S: end of the antecedent and beginning of the consequent.

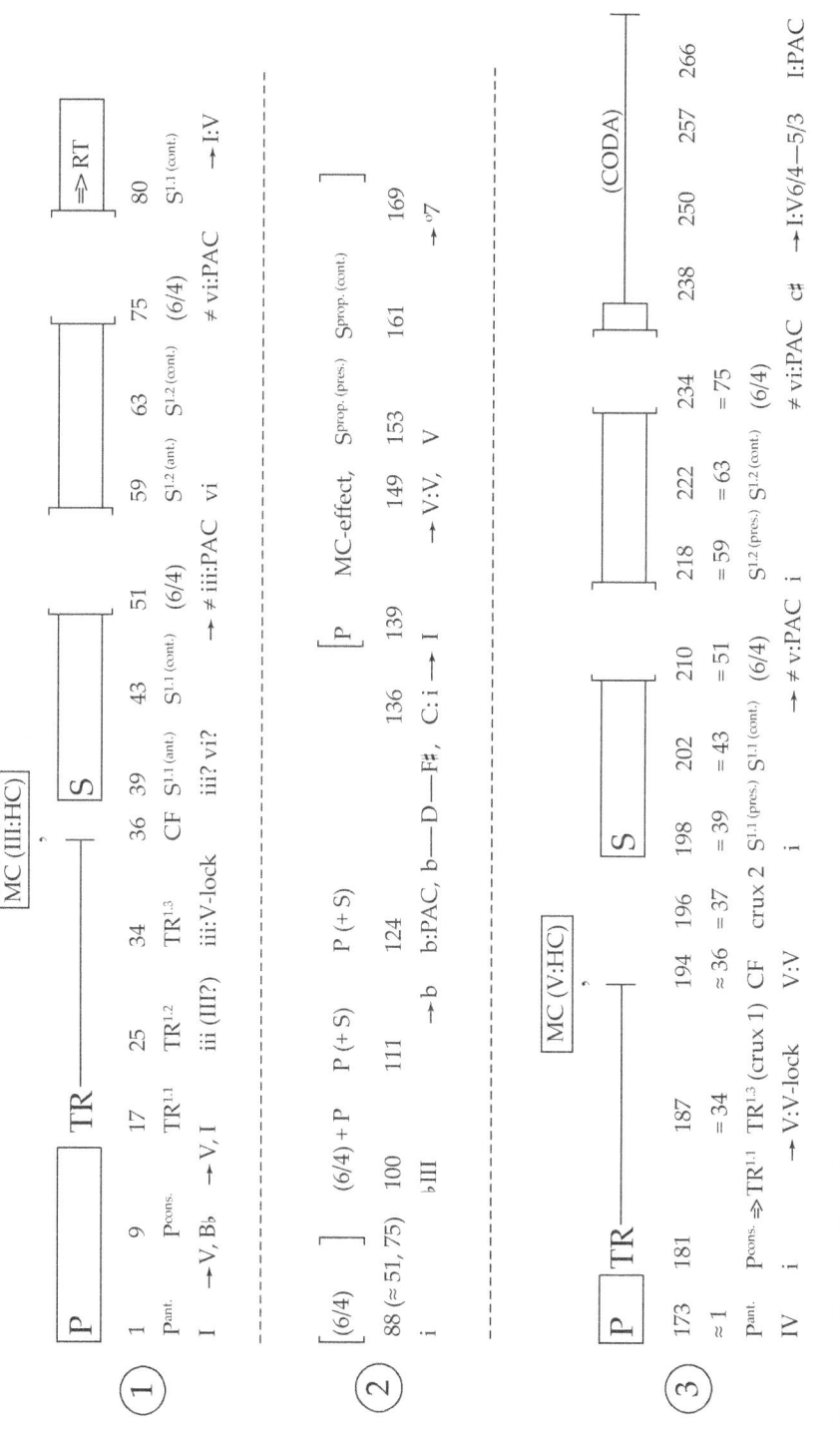

Figure 4.2. Brahms, Piano Sonata in C major, op. 1, i.

most extraordinary rhetorical move of all thus far in an S-space the ambivalence of which has already proven astonishing. Following on the heels of the struggle in mm. 39–50 between E minor and A minor, that is, an A-minor triad over a pedal-point E in the bass voice is surely the ultimate attempt at hedging one's bets, "having it both ways," and staving off a final commitment to one side or the other. In this specific sense, m. 51 should not be regarded as logically and directly continuing from or realizing the implications of the events in m. 50; m. 51 is better understood, rather, as signifying a discontinuity—a stepping outside of, or a turning away from, the S-theme's normative, forward-vectored linear flow in one or another of its possible keys. The specific compositional strategies used to effect this shift, moreover, are the same as those in Schumann's op. 11/iv and in Brahms's own op. 5/v: a durational expansion in the bass that makes room for a rupture in the voices above.

Here, the E in the bass signals the expansion. This is the pitch that was expected at this moment and in this register—the pitch that is "supposed" to be here, following the B7 chord at the end of m. 50. But this E does not simply resolve the foregoing B and then move on. Rather, at the moment of resolution, the E is struck—actually split into octaves—and then sustained across the next eight measures of music as a pedal point. This has the effect of elongating the moment of the supposed cadence—a single moment in time—by projecting it spatially, which in turn has the effect of pulling apart the form and opening up room in which a shift in level of discourse occurs elsewhere in the texture. The shift occurs in the upper voices, in which a rupture signals the intrusion of a separate voice, diegetic instead of mimetic, delivered from outside the first-narrative stream. The rupture, in turn, is signaled by extreme discontinuities in various parameters, including dynamic level (the *pianissimo* at m. 51 signifies "from a distance"), timbre (the *una corda* at m. 51, properly executed, can create a marked distancing effect of its own), tempo marking (the *poco ritenuto* signals a slowing of the pace, as if the narrating agent pauses or lingers), and, most obviously perhaps, register (the D♯5 in m. 50 resolves to an E5 on the downbeat of m. 51, but this E5 is buried in an inner voice by a literally separate and independent voice that emerges from out of nowhere, as if hurled down from on high, on C6 and E6). The tempo marking itself is especially interesting in that while "ritenuto" clearly indicates "slower," it also suggests (deriving as it does from the Italian *ritenere*) "to hold back," "to think," or "to consider." It may well be an unsounding signifier for the narrator's momentary absorption in an interiorized stream of reflection and reminiscence.

The implied narrative thus parallels one seen in earlier examples: a disturbance in the sonata trajectory (here, the tonal tension in the S-theme proper, especially mm. 46–50) functions as a gateway that prefigures a rupture (here the noncadence in m. 51); the rupture then fractures the linear trajectory and signifies the intrusion of a narrating agent who reflects, comments, or tries to stem the crisis. Here, we may wish to hear a certain Romantic longing in the narrator's voice at m. 51—perhaps a looking back over the strained E-minor-A-minor S-trajectory, perhaps a reminiscence on "what might have been" had the sonata taken a different course. In this context, the gradual descent of the superimposed upper voices in mm. 51–54 into the same register as the E5 may signify a long, slow, resigned exhalation of breath—perhaps a grudging acceptance of E as a temporary way station for this highly problematized sonata narrative. This same gesture repeats itself in mm. 55–58 (= mm. 51–54), wondering aloud about but eventually accepting again, as if confirming, the arrival on E major. These last four measures can thus be understood as providing the gateway out of the atemporal stream; a normative consequent ensues at m. 59—a consequent that is parallel to, even while it elaborates on, the antecedent in mm. 39–50. In retrospect, the interpolation appears designed to problematize a tonicized half cadence in A minor that should have appeared in m. 51, where A minor is the key that the S-theme eventually accepts as its own and in which it attempts an EEC, at m. 75. The actual half cadence itself never literally appears on the musical surface; it appears only insofar as the E-major triad in m. 54 finally resolves the B7 chord from m. 50. The entire eight-bar interpolation overwrites the cadence—or spreads it into eight bars instead of just one—and the first narrative continues later, at m. 59, just after the hypothetical cadential moment. In terms of figure 4.1, the situation basically adheres to the internal anachrony model shown in part (b): point A^1/A^2 corresponds to a point in time right before the cadence, whereas point B—the resumption of the consequent—occurs at a point in time just after it; the cadence itself is overwritten, or suppressed and *re*written, by the interpolated atemporal stream. If we choose to hear the interpolation as backward looking, then mm. 51–58 are analogous to one of Genette's internal analepses.

§4. Conclusion

Atemporality in all its forms is a central strategy in the narrative discourse of the Romantic sonata. It is the central means by which the genre achieves its audible separation of story versus narrative time; mimesis versus diegesis; first-narrative versus other, parallel narrative streams. It is the central means, therefore, by which the sonata achieves its identity as *Romantic—novelistic*, in the Schlegelian sense—in the nineteenth century. An awareness of its presence in the Romantic sonata repertoire makes possible a critical interpretation of that repertoire that positively values the apparent formal disorder—that positively values the most idiosyncratic, expressively marked structural and rhetorical discontinuities—so distinctly characteristic of the genre and of the way in which it manifests the aesthetics of the Romantic era.

Notes

1. On the singing style, see Ratner, *Classic Music*, 19. On the "lyrically 'singing' or gracefully *cantabile* S" common in Classical sonatas, especially those of Mozart, see Hepokoski and Darcy, *Elements of Sonata Theory*, 133–35. On "default options" as accounting for the range of compositional choices available to a composer in a sonata's action spaces, see Hepokoski and Darcy, ibid., 9–10.

2. Caplin, *Classical Form*, 61–63.
3. Ibid., 61.
4. Ibid., 39.
5. Some commentators simply assert, without further consideration, that S is in the key of A minor. Examples include Frisch, *Brahms and the Principle of Developing Variation*, 53; and Schubring, "Five Early Works by Brahms (1862)," 199. See also Graybill ("Brahms's Three-Key Expositions," 69), who reads S as modulating, and Zenck ("Classicism vs. the 'New German School,'" 249), who refers obliquely to "the relation of C major and E minor in the choices of the first and second subjects in the first movement of the *Waldstein Sonata* and in Brahms's op. 1/I."
6. Caplin, *Classical Form*, 59.
7. Portions of the op. 58 analysis that follows have previously been published in Davis, "Chopin and the Romantic Sonata."
8. On transition types in the Classical sonata, see Hepokoski and Darcy, *Elements of Sonata Theory*, 95–113. I follow Hepokoski and Darcy, ibid., esp. 94–95, in locating the beginning of a TR at the beginning of a phrase or other formal module, rather than in the middle of that module, regardless of where TR-rhetoric proper seems to emerge.
9. For Hatten, *Musical Meaning in Beethoven*, 15, an *arrival* $^6_4$ is a rhetorically emphasized $^6_4$ chord that has no overt impulse to complete a cadence in the manner of a cadential $^6_4$. See also Klein, "Chopin's Fourth Ballade as Musical Narrative," 45.
10. See Hepokoski and Darcy, *Elements of Sonata Theory*, 26–27.
11. Chopin's use of the fully diminished seventh at m. 19 invites comparison with Beethoven's use of the same sonority in the exposition of the Piano Sonata no. 30 in E major, op. 109, m. 9 (at the *Adagio espressivo*). Hatten (*Interpreting Musical Gestures, Topics, and Tropes*, 169) has described its effect there as a "massive rhetorical disruption" that forms part of a "gesture of radical annihilation"; Kinderman comments on the same passage, as one example of a parenthetical enclosure (see chapter 2, endnote 28). Chopin also uses the fully diminished seventh as a signifier for severe discontinuity again later in this same movement, at m. 65, in the middle of a second S-theme (an "S²") that reverts, in most surprising fashion, to the key of D-major following an apparent v:PAC EEC in m. 56; see Davis, "Chopin and the Romantic Sonata."
12. See Rosen, *The Romantic Generation*, 258–78 on the "dominion over musical composition" (261) of the four-bar phrase in Romantic music. Rosen's discussion has interesting temporal ramifications: he interprets Romantic-period expansions of Classical four-bar phrases not necessarily as conventional phrase expansions per se but rather as hypermetric "fermatas" functioning to effect "expressive suspense" (262).
13. See Hepokoski and Darcy, *Elements of Sonata Theory*, 178–79 on "impossible keys" in Classical-era sonatas.
14. Rosen (*Sonata Forms*, 69) has commented that "Paradoxically, the move to A major at the end of the exposition of this work has the sense of return."
15. In a hearing that has interesting temporal implications and that overlaps especially with my interpretation of mm. 78–99 as reflective or reminiscent, Bozarth ("Brahms's *Lieder ohne Worte*," 374–75) interprets m. 78 as a return to "the sardonic mood that opened the movement," now "in the key of D♭ major," a key that he notes has important links to each of the sonata's previous four movements.
16. For more on movement 1, see part III. Movement 2, incidentally, begins in A♭ major but ends in D♭ major—exactly the same tonal journey articulated in the first movement's modulatory S-theme. The entire sonata, furthermore, can be construed as longing in true Romantic fashion for an impossible, out-of-reach D♭-major paradise. In this context, the celebratory F-major coda at m. 249 in the final movement is a rescue in extremis for the sonata as a whole—an intervention from the outside, a deus ex machina to save the day right at the moment of the final collapse (at, that is, the final return of the F-minor refrain).
17. On the "S⁰" concept, see Hepokoski and Darcy, *Elements of Sonata Theory*, 142–45.

18. Measures 86–93 may also be approached as a single, eight-bar compound basic idea—with a basic idea in mm. 86–89 followed by a contrasting idea in mm. 90–93—rather than a sentential antecedent, because of the lack of a true cadence at m. 93. The expressive point remains the same: this music disengages with the material that comes before it.

19. See chapter 3, endnote 31.

20. Genette, *Narrative Discourse*, 48–49.

21. Schubring ("Five Early Works by Brahms," 199) suggests that m. 51 initiates a new S-theme (calling it the "third main theme"); Frisch (*Brahms and the Principle of Developing Variation*, 53) calls it the "new theme over the E pedal." Jenkins has recently interpreted the event as a half cadence, elided with the downbeat of a new sentence (basic ideas at mm. 51 and 55, continuation at m. 59), in his "Expositional Trajectories Gone Awry."

22. Smith, *Expressive Forms in Brahms's Instrumental Music*, esp. 31–65.

23. See endnote 8.

PART III
Brahms's Piano Sonatas

Brahms's early music, including the three early piano sonatas, has received surprisingly little attention in the secondary literature. In the case of the piano sonatas specifically, this seems to be primarily a result of (1) the view that Brahms's early writing for the piano was problematic and unpianistic and (2) the related view of the sonatas as immature works. In my view, however, all three sonatas are better understood as fully developed manifestations of Brahms's own well-developed Romantic aesthetic: model examples of the Romantic sonata indeed, despite their relative lateness in the context of the Romantic generation proper—which by most accounts is regarded as ending with the revolutions of 1848. These three sonatas comprise representative examples of the same structural and expressive strategies that appear in the Romantic sonatas of Chopin and Schumann as well as strategies that appear—nearly unaltered—in Brahms's later works, including his chamber and symphonic works. That such strategies (if not all features of the surface-level compositional style) in Brahms's early sonatas should be influenced by Schumann specifically is unsurprising, of course, given that these pieces date from a period (1853–54) that finds the young Brahms spending a great deal of time with the elder Schumann, including as a resident in Schumann's home. In Brahms's sonatas as in Schumann's, there appear some of the clearest examples in the nineteenth-century repertoire of what I have characterized as definitively Romantic procedures: a consistent breaking apart or fragmenting of the underlying, fundamentally Classical sonata form via discursive ruptures and digressions that produce multiple layers of temporal and atemporal streams, complicating and enriching an otherwise linear narrative. As such, far from abandoning the fundamental tenets of the Classical sonata tradition, Brahms, as did Schumann and Chopin before him, enters in his piano sonatas into a robust dialogue with—indeed, a critical assessment of—that tradition, therein formulating an expressive vocabulary that is fundamentally Romantic at its core.

Part III proceeds in four chapters that examine selected, formally and expressively problematized moments in Brahms's piano sonatas, with each of the chapters devoted to consideration of Brahms's treatment of one aspect of the sonata process: (1) treatment of the medial caesura, (2) treatment of the S-space, (3) treatment of the development and recapitulation, and (4) treatment of the slow introductions and coda.

5   Treatment of the Medial Caesura

In the Romantic sonata—as in the Classical sonata—treatment of the medial caesura proves to be a critical expressive issue. The first movement of Brahms's Piano Sonata in F♯ minor, op. 2 provides a representative example of how Romantic fragment aesthetics can inform the use of conventions surrounding this most critical of a sonata's junctures. This movement specifically adopts a procedure that can be understood as a hallmark feature of Romantic sonatas in general: this is what I will call a *post-MC interpolation*, in which an MC normative in all apparent respects leads not to a normative S-theme but to a rupture and a deflection into an atemporal stream. S appears later, after an interpolated digression. The procedure is different from, and somewhat more common than, the *pre-MC interpolation*, in which a digression is often staged as an intervention in a crisis within the TR-space itself, before the MC arrives. We have already seen two examples of the latter, in the first movements of Chopin's Piano Sonata in B minor, op. 58 and Schumann's Piano Sonata in F♯ minor, op. 11.

Post-MC interpolations impart a Romantic spin on one of the most important of all of the Classical conventions, right at one of the most important, rhetorically characteristic junctures in the Classical form: the medial caesura, at the seam between the exposition's two halves. The effect is that of splitting open the sonata structure and canceling its forward-vectored temporality at precisely at one of the most markedly forward vectored of all the moments in the form. The Classical medial caesura creates a strong sense of anticipation and should be understood as a rhetorical gesture that boldly announces the introduction of the S-theme—the key player in most Romantic sonata narratives. At a typical MC, implied listeners will hear a "hanging from the precipice" effect, in which the accumulated structural momentum produces a desire to fall forward into the second half of the sonata's expository rotation and take off into the mission of securing the EEC. Denying a sonata exposition this opportunity for forward advance suppresses its Classical teleology in one of the most expressively marked of all possible ways.

In Brahms's op. 2, as indicated in the complete formal diagram of the movement given in figure 5.1, the MC occurs in m. 15, but S does not appear until m. 40. Measures 38–39 may also look like an MC—they articulate a caesura on the dominant in the key of C♯ minor, the key of the S-theme itself—but the gesture there is best understood as an MC-effect that terminates a long, atemporal digression, interpolated between the actual MC and the S and that occupies mm. 16–39.

One of the keys to reading this exposition's structure in this way is recognizing that mm. 9–15 comprise a typical, normative, dissolving-restatement-type TR,

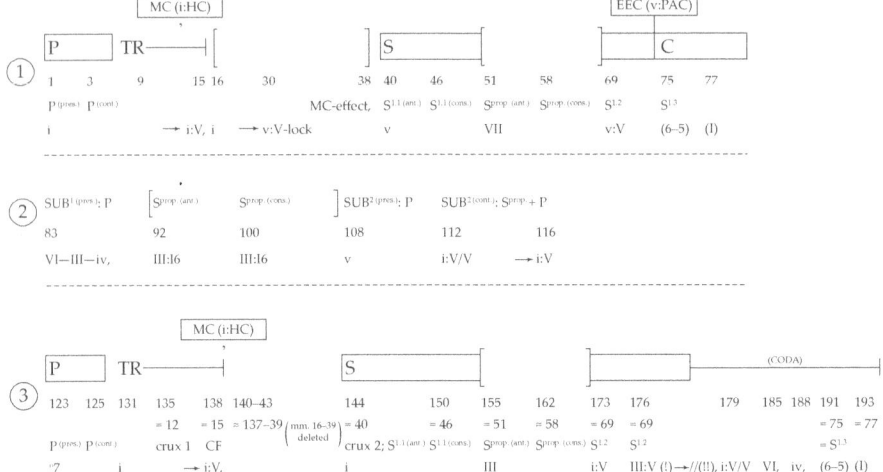

Figure 5.1. Brahms, Piano Sonata in F♯ minor, op. 2, i.

very similar to the dissolving-restatement TRs already seen in the first movements of Brahms's op. 1 (m. 17), Chopin's op. 58 (m. 9), and Schumann's op. 11 (m. 95). The TR here in op. 2 is in dialogue specifically with the dissolving-consequent principle: it follows from an eight-bar, sentential-antecedent P that includes a presentation module in mm. 1–2 (with sequential one-bar basic ideas) followed by a long continuation sounded entirely over a dominant pedal; and it opens in typical fashion by restating the head-motive from P (m. 9 = m. 1) before dissolving into TR-rhetoric and modulating to the key of the relative major. The dissolution occurs almost immediately: the four-octave A at m. 9 b. 3 sustains across the bar line into m. 10, interrupting or annulling the sentence format established earlier (compare what happened to the same A from the end of m. 1), and a modified version of the second basic idea follows in m. 10, now on the submediant, D major. D major is promptly reinterpreted as subdominant in the relative A major, and the dominant in that key arrives, on schedule, so to speak, in m. 13. Measure 14 b. 1 constitutes a moment that could, on a first hearing, be a half-cadential arrival—a III:HC that in fact very well could function as the MC.[1]

The first fourteen bars of this movement thus comprise a normative, compact, concise opening of a sonata exposition entirely Classical in its formal proportions. But in the moments immediately following the downbeat of m. 14, this Classical exposition goes awry in characteristically Romantic fashion. No sooner does the TR propose a III:HC MC at m. 14 b. 1 than it pauses to reconsider the choice, then reneges entirely and makes a staged about-face. Measures 14–15 "back up" through the tonal structure just traversed: the E-major triad on the downbeat of m. 14 steps down in the middle of the measure, with all its voices moving in parallel motion, to a D-major triad. This D-major triad is then reinterpreted such that it reverts to its original harmonic function, in effect backsliding from subdominant function in A major to its original role as submediant in F♯ minor. Then it steps down again, at the downbeat of m. 15, onto an implied root-position, C♯-major triad—the dominant, back in the home key of F♯ minor. Measure 15 b. 1 constitutes the real, TR-ending MC-moment—a i:HC MC that replaces the III:HC MC proposed just three beats earlier. The proposed modulation and, with it, the positively inflected, Arcadian key of the relative major has been rejected and suppressed. The rhythmic gesture in m. 14 acquires a heightened expressive significance in this context, in that the typically Brahmsian hemiola created when the D-major triad appears not on b. 2, as might have been expected, but on the fourth eighth note in the measure can be heard as connoting a slight hesitation—a sense that the D-major triad comes "too late" and is thus detached or separated from the chord on the downbeat.

The strikingly Romantic cancelation of forward motion associated with post-MC interpolations follows. The MC leads not to a normative S but rather to a deflection—a rhetorical equivocation, one that opens up a hole into which a twenty-four-bar block of music is interpolated from outside the first-narrative stream. The situation is an exceptionally clear example of a ruptured atemporality: expressively marked discontinuities in multiple parameters invite a reading in which one musical event should not necessarily be understood as following unproblematically from another within a single, unified, coherent narrative-temporal stream. In this instance, discontinuities emerge in register, dynamic level, and texture: the collapse at the downbeat of m. 16 onto a low-register, *pianissimo, mezza voce*, monophonic F♯ literally connotes the intrusion into the sonata structure of a separate voice, different from that of the movement's first fifteen bars. This new voice can be construed as the diegetic voice of a revealed subjective agent—the narrating protagonist—staged here as intruding on the mimetic narrative and suspending the story in order to take time to diegetically reminisce, reflect, or comment on the course of events. The interpolated block of music that follows then proceeds to compose out a musical analog for an atemporal achrony—a disturbed, troubled excursus during which the narrator (perhaps commenting on the foregoing Classical sonata exposition and its rejection, perhaps agitated by the suppression of the modulation to the relative major) adopts an alienated stance toward the rhetorical discourse of the exposition proper even while also glancing proleptically forward toward S and analeptically backward toward P.

This specific expressive content is signaled by what amounts to a staged breakdown of the sonata's thematic rhetoric within the interpolation itself. That is, the initial motive at m. 16 obviously looks forward to the head-motive of the S-theme at m. 40; note the arpeggiation in both instances of a minor triad embellished with a lower-neighbor ♯$\hat{4}$ leading upward to $\hat{5}$. But at the same time, the rhetoric is that of dismissal: this music immanently rejects any notion on the part of the implied listener that it might function as the sonata's secondary theme. On the contrary, listeners who correctly apprehend m. 15 as the MC and expect the S-theme to follow will hear the material at m. 16 as a markedly disaffected "anti-S," so distant is its rhetoric in every way from that of the first-level-default, lyrical, Arcadian, nineteenth-century *Gesangsthema* S.² The tonality suggests a crisis of continuation: the bass returns immediately at m. 16 to the tonic F♯, which may signify a glance backward toward the P-theme or may manifest the inescapable pull of the sonata's home tonic—the same force, perhaps, that contributed to the tonal backtracking in mm. 14–15; and the music that ensues oscillates between tonic and dominant in F♯ minor (see mm. 16–17 and 18–19) in an effort to avoid proceeding forward into a secondary key. Related is the creeping back into play of P-based material at m. 23: the sonata pathway has been lost, forward motion has been intentionally suppressed, and the narrator is reluctant to look ahead to what might come next in the wake of the rejected modulation to the relative major. And the thematic syntax becomes muddled: m. 16 appears to initiate a sentential presentation (in which mm. 16–17 and 18–19 comprise two two-bar basic ideas), but rather than proceeding with a normative continuation, the sentence runs aground, with the basic idea persisting into mm. 20–21 and even beyond—looping back onto itself as if futilely groping for (or, again, intentionally avoiding) the trail back to sonata viability. In fact, clear continuation rhetoric does not appear until m. 28, where there ensues a spinning out of the P-based motive in the right hand and a change of articulation in the left, all marked *poco stringendo*. The continuation can be thought of as initiating an exit strategy and signaling a gateway out of the interpolated stream, where the gateway effect accrues primarily from the tonal motion: the bass retreats to a G♯ pedal—dominant of the impending tonic, C♯ minor—and the terminal MC-effect arrives in mm. 38–39.

Thus, in retrospect, this is a sonata narrative in which a P-TR-MC complex first proposes, then rejects, a Classical sonata structure and, with it, a modulation to the relative major; the narrator then intervenes, unable to maintain the requisite emotional distance; and finally the narrator yields and the sonata continues. Note that the movement's recapitulation (on which more below, in chapter 7) confirms that this is an appropriate reading of the exposition's pre-S trajectory: there, the MC arrives in mm. 137–38 (= mm. 14–15), mm. 138–39 compose out the original fermata from m. 15, mm. 140–43 comprise a varied repetition of mm. 137–39, with a dominant in mm. 142–43, and S launches in m. 144 (= m. 40)—thus omitting altogether the original atemporal digression from mm. 16–39.

* * *

A similar example of a post-MC interpolation occurs in the first movement of Brahms's Piano Sonata in F minor, op. 5. In fact, this very interesting movement is one of Brahms's most complex and highly fragmented, comprising multiple voices residing in multiple narrative-temporal streams and creating a complex network of expressive meanings. The exposition includes not only a post-MC interpolation but another atemporal digression as well, this one situated between the P- and TR-spaces, as shown in the formal map of the movement given in figure 5.2.

Consider the first interpolation in more detail before moving on to the post-MC interpolation. P opens at m. 1 with loose sentence rhetoric, where the use of

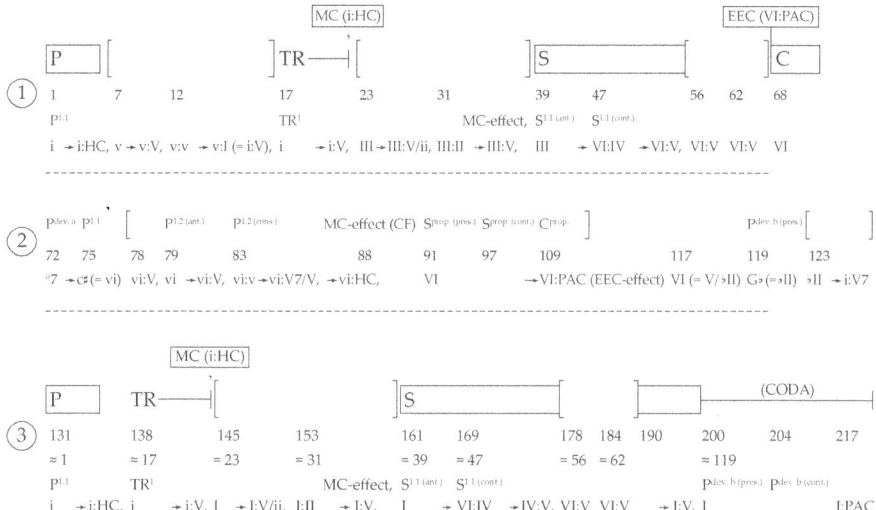

Figure 5.2. Brahms, Piano Sonata in F minor, op. 5, i.

one-bar basic ideas recalls the sentence strategy heard at the opening of op. 2/i. The theme arrives in m. 6 on a i:HC, which suggests that these measures will function as an antecedent from which a consequent—perhaps a dissolving-consequent TR—will follow. TR does indeed follow, but its appearance is delayed until m. 17; when the TR does materialize, furthermore, it does not dissolve but instead simply repeats the P-theme intact, with an extra flourish before the terminal i:HC in m. 22—a cadence that now functions as the expositional MC. That mm. 17–22 function as the TR is a critical aspect of the form that may not be entirely obvious, partly because of the separation of these six bars from the P-theme itself and partly because aspects of TR-function are rhetorically suppressed.[3] But there are at least two important rhetorical markers of a TR at m. 17: this music is in dialogue with the common practice of opening the TR as a counterstatement to P; and, related, the *forte* dynamic here suggests the "*forte* affirmation" effect characteristic of many eighteenth- and nineteenth-century transitions.[4] These signals imply that m. 17 is the TR-opening, and that a TR-dissolution, and perhaps a modulation, will logically follow. When the ensuing module refuses to dissolve or modulate but instead restates the P-theme almost exactly, this should not be understood as calling into question the identity of m. 17 as the beginning of the TR but rather may be understood in terms of the resetting the clock strategy: mm. 1–6 comprise a normative P-antecedent, mm. 7–16 an unexpected overwriting of the anticipated consequent, and mm. 17–22 a repetition of the original antecedent—a second attempt at P, as it were, in an attempt to remedy a problematic situation. It may also be understood as a suppression of aspects of normative TR rhetoric or, indeed, as a suppression of the entire TR itself, in favor of holding on to the P-theme, retaining the key of the tonic, and refusing for as long as possible to move forward through the obligatory sonata processes.[5] The latter reading foregrounds a latent rhetoric of suppression underlying the movement's exposition.

Either reading of the TR foregrounds mm. 7–16 as an expressively charged passage. Specifically, m. 7 signifies a rupture involving striking discontinuities in register (note the drop by one octave from m. 6 to m. 7), dynamic level (the collapse to *pianissimo*), and rhythm (the regrouping at the level of the eighth note brought about by the left-hand triplets, which conflict with the duple groupings both in mm. 1–6 and in the right hand in mm. 7–16).[6] The rupture itself signals that, far from a normative consequent to the foregoing antecedent, mm. 7–16 instead suppress the consequent that should have been present instead and replace it with a new, independent period. The next ten bars comprise their own antecedent-consequent pair of five-bar sentences in C minor, 1 + 1 + 3 measures each. The antecedent's initiatory C minor comprises a modally decayed form of the C major in m. 6; the consequent's initiatory G minor in m. 12 is likewise a modally decayed form of the G-major triad in m. 11; and the consequent concludes by recapturing the C-major triad from m. 6 when it arrives on a Picardy-inflected PAC in m. 16. As such, mm. 7–16 momentarily suspend the sonata-in-progress in favor of an interpolated, diegetic excursus in the suddenly audible voice of the narrating protagonist. The digression can be heard as highly interiorized, in that it gazes deep into the inner reaches of the lyric agent's consciousness: the pulsating triplets comprise an indexical sign for the narrator's own heartbeat; and what that agent narrates is colored by fear or doom, in that the triplets invoke the characteristic Beethovenian fate motive. The passage may connote a shift into a hazy, reminiscent dream space, in that the grouping conflict on the rhythmic surface lends an ethereal, floating quality—as if the music has come unmoored and is no longer firmly grounded in a stable, rhythmic-metric reality. And the interpolation can be thought of as a musical analog for an anachrony, specifically a prolepsis: the presence of C minor at m. 7 suggests that the narrator peers forward into the abyss of the F-minor sonata-to-come and sees therein a darkened, tragic minor-minor exposition (with an F-minor P and a C-minor S) in which the potential for a relative-major Arcadian paradise is painfully suppressed.

The post-MC interpolation—the exposition's second interpolation—appears in m. 23. Just as in the first movement of op. 2, the MC in m. 22 should be understood not as leading directly to a normative S-theme but instead as producing a rupture. S itself does not appear until m. 39, where there enters a normative, prototypical *Gesangsthema* in the highly idealized key of the relative major, A♭—the musical analog for the pastoral narrative's characteristic retreat into a vision of the lost Arcadia. This means that mm. 23–38 should be understood as another rhetorical equivocation—another disaffected "anti-S-theme," that is, analogous in its expressive meaning to mm. 16–39 in op. 2/i. Here again, the equivocation delays the MC's forward-vectored impulse, S is postponed until later than expected, and the narrating protagonist intrudes diegetically into the story with a detached, reminiscent rumination. There are obvious differences in the surface-level compositional strategies here and in op. 2—here, the interpolation booms forth aggressively, *forte*, *fest und bestimmt* ("firm and determined"), forcibly overwriting the *Gesangsthema* S, while the op. 2 interpolation collapsed to a hushed, *pianissimo, mezza voce* whisper—but there are notable similarities as well. The op. 2 interpolation looked at once proleptically forward and analeptically backward, and the op. 5 interpolation behaves similarly: the tonality looks forward by proposing the relative major as a local key center and throwing off the threat of the minor dominant that loomed earlier, in m. 7; the melody looks forward, in that it suggests the melody of the S-to-come in m. 39 (the C-B♭-D♭ in mm. 23–24, $\hat{3}$-$\hat{2}$-$\hat{4}$ in A♭ major, will eventually become C-B♭-E♭, or $\hat{3}$-$\hat{2}$-$\hat{5}$, in mm. 39–40); the bass voice looks backward by continuing to dwell on the one-eighth-plus-two-sixteenths idea—the most characteristic motive from the P-theme; and the formal organization looks forward, in that mm. 23–30 and 31–38 become, in retrospect and upon hearing m. 39, two compound basic-idea statements in a large sentence the boundaries of which transcend the localized formal seams and provide a more traditional sense of continuity at a deeper level—compensation, perhaps, for a starkly disjointed surface.

Notes

1. Others have read the transition as beginning at m. 16 rather than m. 9. Frisch (*Brahms and the Principle of Developing Variation*, 53) hears a structure comprising P, mm. 1–15; TR, mm. 16–39; S, mm. 40–68; and codetta, mm. 69–82. Dickensheets ("The Nineteenth-Century Sonata Cycle as Novel," 134) reads the layout similarly, at least with regard to the TR, which she also hears as beginning in m. 16. Newman (*The Sonata since Beethoven*, 333) refers, cryptically, to "second theme of op. 2/i (mss. 10–71)," which comes shortly after a comment that op. 2 is the "wildest, most bombastic, most declamatory, least playable, and structurally least successful" of any of Brahms's sonatas.

2. A similar rhetoric of S-rejection also informs the first movement of Schumann's Piano Sonata in F♯ minor, op. 11 in the interpolated mm. 107–22 that follow the potential MC-proposal in m. 106.

3. Frisch (*Brahms and the Principle of Developing Variation*, 37) reads mm. 1–22 as a P-theme comprising "a tripartite opening period" in which mm. 7–16 occupy a contrasting middle section; he reads the TR as beginning at m. 23. Bozarth ("Brahms's *Lieder ohne Worte*," 371) likewise reads TR as beginning in m. 23.

4. Hepokoski and Darcy, *Elements of Sonata Theory*, 93–116 (esp. 93–95).

5. The TR-suppression itself is also in dialogue with Classical precedents: see ibid., 115–16.

6. Bozarth proposes (convincingly, in light of Brahms's interest in the novels of E. T. A. Hoffmann) that m. 7 initiates a shift toward the opposite side of the dual "Brahms-Kreisler personality," where mm. 7–16 represent the poet-composer's more introspective side and mm. 1–6 the more extroverted side; see Bozarth, "Brahms's *Lieder ohne Worte*," 370–71. See also Floros, *Brahms und Bruckner*, 84–98. For more on Hoffmann and his relevance, see Dickensheets, "The Nineteenth-Century Sonata Cycle as Novel"; and Dickensheets, "The Topical Vocabulary of the Nineteenth Century," 136–37.

6 Treatment of the S-Space

In the Romantic sonata, the S-space is typically a central feature of the sonata's dialogue with conventions of the pastoral narrative. Two specific issues are important in this regard: eighteenth- and nineteenth-century conventions surrounding the tonal and modal choices for S in minor-mode sonatas; and the pastoral as a narrative archetype for the Romantic sonata, and, in this context, the special significative potential carried therein by the S-theme.

First, on tonal and modal choices for S, the principal expressive concern is the Sonata Theory concept that minor-mode sonatas carry with them an extraexpressive "burden" that major-mode sonatas do not: minor-mode sonatas can be understood expressively as seeking to transform their minor mode into a brighter, more hopeful, transcendent major.[1] The choice of key, and mode, for the secondary theme in the exposition plays a vital role in this expressive formulation. Two normative options are available: the relative major and the minor dominant. To choose the relative major is to establish the means by which the minor-mode burden will be cast off later: the choice forecasts that the recapitulatory S will appear in the major tonic and that the expressive narrative will be one of triumph or emancipation, in which the promise of the major overcomes the bleak pessimism or dark tragedy of the minor. If the recapitulatory S appears instead in the tonic minor, or if it opens in the tonic major and then collapses to minor, the narrative can be understood as tragic or defeatist, with the major overcome by the minor. On the other hand, to choose the minor dominant for the expositional S is to fatalistically refuse even to explore the possibility of major-mode relief from the weight of the minor; the choice forecasts from the outset that the recapitulatory S will appear in the tonic minor and that the sonata will likely come up short (in what can be described as *modal failure*) in its quest to secure major-mode transcendence out of minor-mode desolation.[2]

Related is the question of appropriate expressive correlations for the major/minor opposition in a nineteenth-century sonata. In the Classical style, it is fundamental that the major/minor binary opposition correlates with positive/negative or with a range of consistent, but more culturally or historically specific, values: confidence/withdrawal, joy/melancholy, triumph/resignation, and so on.[3] These expressive conventions continue to inform the music of the nineteenth century. That is, the expressive correlations for the major/minor opposition in the Romantic period should be regarded as normatively consistent with the positive/negative correlations established in the Classical era;[4] the fact that there are more minor-mode Romantic sonatas than there are minor-mode Classical sonatas does not mean that the minor mode becomes expressively neutral in the nineteenth century or that the major/minor opposition no longer correlates with positive/negative. In fact, the increased frequency with which the minor mode appears in the nineteenth century is readily explainable within the world of Romantic aesthetics, in which the minor mode has an obvious expressive value: it becomes a tool for expressing the darker, more melancholy, self-critical impulse characteristic of Romanticism, in which the imperfections of the present trigger psychological turns inward and longings for retreat toward the idealized Arcadian paradise. Other commentators have made similar observations and have accorded similar weight to the minor mode in Romantic music: the major/minor-positive/negative mapping is central in, for example, Michael Klein's readings of Chopin's first and fourth Ballades, and in Peter Smith's readings of expressive trajectories and expressive genres in Brahms's sonata forms. For Smith, the opposition plays an important role particularly in the *per aspera ad astra* plot archetype—heroic tales of overcoming adversity similar to those characteristic of Hatten's tragic-to-triumphant expressive genre. Such plot types are common, according to Smith, in music of Brahms, especially in pieces in C minor, in which Brahms was working firmly within an expressive tradition that dates to the early nineteenth century and to Beethoven's Symphony no. 5 in C minor, op. 67.[5]

Second, on the pastoral as a narrative archetype in the Romantic sonata, consider that, as mentioned, the sonata can be regarded as the generic locus for the pastoral in music, just as, for example, landscape painting or lyric poetry are generic loci of the pastoral in art and literature. This is because the sonata provides an ideal musical-structural context in which the most critical aspects of the pastoral narrative can be mapped onto the most salient features of a musical form. The sonata's oppositions of themes (P versus S), keys (especially minor tonic versus relative major), and styles or topics (aggressively declamatory versus arrestingly lyrical, for instance) conveniently map onto the pastoral's themes of retreat/return, perfect/imperfect, present/past, and so on. The central musical facet of almost every such mapping is the opposition of a tonic-key, often minor-mode, restless, agitated, angular, *forte* P-theme and a maximally contrasting, nontonic, relative-major, lyrical (*dolce* or *bel canto*), piano S-theme of the type known as, as noted already, a *Gesangsgruppe* or *Gesangsthema*.[6] This P-S opposition is fundamental to the expressive language of Romantic music: it was available in the Classical sonata, but in the nineteenth century, in the era dominated by Romantic sensibilities, it became one of the definitive rhetorical features of the genre. By midcentury, it had acquired the status of a normative, first-level-default option governing the formatting of P and S, such that the contravening of the norm invites hermeneutic interpretation. That is, the choice of any S-type other than the *Gesangsthema*, and the choice of any key for S other than the relative major, should be understood in a Romantic sonata as some form of an expressively marked overwriting of the normative expectations engendered by the genre itself.

The opposition between maximally contrasting P- and S-themes in the nineteenth-century sonata should be regarded as charged with expressive meaning.

This has long been recognized in music criticism. As Adolph Bernhard Marx famously observed in 1845, that meaning can be couched in gendered terms: masculine (*Männlichen*) versus feminine (*Weibliche*), or, in the language of Hepokoski and his critique of Marx, the tormented, male-in-crisis P versus the self-assured, comforting, redemptive female S.[7] Such gendered metaphors may be entirely appropriate for a number of the most well-known examples, as Hepokoski has discussed; many of these are either programmatic or linked to an opera, and many do appear to imply a correlation between a male-character P and a female-character S. These include, among others, Beethoven's Overtures to *Coriolan*, op. 62 (1807) and *Egmont*, op. 84 (1810), Weber's Overture to *Der Freischütz* (1821), and Wagner's Overture to *The Flying Dutchman* (1843). But the gendered metaphors cannot fully explain every case; even the *Coriolan* and *Egmont* examples are more complicated, as is, for instance, a seemingly obvious example like Tchaikovsky's *Romeo and Juliet* overture. Nor can they necessarily explain similar thematic, stylistic, and topical oppositions that crop up frequently even in more purely "absolute" sonatas that are not associated with specific characters or with a parallel program or text.

My view is that the characteristic oppositions in the pastoral narrative can provide a more productive way of framing the expressive meaning of the opposition. Romantic sonata narratives, especially those in the minor mode, can be heard as normatively premised on the opposition of a P-theme that correlates broadly with an external, present reality and an S-theme that correlates, also broadly, with a construction of the image of Arcadia—where Arcadia is, generally speaking, an internalized, unreal but intensely desirable, idealized, nonpresent time, place, personage, or expressive state toward which the narrative retreats and from which it eventually returns. S thus signifies a more perfect, more beautiful alternative to the flawed present of the P that comes before it; it signifies a wishful turn toward the past (a distant memory, perhaps) or a hopeful glance toward the future (a hypothetical, imagined Utopia). Central to these narrative strategies are the tonal and modal choices for S and the related issues of expressive correlations for the major/minor opposition. That is, an S-theme in the normative key of the relative major manifests the image of the Arcadian ideal and suggests that the narrative involves a retreat from a real, tangible present (P), to an imagined nonpresent (S), and back again. An S-theme in the minor dominant, on the other hand, signifies a tragic or catastrophic suppression of the longed-for, imagined idyllic world and suggests a narrative involving a fatalistic tale of shortcoming, rejection, or outright failure. Other key choices invite various combinations of these two possibilities. S-themes in the major mediant or major submediant, for example—not uncommon in nineteenth-century sonatas—might be understood as achieving the "right" mode but the "wrong" key and thus as signifying transgressive "false positives": heavily ironized, poignant, impossibly beautiful paradise worlds that stand in for the true Arcadia, itself forever lost, unreachable, or unrecoverable.

Very importantly, note that to claim that the S in a Romantic sonata narrative normatively signifies the image of Arcadia and thus a beautiful memory of the past or an idyllic image of an imagined future is not the same as claiming that S itself constitutes an atemporal analepsis or prolepsis. One should not infer that a minor-tonic P is temporal and a relative-major S is atemporal and outside the boundaries of story time.[8] Rather, any normative S-theme should be regarded as a temporal element in the story proper, an integral part of the narrative of retreat and return on which the sonata is premised. Any sense of the past or of a past tense, for example, connoted in the S-theme is part of that story—part of the mimetic, first-narrative content and therefore not the same as the past tense invoked in the various musical analogs for analepses, prolepses, or shifts in the narrative-rhythmic pace. These latter examples of past tense all involve the change of tense that accrues from the revelation of the implied narrator who tells the tale, one who steps outside mimetic story time in order to comment diegetically on the ongoing story-in-progress as it unfolds. In fact, this discursive situation helps account for the most common locations in which atemporal digressions occur within Romantic sonata structures: many appear, as mentioned, in the run-up to the S-theme—in the TR or in the space around the MC; many others appear within the S-space itself, including in the space around the EEC or ESC. Many, therefore, result from the narrator's own inner (emotional or psychological) struggle to deliver the part of the story—the paradisiacal S—that is at once the most beautiful, the least tenable, the most painful, and the most difficult with which to come to terms.

Some commentators have already suggested that the pastoral is an appropriate narrative archetype for the Romantic sonata and, more broadly, for other Romantic genres that allow for large-scale contrasts among themes or formal modules (including Chopin's Ballades, certain Romantic character pieces, or many Romantic lieder). Smith implies as much, in that a number of his readings of expressive content in Brahms's sonata forms are informed by the expectation for *Gesangsthema* S-rhetoric and by the fulfillment or the overriding of this expectation.[9] Seth Monahan similarly construes Mahler's sonata narratives as premised on a P-S opposition that he describes in terms of an "objective or situational" P that maps onto "the 'world' in which the drama unfolds," and a contrasting, "subjectivized" S normatively imbued with "hyperbolized affective traits suggesting a musically embodied persona, negotiating that world and reacting to its stimuli."[10] Michael Klein invokes the pastoral specifically, which he argues is an appropriate narrative archetype for Romantic music because interior themes in that repertoire (Klein's concern is Chopin's large works, including his sonatas) often correlate with "a difference from the ontological reality of the surrounding musical material: past as opposed to present, interior as opposed to exterior, there as opposed to here," and so on.[11]

* * *

A good initial musical example that illustrates these issues is the temporally fragmented S-theme in Brahms's op. 2/i, beginning at m. 40. Here, the implied composer chooses the darkened world of the minor dominant (C♯ minor) for the key of S. Within the pastoral framework, this choice can be understood as a suppression of the Arcadian ideal that engenders a narrative of hopelessness and impossibility, tempered, as we shall see presently, by wishful reminiscence. S comprises a period, with a six-bar antecedent aiming at the dominant (mm. 40–45: $S^{1.1\ (\mathrm{ant.})}$ in figure 5.1) followed by what the implied listener at first assumes will be a six-bar consequent aiming at the tonic (hypothetically mm. 46–51: $S^{1.1\ (\mathrm{cons.})}$). The unusual length of both modules results from the presence of asymmetrical, three-bar basic ideas (mm. 40–42, 43–45, etc.): each contains a head comprising, first, four beats of an aggressive, rising figure closely related both to P and to the interpolated material from m. 16 (note the similar shapes); and, second, a tail comprising five beats of a contrasting, descending, sighing figure (note the succession of *pianto* appoggiaturas). These basic ideas encapsulate the struggle that will mark the S-theme as a whole, in that each basic idea comprises a sinister, *piano* head that suppresses the normative, lyrical, Arcadian *Gesangsthema*, followed by a more lyrical, oppositely contoured (descending instead of ascending) *forte* tail that cues an outburst or a shout and that attempts to assert the desired S-rhetoric. Any number of expressive implications may follow: Arcadian unreality tries to shine forth from the darkness of present-day reality; a nonpresent paradise is destined to remain forever unachievable within the unremitting demands of life's exigencies. In fact, such readings follow from the narrative articulated thus far in the exposition as a whole, in which a menacing, minor-mode P gave way to a TR that sought a better world and modulated to the relative major before reconsidering and fatalistically backing up to the minor tonic, triggering a crisis of confidence in which the narrator intervened to look back over what happened and try to summon the will to continue.

Such a narrative of hopelessness and loss continues to inform the series of interesting events that follow—including the impending digression into atemporality. The digression itself comprises a ruptured atemporality followed by an interpolated excursus inserted just before the end of the S-theme's consequent module—which opens, as mentioned, at m. 46, in C♯ minor, with a varied restatement of the basic idea from m. 40. The consequent moves onto predominant harmony (V of V) in its third bar, m. 48, then continues on to dominant harmony in m. 49 in anticipation of what the implied listener can easily imagine will be a i:PAC in C♯ minor at m. 51. The implied listener assumes, furthermore, that such a cadence, were it to occur, would be the exposition's EEC—an EEC that would secure the key of the minor dominant and nail shut the door once and for all on the Arcadian A major—itself but a distant memory anyway at this point. But, as in the TR, such doom proves too painful for the narrator to handle. Once again, there emerges a crisis of continuation in which the narrator forgoes the requisite distance and emotional detachment in favor of suspending the tale and commenting directly. Mimesis gives way to diegesis in a striking rupture that rips open the S-theme right at the very moment at which the implied listener expects the C♯-minor cadence. A non sequitur in the middle of m. 50 generates rhetorically underscored discontinuities in the voice leading, tonality, dynamic level, and expressive topic: all voices leap upward, unexpectedly, at m. 50 b. 2, onto a B♮—lowered $\hat{7}$ in the key and thus an expressive reversal or suppression of the leading-tone B♯ that had sounded just one beat earlier; B♮ is immediately reinterpreted as $\hat{5}$ in E major, and the bass leaps at m. 51 b. 1 onto E; and, at the last eighth note of m. 50—literally at the last possible second—the bellicose *fortissimo* from the tail of the basic idea plunges suddenly to a sweet, expressive *piano*.

What follows is extraordinary: into the hole opened up by the rupture, the narrator inserts what amounts to a proposal for an alternative, "better," more idealized S-theme, the mode and the well-formedness of which compensate for the imperfections of the minor-dominant theme from m. 40. That is, the proposed new theme that appears at m. 51—S$^{\text{prop.}}$ in figure 5.1—manifests a stylistically normative, arrestingly lyrical *Gesangsthema* in the major mode that sings forth as a sentence based on a much more typical two-bar, instead of three-bar, basic idea (mm. 51–52).[12] The tonality is also heavily marked: the brightened E major would seem to signify a momentary glimpse into the Arcadian paradise, but E major is the relative of C♯ minor, the minor dominant, and not of the sonata's home tonic, F♯ minor. Thus, E major is not the Arcadian paradise itself—which would have appeared in the key of A major—but rather a substitute: an illusory, fantastic, dreamlike figment of the narrator's imagination, an image of sheer impossibility thrown down into the sonata as an escape from an agonizing story of paradise lost. In fact, the new E-major theme grows directly out of the original basic idea's tail portion (see mm. 41–42)—a tail that was itself an attempt to break away from the aggressively rising, P-based head (mm. 40–41). Such a motivic relationship underscores a reading of the theme as signifying self-extrication from present reality via a flight into an alternative dream space.

Other rhetorical aspects of the E-major theme connote a certain irony and untenability. Like any dream, as beautiful and attractive as it may be, it remains fleeting and unsustainable. Its tonality is especially tenuous: the sonata exposition simply cannot continue, and there can be no EEC, in the "wrong key" of E major. The pulsating triplets at m. 51 again comprise a musical token of the narrators' anxious heartbeat and thus an inward-looking sign of the narrator's consciousness; deep unease lurks beneath a more tranquil surface. The theme's sentential antecedent, furthermore, seems to be cut off before it can reach its normative half-cadential conclusion: a fully diminished-seventh chord arrives in m. 57 (and becomes a V♮9 by the measure's end), in the seventh instead of the eighth bar of what might otherwise have been a normative, eight-bar sentence. A sentential consequent then appears in m. 58 and intensifies the latent angst: the left hand's heartbeat triplets now comprise a quicker, more agitated (note the *più agitato*) reference to a series of dissonant upper neighbors (C♯, m. 58; D♮, m. 59; C♮, m. 60; etc.), and the gap-producing rests on the downbeat of mm. 59 and 61 perhaps correlate with a quick, apprehensive inhalation of breath—a gasping for air, maybe in response to fear of the theme's imminent dissolution. That fear proves justified because the consequent begins to dissolve almost as soon as it begins: it decays to E minor in m. 60; enters an ascending sequence in m. 62–65 (observe the 6-6-6-6 linear intervallic pattern above the ascending E-F♮-G♮-A bass); gets stuck, so to speak, at m. 66, which duplicates m. 65, save for the changing of C♮ to C♯ and the attendant shift to an A7 chord; repeats m. 66 literally in m. 67, remaining in a holding pattern with the outcome hanging in the balance; and finally wakes up and finds a way out at m. 68, where the A7 chord is enharmonically reinterpreted as an augmented sixth in C♯ minor. Thus, the dream collapses. The structural dominant—dominant of the original S, in C♯ minor, and not of the proposed S in E major—arrives in m. 69 in the form of a cadential $^6_4$ over G♯ in the bass, just as the original S-theme material makes its return; reality reappears and squelches the proposed image of paradise. Incidentally, this is another situation in which the interpolated material could be removed without disturbing the larger outlines of the narrative (as in, for example, the first movement of Chopin's op. 58 or the finale of Schumann's op. 11): the implied listener can easily imagine a recomposition in which m. 69 was connected backward to m. 50 and the intervening material deleted, such that the $^6_4$ chord that arrives in m. 69 is the very cadential signal that the S-theme had been looking for all along.

As such, the exposition has been broken apart and split open—fragmented in true Romantic fashion right at one of the most forward-vectored of all the moments in the entire form: the approach to the EEC.[13] The EEC itself arrives in m. 75. But the cadence, when it does arrive, proves characteristically problematic, and as such, it resists a simple, straightforward interpretation. The problem is that an upper-neighbor A ($\hat{6}$) intrudes into the expected tonic triad before resolving downward by half step onto the obligatory G♯ ($\hat{5}$), which makes fleeting appearances at the ends of mm. 75–76 before being secured permanently in m. 77. Perhaps in some contexts an embellished cadence may not raise eyebrows, but here, it seems that to insert an upper neighbor into the tonic triad at the very cadence-moment itself signals a gesture that rhetorically undermines the stability of the EEC. In some sense, this neighbor can be regarded as a milder, gentler form of the sharper discontinuity—the full-fledged rupture—invoked at the EEC in op. 1; it may constitute a more transitory nod toward cadential uncertainty, in the form of Sonata Theory's *attenuated EEC*, rather than full-fledged cadence failure via a rupture and a shift of discursive level.[14] Its expressive meaning might be read in several ways, all of them probably related to the interpolated E-major excursus that dissolved moments before: perhaps it signifies the tremor associated with the dreaded fulfillment of fate (a reading that would be consistent with the Beethovenian triplet figures—fateful tolling of the bells—in mm. 75–76, bb. 1–2); or perhaps the upper-neighbor A specifically signifies the lingering presence of the narrator's consciousness, revealing a reluctance to uncritically consent to tragic, minor-dominant reality in the wake of the interpolated, major-mode reverie. (The upper-neighbor A itself may even look back specifically toward the relative major, A major, that never materialized.) Perhaps, then, one should hear the upper neighbor as a distant echo of the narrator's own voice, fading into the distance as the story moves on and leaves behind any hope of recovering the Arcadian dream. The full arrival of the C♯-minor tonic, which is secured by m. 77, would thus correlate with crushed dreams of an idealized Utopia—an idealized, Romanticized image of paradise crushed by a stark, desolate reality.

All of these events have ramifications for what happens in the recapitulatory S-space in the same movement. The key point in this regard is that the recapitulatory S refuses to adhere to the narrative trajectory laid out in the expositional S: it discards the exposition's equivocal, attenuated EEC, leaving in its place a recapitulation and, indeed, a sonata as a whole that comprises a Romantic fragment, incomplete and broken via outright collapse and failure.

The treatment of the atemporal digression in the recapitulation differs from that of the exposition in important ways. In the recapitulation, S opens at m. 144 (= m. 40), in the tonic F♯ minor and following, as mentioned, a twice-repeated MC (mm. 137–43) and an ellipsis that skips over the original post-MC interpolation (originally mm. 16–39). S then tracks almost exactly through its expositional precedent: it opens with an incomplete period (mm. 144–54, = mm. 40–50) in which a rupture (m. 154 b. 2, = m. 50 b. 2) overwrites the terminal cadence, then proceeds into an interpolated, diegetic dream space and a new, major-mode S-proposal that comprises its own well-formed sentential antecedent (mm. 155–61, = mm. 51–57) and sentential consequent (beginning at m. 162). Note especially the tonality: because of the tonal level of the recapitulatory S (tonic, F♯ minor), the $S^{prop.}$ now appears in none other than the key of the relative major—the very key that was proposed but then lost in both the expositional and recapitulatory TR-zones. Note also that in the interpolation's consequent module at m. 162, the pulsating triplets that originally appeared in the accompaniment (compare m. 58) have now been suppressed and overwritten by a rising, portentous figure that was first heard in the exposition's post-MC interpolation (compare the bass in m. 16, for example). This is a striking expressive move, the rhetoric of which probably signals a disturbance and prefigures imminent disaster: perhaps this is a haunting remnant of the protagonist's consciousness, which had been suppressed earlier (when the post-MC interpolation was deleted) but which now intrudes ever so softly and subtly back into the discourse; perhaps this is an overt signal of the obvious, namely that the dream—the proposed S in the relative major—is again unsustainable and that reality will eventually return and overwhelm the imagined Arcadian idyll.

The same exit strategy as was heard in the exposition then ensues at m. 172 (≈ m. 68), which arrives on an augmented sixth that gives way to the return of the first narrative and to the structural dominant in m. 173 (= m. 69). At this point, there is no reason for the implied listener not to assume that this structural dominant will give way to the final ESC-cadence, which should appear (given the expositional precedent) in m. 179. But there follows instead a startling series of events in which the recapitulation jettisons the expositional trajectory. The recapitulation collapses, in fact, seizing on the latent expressive implications of the exposition's attenuated EEC and magnifying them in order to derail the sonata at the last possible moment. A structure that earlier had signified grudging acceptance now signifies overt rejection. As mentioned, mm. 173–75 point unproblematically toward a i:PAC EEC, just as did mm. 69–71. But at the very moment at which the final drive toward the cadence is expected, the progression is overwritten by a reversal and an apparent descent of the protagonist into near-pathological irrationality. The critical event occurs at m. 176, which, rather than pushing forward, instead backs up and reiterates the cadential $^6_4$ from m. 172, as if to engage with the "one more time" technique. But the cadential $^6_4$ at m. 176 hardly signals a normative repetition of the cadential progression. Most astonishingly, the chord is an A-major triad over an E in the bass; this is a cadential $^6_4$, that is, in the Arcadian relative major, a key that has been proposed but then lost no fewer than three times over the course of the entire movement. Its appearance here surely signifies sheer despair: any prospect of recovering the A-major paradise is now completely lost, and any appearance of A major at this point in the narrative is destined to be but a faint flicker—an absurd fantasy, tragic in its hopelessness.

Everything that follows must be understood in the wake of this last-ditch grasp at the A-major specter. First, mm. 176–78 recompose mm. 172–74 (= mm. 69–71 again). Second, whereas the final cadential progression (music that was originally expected at m. 176, = m. 72) should now be expected to follow at m. 179, that progression is still not allowed to materialize: m. 179 blocks the cadence by careering onto a V of V in F♯ minor, and the anticipated cadence is overwritten by new material. This is perhaps the most remarkable event of all within a recapitulation the ending of which has already proven torturous. It signals a devastating, eleventh-hour breakdown of the entire sonata structure, which is now destined for failure. In fact, at m. 179 the narrative is simply discarded altogether; the incomplete sonata-space is abandoned in favor of an extrastructural coda. This is the meaning of the otherwise puzzling double bar at m. 179, a powerful, unsounding notational signal that sonata-space proper should be regarded as having come to an end. Thus, the movement's final rotation comprises a nonresolving recapitulation: a PAC ESC fails to occur at the location predicted within the expositional rotation; the cadence has been written out of existence by the deflection onto new material at m. 179. The fact that the cadence does eventually appear, later, at m. 191 (= m. 75), is a separate issue: this cadence occurs too late to save the structure from collapse. Perhaps the ESC can even be regarded as overwritten—or as doomed to oblivion—as early as the last-second grasp at the A-major $^6_4$ chord in m. 176. In fact the double-bar line (and the coda's downbeat) might well have appeared at that bar instead of at m. 179; that it does not appear until three bars later seems to underscore the reading of mm. 176–78 as a momentary hallucination, futile and desperately confused. The narrative ends in utter tragedy: the turbulent coda proposes but evades closure twice (moving V-VI in mm. 184–85, then V-iv in 187–88) before finally producing it in mm. 191–93 (= mm. 75–77)—pounding the stake into the heart three times, as it were, to assure that the last breath of life is squeezed from the Arcadian dream. The movement ends with two faint, breathless, *piano* (*una corda*) gasps.

* * *

These issues play out musically in different ways in two additional examples: the S-themes from the first movement of Brahms's Piano Sonata in F minor, op. 5, and the last (fourth) movement of Brahms's Piano Sonata in F♯ minor, op. 2. In op. 5, S commences in m. 39, as shown in figure 5.2, with the $\hat{3}$-$\hat{2}$-$\hat{5}$ gesture—now fully formed in A♭ major—that was forecasted in the post-MC interpolation, mm. 23–38. This theme is a touchstone example of a Romantic *Gesangsthema* S, proving ultimately to be a musical image of a beautiful but impossible, unreal, and ultimately unrealizable Arcadian paradise that remains forever out of reach amid the flaws and limitations of a contemporary, imperfect world. Note first that the $\hat{3}$-$\hat{2}$-$\hat{5}$ gesture itself imbues the theme with an additional, highly rhetorically charged layer of meaning: it bears an expressively rich intertext with Beethoven, comprising a conspicuous allusion to the familiar $\hat{3}$-$\hat{2}$-$\hat{5}$ that opens the A♭-major slow movement of Beethoven's Piano Sonata in C minor, op. 13 (the "Pathétique"; surely, the fact that the motive appears here in the key of A♭ major should not be dismissed as mere coincidence). And if this reference seems but a transient, evanescent glint even for implied listeners schooled in the Beethoven sonatas, the opening of the second movement of Brahms's op. 5 confirms that what was flashed in front of our ears in the first-movement S-theme was no mere figment of the aural imagination. That is, in extraordinary fashion the Pathétique allusion that was broken off after only three notes in the first movement completes itself later—in the same key, no less—in mm. 2–4 of the second movement. Example 6.1a shows the complete Pathétique antecedent, in which the $\hat{3}$-$\hat{2}$-$\hat{5}$ motif is a basic idea that proceeds to a descent through D♭ to C ($\hat{4}$ to $\hat{3}$, pulled downward by the force of gravity), a rising arpeggiation, and an arrival on $\hat{5}$.[15] Example 6.1b shows how the same melody is fragmented across the first two movements of Brahms's op. 5. The three-note basic idea appears in mm. 39–41 in the first movement, but proceeds there (see mm. 42–43) not to the more natural descent through $\hat{4}$ and $\hat{3}$ but instead to a gravity- (and Beethoven-) defying ascent through F♭ and G♭. Only in the second movement does the figure resume from where it left off, completing its $\hat{4}$-$\hat{3}$ descent (now embellished in mm. 2–3), its upward arpeggiation (m. 3), and its arrival on $\hat{5}$ (m. 4, now reached via an exclamatory upward leap that replaces Beethoven's original, downward $\hat{2}$-$\hat{5}$ relaxation). The expressive meaning is clear: if the first-movement S connotes a vision of a glorious Arcadian paradise forever lost to time, and if the second movement comprises a reminiscent, wishful look backward toward the same paradisiacal vision, then this is a paradise inhabited by Beethoven himself.

 S proceeds to engage with aspects of the pastoral narrative via a heavily marked tonal trajectory, a rhetorical breakdown, and a momentary deflection into atemporality. Regarding the tonal trajectory, the most important point is that S modulates and fails to close in the same key in which it started. A sentential presentation module (mm. 39–46) signals almost immediately that the key of the relative major will be untenable: mm. 42–44 tonicize G♭ major (note the inner-voice C♭ in m. 42), while the ensuing continuation stages its initiatory G♭-major triad not as a tonic but as the subdominant in D♭, with the upper voice spiraling upward from B♭ (m. 47), through C♮ (m. 48), and then through a segment of the D♭-major scale (mm. 49–51). The goal is a twice-repeated predominant-dominant progression in the newly acquired key

142 | Sonata Fragments

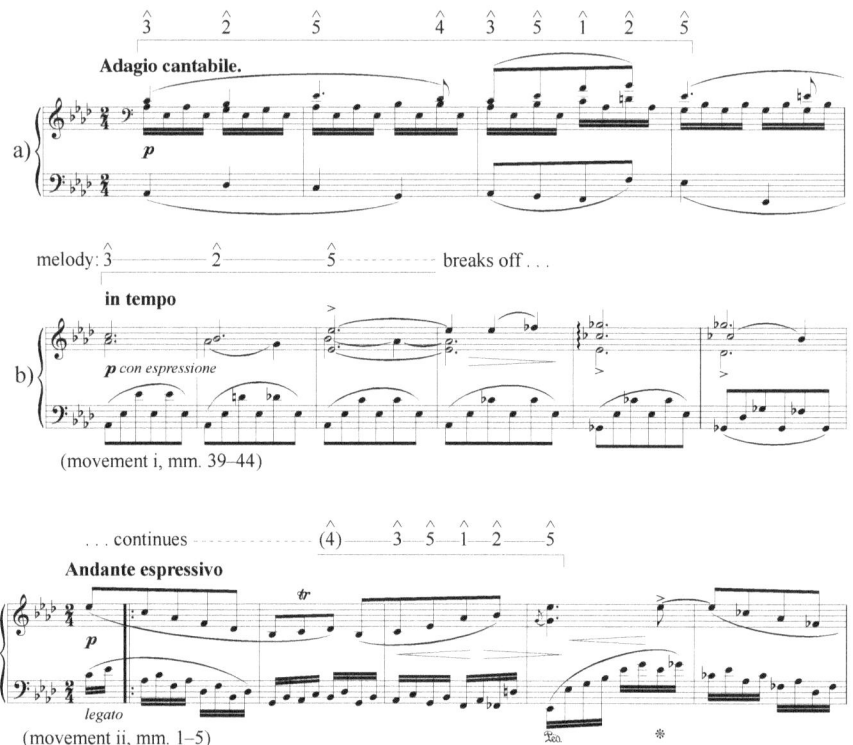

Example 6.1. a) Beethoven, Piano Sonata in C minor, op. 13 ("Pathétique"), ii, mm. 1–4. b) Brahms, Piano Sonata in F minor, op. 5, i (mm. 39–44) and ii (mm. 1–5).

of D♭, in mm. 54–55 (where m. 55 comprises a "one more time" repetition of m. 54). Clearly a cadence—presumably the EEC, in D♭—is imminent.

In a pastoral-narrative context, the modulation can be understood as signifying an inability or unwillingness to hold on to the idealized key of the Arcadian relative major; a beautiful memory, so painstakingly reconstructed during the post-MC interpolation and the initial bars of S (a memory of Beethoven himself?), passes away quickly, as an ephemeral, ineffable vision. The meaning is laden with irony, moreover, in the sense that, as mentioned, major-submediant (and, similarly, major-mediant) S-themes imply rejections or denials of the first-level default key of the relative major and, as such, invoke a certain false positivity: these are S-themes in the "right mode" (the major mode) but the "wrong key" and, as such, can be understood as signifying a substitute paradise world that stands in for the real Arcadia, intensely desired but tragically inaccessible. Modulating S-themes imply similar meanings: an S that opens in the idealized relative major but then modulates away, and perhaps even cadences in some other key, suggests a narrative that includes a brief, fleeting appearance of an Arcadian image right at the outset of the S-space, followed by a slippage, with the image disappearing into oblivion. Such interpretations are more apparent in situations in which the modulation is to the key of the minor dominant and thus carries with it a negatively inflected sense of modal breakdown or failure. But the interpretation is viable even in scenarios that involve no modal decay, as in op. 5: here, any positive sheen on the modulation from A♭ major to (an equally positive?) D♭ major should be regarded as but a surface glow, one that produces a falsely positive, ironic masking of the fact that D♭ remains a wrong-key, fantastic impossibility and that the true Arcadia world, A♭ major, has fragmented and disintegrated, hopelessly lost to time.[16] In this specific instance, it may be possible to think of D♭ major in terms of its proximity to C: D♭ may be an "overshooting" by a half step the minor dominant, C minor—the more common tonal goal of modulating S-themes—such that D♭ major is a naïve, futile attempt to deny the reality of the A♭-major loss and avoid the potential trauma associated with a dark, C-minor abyss.

Such expressive content may explain the striking rhetorical breakdown that follows. S comes apart at the seams before deflecting into an atemporal interpolation—the third in this highly fragmentary exposition—at the moment of the expected EEC, at m. 56. The cadence moment comprises a good example of conflated atemporality types, like what happened at mm. 51 and 75 in Brahms's op. 1/i: at m. 56, the bass voice signals a durational expansion by obstinately refusing to resolve to D♭ ($\hat{1}$), instead hanging on to the A♭ ($\hat{5}$) from m. 55. A♭ is then projected spatially, as a pedal point that provides space for a rupture. At the moment of expected cadential resolution, the dynamic level plummets from *forte* (in m. 55) to *piano* (m. 56) and the bass voice leaps up, such that the A♭ in m. 56 is one full octave higher than in m. 55; the effect is that of the bass having dropped completely out of the texture, leaving the music that remains behind suspended vertiginously in midair. The rupture thus overwrites the expected D♭-major cadence and, as such, implies a refusal or an unwillingness of S to commit to a straightforward, unproblematic cadence in a key other than that which was desired to begin with—here the relative major, A♭. The A♭ pedal point proceeds to support a twelve-bar interpolated digression, mm. 56–67, where the lingering A♭ itself is a vestige—the sole, glimmering remnant amid a broken world—of the key that was lost in the modulation moments earlier. The narrator refuses to relinquish the beautiful memory of the relative-major Arcadia and move on with the story; mimesis shifts to diegesis and the narrator intrudes anxiously, suspending storytime teleology in order to linger in a reminiscence. The interpolation's restless, scurrying, hemiola-inflected melody may signify the narrator's own unease, while the agitated, pulsating lower voice comprises another musical icon of the narrator's inner heartbeat, throbbing with distress and disappointment.[17] A PAC in D♭ major—the cadence that should have occurred at m. 56—finally materializes in m. 68 and marks the return of first-narrative temporality. The cadence includes an added $\hat{3}$, F, in the top voice, suggesting a weakened, attenuated capturing of a D♭-major pseudoreality.

The S-theme in the finale of op. 2 (refer to figure 6.1) engages with the same expressive issues using many of the same musical strategies, including a heavily marked tonal environment, a rhetorical breakdown, and an atemporal digression. Perhaps the most notable expressive feature of this expositional S is its key: that of the minor, not the major, mediant. It thus plays a central role in a highly deformational minor-minor exposition, with P in F♯ minor and S in A minor; the situation can be understood as a direct consequence of the suppression of the Arcadian relative major that occurs throughout the sonata as a whole, especially its first and last movements. The rhetoric of suppression emerges in the thematic rhetoric as well: S refers to a rustic, *style hongrois* topic—a Gypsy dance—that overtly suppresses the normative, *Gesangsthema* S-type.[18] The exotic dance topic may be a gesture toward grotesquerie that mocks, with a sardonic irony, the Romantic *Gesangsthema* convention, perhaps even with an air of self-deprecation. Note the interesting choice to retain the three-sharp key signature at m. 71: this may be an unsounding signal that A major is really the desired key; A minor is an interloper, intruding where it is not welcome.

The theme proceeds toward a cadence in A minor, veering onto the Neapolitan at m. 84 and apparently signaling an imminent ♭II-V-i cadential progression. But forward progress then stalls: mm. 85 and 86 repeat m. 84 exactly, and the theme

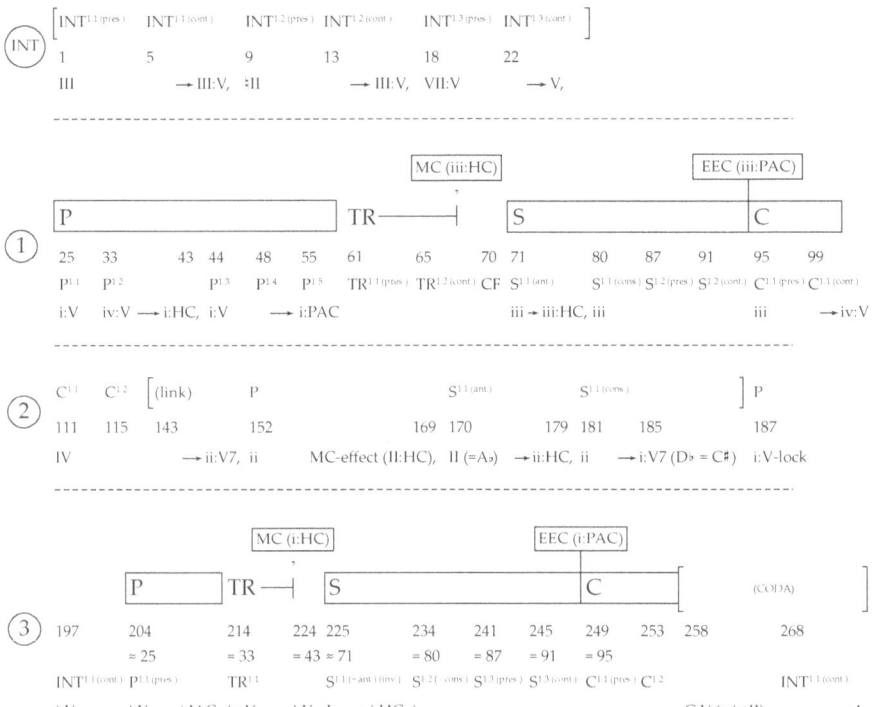

Figure 6.1. Brahms, Piano Sonata in F♯ minor, op. 2, iv.

gets stuck, as it were, unable to continue toward the forecasted cadence, perhaps because the momentarily revealed lyric subject finds himself questioning whether an A-minor EEC can really be viable. Measure 87 initiates what amounts to a rescue operation as an attempt to avoid a complete S-breakdown: a presentation module in mm. 87–90 ($S^{1.2\ (pres.)}$) leads to a normative continuation in m. 91; the phrase rhythm slows markedly around m. 93, on the final approach to the cadence; and the EEC appears in m. 95. The cadence itself is anything but straightforward: in an extraordinary act of naïveté consistent with the S-theme's rustic, low-style simplicity, it introduces a surprising Picardy third, C♯, yielding an ephemeral impression that the EEC has in fact been secured in the modally corrected key of A *major*. The gesture is almost certainly best regarded as a surface-level effect (thus the "iii:PAC" instead of "III:PAC" in figure 6.1)—a vain effort to write over the inevitable A-minor EEC and replace it with a more positive, more hopeful, but ultimately futile, A major. Indeed, A minor persists: a portentous, tolling-of-the-bells $C^{1.1\ (pres.)}$ gesture booms forth immediately in m. 95 with the signature anapestic, Beethovenian fate rhythm (⌣⌣⌣/), silencing with a grim minor mode any inclination toward believing that the EEC occurred in the major mode.[19] The Picardy gesture may be understood as another wishful, reminiscent look backward—an ironic "if only" gesture that glances specifically, perhaps, at the lost A major from the first movement's development section or at the finale's A-major slow introduction (see below, sections 3 and 4, respectively).

In this movement's recapitulatory S, the tonal trajectory becomes problematized to an extent that it triggers a full-fledged rhetorical breakdown and temporal rupture. S appears there in the tonic major at m. 225 (≈ m. 71), apparently achieving the hoped-for minor-to-major emancipation. But, in fact, the recapitulatory S comprises one of the most ironic of all imaginable moves: the theme appears in *inverted* form, thus standing on its head the *style hongrois* folk dance. Far from realizing a major tonic that rescues the narrative from minor-mode failure, this inverted S connotes another descent into sardonic self-deprecation. The theme laughs at itself, as it were, mocking its own futility and thumbing its nose at F♯ major.

Such a reading accounts well for what happens next: the major mode proves unsustainable, and a complete breakdown occurs in the consequent module, beginning at m. 234. Strict *correspondence measures* resume (m. 234 = m. 80);[20] S reverts to its original, uninverted form; and the mode crumbles into a tragic F♯ minor that belies whatever rustic innocence might remain, in what now sounds like a menacing, troubled dance theme. ESC arrives in m. 249, complete with the Picardy third from the original EEC; here, as in the exposition, major-mode stability is canceled immediately by the minor-mode tolling of the bells in mm. 249–50. A new $C^{1.2}$ module appears in mm. 253–54 and glances at B minor before sliding—braking precariously—into a new module at m. 258. Formally speaking, m. 258 initiates the movement's coda. But the move is also central in an expressive sense: mm. 255–58 bring the sonata operation to a skidding stop and, in the process, effect a swerve completely off the sonata road. These four bars thus constitute a gateway passage that prefigures a rupture at m. 258, where the initiatory, declamatory INT$^{1.1}$ $^{(pres.)}$ motive from the slow introduction is hurled down right in the middle of the ongoing C-space, in the bass (*marcato il basso*) and at a *fff* dynamic (the loudest in the entire movement). The discontinuity is simultaneously underscored by a shift to the tritone-related C major, one of the most distant of all possible key choices, where such a shift is consistent with Brahms's use of the Neapolitan (♭VI-♭II-♯IV/♭V) complex to signify a disturbance in the narrative, often in the form of a deflection into a composed-out moment of contemplation or reminiscence. Measure 258 thus comprises a veritable paroxysm in which the narrating agent suddenly suspends sonata action in order to assume the role of a deus ex machina in an eleventh-hour rescue. Having failed to secure the major tonic and fend off a tragic minor-mode ending, the narrator jettisons first-narrative temporality; the sonata proper is over.

Additional Interpretive Considerations

Many of these interpretive issues surrounding the treatment of the S-space in a Romantic sonata raise additional concerns that inform an approach to interpreting Romantic music more broadly. First, consider that numerous instances arise—beginning most obviously with music of Beethoven and continuing in music of Chopin, Schumann, and Brahms—in which it may be tempting to link the expressive narrative to aspects of the composer's biography. This is true of the narratives in, for example, the first movements of Brahms's opp. 2 and 5. Such connections should be drawn cautiously; expressive narratives—in the sense of the music's emplotment of a series of ordered, expressive states—exists regardless of whether it can be correlated with the life story or with any other historically authentic accounts conveyed consciously or intentionally by the actual composer.

Consider specifically the case of Brahms's op. 2. Biographical correlations seem particularly apropos in light of that sonata's dedication, "*Frau Clara Schumann verehrend zugeeignet*" ("adoringly dedicated to Frau Clara Schumann"). These five words can be regarded as an invitation into the well-known, often-repeated story of a young man—Brahms himself—who desires a married woman—Clara—superior in age as well as in cultural and artistic sophistication. The young man intensely desires the woman, but the longed-for relationship proves impossible due to his friendship with her husband, Robert. As such, the man—his masculinity suppressed—must find a way to deal psychologically with his circumstances by making the relationship more normal and more emotionally stable, at least in part by setting aside whatever physical desire he may feel for the woman and processing whatever trauma might accrue. Failure to do so successfully may pose a risk to his artistic career, not to mention his psychological health and well-being. In the end, he is successful, though the process is painful: he closes the book on the possibility of the (fully consummated) relationship he may have initially desired. He closes it unwillingly at first, but he closes it nevertheless, firmly and with confidence.[21]

Such a story can easily be mapped onto the movement's pastoral narrative. The F♯-minor P, correlating with a real-world present, would be understood as signifying Brahms's situation in the Schumann home, with all the complexities that situation presents to him. A relative-major S—the Arcadian paradise to which there is a retreat and from which there must be a return—would map onto Clara: the desired woman, the need for a relationship, the pleasure such a relationship might bring. A minor-dominant S would suppress the relative major and stifle the Arcadian fantasy, correlating with the unavailability of the desired woman and with the impossibility of the desired relationship. Thus, the movement's specific narrative trajectory is one in which Brahms assumes his role in the Schumann home and begins to seek Clara (P, followed by TR seeking the relative major), then second-guesses whether the desired situation is truly viable (TR reconsiders, then backs up; the narrator—who obviously can now be conflated not only with the implied but also with the *actual* composer—steps in to reminisce and contemplate the situation, in the post-MC interpolation). It is not; ideals of masculinity are suppressed (S, in the minor dominant). The situation triggers a certain amount of regret and looking back on "what might have been" (the false-positive, E-major S-proposal) as well as, later, a full-fledged, reminiscent daydream (in the form of an A-major S-proposal, in the development, m. 92) of what a better place the world might be if the anticipated relationship had really been possible. The daydream eventually gives way to the harrowing realization that the relationship is doomed to untenability (dissolution of the developmental $S^{prop.}$, followed by an off-tonic, fully diminished-seventh recapitulation in m. 123). After several last-ditch attempts to process the trauma by reimagining the dream and then letting it go once and for all (the recapitulatory S-space interpolation in A major, m. 155; and the wishful deflection at m. 176 onto a cadential $^6_4$ in A major just before the ESC), Brahms nails the door shut forever (the violent coda).

Of course, Brahms completed this sonata in November 1852, nearly a year *before* meeting the Schumanns at their home in Düsseldorf in late September 1853.[22] Even so, the lessons such a hermeneutic exercise provides are not easily dismissed. The ease with which this movement's musical narrative maps onto this particular biographical narrative speaks not so much to any autobiographical authenticity immanent in the movement itself but rather to the presence of a constellation of aesthetic concerns shared among all Romantic artists and routinely foregrounded in their artworks. These include concerns for the imperfections of the present; for the loss and impossibility of recovery of a more perfect golden age; for highly personalized, interiorized forms of trauma and emotional distress; and for dreams and reveries that provide escape routes, even if only imagined, into idealized spaces—and where the retreat to such spaces constitutes the specific psychological means of coping with the suffering brought on by the shortcomings of the existential present. Such archetypal narratives should be regarded as more central in the Romantic imagination and in the interpretation of Romantic art than any specifically autobiographical narratives that may accrue, whether in this or in any other sonata movement.

Second, and more broadly, observe that interpretations of any of a sonata's surface-level structural features and events are complicated by their stylistic and historical context. This issue comes to the fore especially when considering treatment of the S-space in Romantic sonata movements. Interpretations of cadences—especially EECs and ESCs—can be particularly problematic. Consider, for example, the undermined EECs in opp. 2/i, 2/iv, and 5/i, and even (referring back to chapter 4) at m. 75 in op. 1/i. Expressive interpretations of such events depend upon an interpreter's flexibility with respect to what constitutes a "cadence" in the music of Brahms, or perhaps upon an interpreter's views on whether the Sonata Theory concepts of cadence failure, expositional failure, or sonata failure are appropriate for describing nineteenth-century sonata practice. Either issue is considerably more straightforward in the Classical sonata than in the Romantic sonata: Classical S-themes can be said to have an obligation to produce a full PAC in the secondary key, where anything less than a full, unambiguous cadence delays, undercuts, defers, or cancels the tonal closure of the expositional S-space and of the exposition as a whole.[23] But these issues become more complex in the Romantic sonata, in large part because some would maintain that the highly diversified stylistic and tonal language of the post-Beethovenian nineteenth century necessitates admitting a wider range of possibilities for the kinds of events that are understood as *cadential*. Such views almost invariably follow from the fact that Brahms and others in the period frequently—much more frequently than did Classical composers—introduced various forms of cadential complications at moments at which a PAC may have been expected. Some recent commentators have proposed elaborate typologies to account for the expanded range of options invoked by nineteenth-century composers at cadence moments.[24] Such thinking leads to the possibility that the ostensible EECs in question should be regarded not as undercut cadences or as outright cadence failures but rather as substitute, stand-in PAC events—in each case not a cadence in the Classical sense but a cadence nevertheless, rather than some sort of evaded, overwritten, or missed PAC. After all, it is possible, as mentioned, to rationalize the cadences in op. 1/i and 2/i as composing out, respectively, a $^6_4$-$^5_3$ or 6-5 appoggiatura figure in the upper voices above a sustained bass pedal point. Perhaps in this sense either event can be regarded as a normative, typical cadential event within the constraints of a specific style—within, in this case, Brahms's personal musical language. Perhaps either moment would thus be best regarded as cadential, even though the same or similar situation in, say, the music of Mozart or Beethoven would not be understood as cadential in an equivalent sense.

If this and other comparable cadence situations raise questions about the viability of concepts such as expositional or sonata failure as interpretive rubrics for the Romantic sonata, similar questions also arise in the context of, for example, nineteenth-century tonal schemes—including those involving secondary themes deployed in deformational, "incorrect" modes or keys (any keys, that is, other than the major dominant in a major-mode sonata, or the relative major or minor dominant in a minor-mode sonata). Questions of whether any such situations should be regarded as deformational and expressively marked in the Romantic sonata is a subject of debate in what has become known as *deformation theory*,[25] with much of that debate underpinned by a single, broader question: that of just how far generic norms and deformations associated with Classical, eighteenth-century sonata practice may be carried forward and used to regulate the interpretation of sonata practice in the post-Classical world of nineteenth-century Romanticism. On one side is the view that a feature that may once have been deformational is no longer deformational as such once it becomes common, predictable, or expected within some circumscribed frame of reference (music of a given composer, music of a specific stylistic or historical period, and the like); on the other is the position that the routine use of a particular deformation constitutes not a conversion of that deformation into a norm but rather a composer's "customization" of a norm "for his own use"—a regular, repeated subversion of a norm using what becomes a common, familiar deformational strategy.[26] In the latter view, a deformation remains deformational regardless of the degree of commonality it acquires in any musical environment—resulting in, among other consequences, the possibility of a paradoxical situation in which a deformation—expositional or sonata failure, for instance—becomes a first-level default.[27]

The problem of choosing the "correct" side in this debate can be intractable. In fact, the issue itself is intractable, specifically because the norms of any semiotic system are, at any given moment in historical time, constantly in flux: identifying and understanding them requires positing a synchronic definition of a norm, which is in fact diachronic and subject to constant reinterpretation and change.[28] Even so, the problem at hand can be further nuanced and better understood—and in the process, we can move beyond oversimplified questions of who is "right" and who is "wrong"—by attending to the various levels on which readers read and interpret texts. Especially helpful in this regard is the literary criticism of Peter J. Rabinowitz, who has expanded on Booth's concept of the implied reader in order to build a robust interpretive model that more fully accounts for an implied reader's (nevertheless synchronic) range of beliefs and values.[29] Specifically, Rabinowitz distinguishes between two types of implied audiences for whom an implied author writes: one is the *authorial audience*, the other the *narrative audience*. The authorial audience is the hypothetical ideal audience for whom authors rhetorically design their texts: authors assume that members of this hypothetical audience possess certain beliefs, a certain amount of historical knowledge, and a certain level of familiarity with rhetorical, generic, and other conventions. Authors make their artistic choices based in part on these assumptions, and their artistic success will depend in part on whether their assumptions are accurate.[30] The narrative audience, on the other hand, is an "imitation audience": this is the audience "inside the narrative" that readers pretend to join when they read. Members of a narrative audience believe that a work of fiction is really a history: they believe that the characters are real and that the story really happened.[31] Actual readers can always inhabit both audiences; in fact, they must inhabit both audiences at one time or another in order to successfully interpret a text. In this sense, a reader can take a variety of interpretive positions, without any of them being necessarily "right" or "wrong," or "accurate" or "inaccurate." Rather, text-adequate interpretation depends on readers using the knowledge of the authorial audience to correctly apprehend the beliefs and values of, and to become members of, the narrative audience. Difficulties arise mainly when readers try to draw conclusions or make interpretations that are not appropriate to the stance from which those interpretations are made.

Some examples will be helpful. Rabinowitz uses Tolstoy's *War and Peace*, in which the narrative audience is required to believe that Moscow was destroyed in 1812 and that Natasha, Pierre, and Andrei are real people, while the authorial audience knows that only the burning of Moscow is a historical fact.[32] He also points to fairy tales: the narrative audience for Cinderella, for instance, needs to pretend to believe in fairy godmothers, while the authorial audience is aware that the genre is the fairy tale and knows that such things are not real; readers wanting to reasonably interpret the story and account for Cinderella's actions must temporarily inhabit the narrative audience or else be forced to assume that Cinderella is "a neurotic, perhaps psychotic, young woman subject to hallucinations."[33]

None of these principles are limited to literature. The narrative audience, for example, for Pablo Picasso's "Reclining Woman with Large Hand" (1945) or his "Reclining Woman Reading" (1960) accepts that these are images of women and pretends to enter the world of the pictures, from which vantage point the paintings' sensuality can be appreciated; the authorial audience, on the other hand, knows very well that real women look nothing like the women in these pictures, regardless of the fact that Picasso often—almost always, in fact—represented his women in such ways. But this same authorial audience, on the other hand, is in a position to attend to the technical strategies Picasso employed in creating the pictures and in treating his subjects deformationally, for expressive effect, just as the authorial audience for Cinderella can attend to the ways in which the story treats the generic conventions associated with the fairy tale.

All of these situations are complicated, furthermore, by the presence of a third audience: the *actual audience*, members of which must possess the knowledge and skills necessary to join the authorial audience.[34] Actual audience members who are not aware of the generic or historical contexts for Picasso's works, for example, or who do not understand his technique, or who have not seen enough of his work, may well decide simply that he lacked the technical capacity to accurately render the figure of a woman, obviously missing the point of the texts entirely. The gap between actual and authorial audiences can be narrowed, or closed completely, by education and training. But narrowing the gap between authorial and narrative audiences is largely a decision of readers who choose, consciously or unconsciously, to ask themselves, "What sort of person would I have to pretend to be—what would I have to know and believe—if I wanted to take this work of fiction as real?"[35] Adopting such a stance is clearly something like adopting the pretense traditionally known as the "suspension of disbelief," but the paradigm is richer: in reading texts, a reader both suspends and does not suspend belief at the same time.[36]

Rabinowitz's approach can be transferred to Romantic music and used to shed light on various interpretive challenges. One who argues, for example, that an "epistemically specific" approach to music of Bruckner renders historically inappropriate the concept of a nonresolving recapitulation as deformational,[37] because in Bruckner's language, such procedures are so common that they rise to the status of a first-level default option, is inhabiting the authorial audience and seeking to understand Bruckner's compositional technique—in a way that is not unlike how an authorial audience would seek to understand the facts required to read *War and Peace* or take stock of Picasso's technical procedures. Another who observes the fact that Brahms or other nineteenth-century composers often evade or otherwise introduce various equivocations at moments in which a more Classical PAC might have been expected and, following from this, chooses to categorize ranges of cadence events according to typologies of available options is likewise inhabiting the authorial audience and seeking to account for compositional procedure.[38]

But, as in narrative fiction—as in *War and Peace* or the paintings of Picasso—the end result in the act of interpretation will be different depending on which audience one inhabits. From the point of view of the authorial audience, an equivocal cadence in Brahms may not be unusual in any way; from the point of view of the narrative audience, however, an equivocal cadence can be just that—an equivocation that comes up short of securing tonal closure at a level that a normative PAC (which is understood as possible but not present) would have attained. Similarly, authorial audiences understand, and expect, that expositions and recapitulations in Romantic sonatas will not usually achieve tonal closure in the Classical sense; narrative audiences understand that such expositions and recapitulations have not fulfilled their generic obligations. For authorial audiences, S-themes in the keys of the mediant and submediant may not be surprising; for narrative audiences, the only acceptable, expressively unmarked option for the S in a major-mode sonata will be the major dominant. Importantly, the *frequency* with which any strategy or scenario—an evaded cadence, a nonresolving recapitulation, an S-theme in the key of the mediant—arises within a given stylistic or historical context is a separate issue from that of how to interpret that scenario from the point of view of a given audience. Just because Picasso almost always paints women in a particular way does not mean that we should conclude that this is what women really look like, or that Picasso's more realistic representations must have the same expressive significance; similarly, just because Brahms, Mahler, or other nineteenth-century composers often equivocate at the moment of an expected PAC does not mean we should assume that the events we find in place of those PACs must substitute for them and acquire an equivalent expressive meaning.

Rather, cadence failure and, related, sonata failure should be understood as having obvious value in the Romantic-aesthetic world in which Brahms was writing. Such forms of staged failure—fragmentation of a more perfect whole so as to produce infinite openness in lieu of tidy closure—far from being "failures" in the most traditional sense, provide powerful tools for the expression of a characteristically

Romantic skepticism toward Classical and Enlightenment values of clarity, balance, symmetry, logic, and rationality. They masterfully encapsulate the artistic spirit of Romanticism by looking back on an idealized, lost Arcadian paradise (the Classical sonata tradition) and rethinking that vision within a view of a present-day, fragmentary world marred by imperfection.

Notes

1. Hepokoski and Darcy, *Elements of Sonata Theory*, 306–17.
2. On modal failure, see ibid., esp. 178–79 and 310–12.
3. Ibid., 306–10 provide a more nuanced discussion. See also Rosen, *The Classical Style* (passim, including 254–56). This view of an expressive opposition between major and minor has a long history that dates from work of eighteenth-century theorists: see Ratner, *Classic Music*; Steblin, *A History of Key Characteristics in the Eighteenth and Early Nineteenth Centuries*; and Wheelock, "*Schwarze Gredel* and the Engendered Minor Mode in Mozart's Operas."
4. For historical views of the expressive duality of major and minor in the nineteenth century, see Harrison, *Harmonic Function in Chromatic Music*, 215–322.
5. Klein, "Chopin's Fourth Ballade as Musical Narrative"; Smith, *Expressive Forms in Brahms's Instrumental Music*, 178 and, more broadly, 214–70. On the tragic-to-triumphant expressive genre, see Hatten, *Musical Meaning in Beethoven*, 79.
6. On S-types in the Classical sonata, see Hepokoski and Darcy, *Elements of Sonata Theory*, 131–39. On the P-S contrast in the nineteenth century, see Hepokoski, "Masculine-Feminine."
7. Marx, *Die lehre von der musikalischen Komposition*, III:282 (cited and translated in Hepokoski, "Masculine-Feminine," 494). For Hepokoski's language, see Hepokoski, ibid., 498. See also Burnham, "A. B. Marx and the Gendering of Sonata Form"; and see McClary, *Feminine Endings: Music, Gender, and Sexuality*, esp. 53–79, for an extended (and provocative) discussion of these and other gender issues in the sonata form.
8. Monelle's descriptions (*The Sense of Music*, 81–114) of a sonata's themes, including its S-theme, as manifesting a temporally arresting "lyric time"—as opposed to the temporally forward-vectored "progressive time" of transitions and development sections—raise separate issues, most of them more phenomenological than are the issues of narrative structure and discourse with which I am concerned here.
9. Smith, *Expressive Forms in Brahms's Instrumental Music*, passim (including 10, 123, 160, and 173).
10. Monahan, "Success and Failure in Mahler's Sonata Recapitulations," 40.
11. Klein, "Chopin's Fourth Ballade as Musical Narrative," 32. As mentioned, many such interior themes in music of Chopin take the topical form of nocturnes or other character pieces (pastorales and others). Klein notes that the nocturne specifically suggests the possibility of a gendered reading, where the nocturne signifies a feminine subject or a generic femininity. See also Petty, "Chopin and the Ghost of Beethoven," 286; and, on the gendering of Chopin, Kallberg, *Chopin at the Boundaries*, 30–86.
12. Frisch, *Brahms and the Principle of Developing Variation*, 53, hears the same series of events similarly, writing that in m. 50 "a jarring B♮ ruptures the G♯-major harmony and forces a modulation to E major," and he likewise observes the well-formedness of the phrase rhetoric beginning in m. 51.
13. Dickensheets ("The Topical Vocabulary of the Nineteenth Century," 132–36) has also emphasized the *novelistic* (in the Schlegelian sense of *fragmentary*) quality of the movement. Aspects of her reading overlap with my own: she hears the narrative in the S-space as one that

"begins with the protagonist [that is, the P-based material in m. 40] in a new guise, moves to the lady [the E-major theme, m. 51: the "noble lady of high breeding and honor" mentioned in the poem on which the second movement is based], and returns to the protagonist [modulates back to C♯ minor]—creating at least the strong possibility that the lady is merely an idealistic dream."

14. The attenuated EEC is an apparent cadence rhetorically undercut in one or more of its parameters, so as to undermine or call into question its power to provide full structural closure. See Hepokoski and Darcy, *Elements of Sonata Theory*, 169–70.

15. For "gravity" in this context, see Larson, *Musical Forces*; and Hatten, "Musical Forces and Agential Energies." Hatten discusses the Beethoven op. 13/ii melody in his "Melodic Forces and Agential Energies."

16. Especially interesting in this context is McClary's reading (*Conventional Wisdom*, 123) of the submediant as standing "for Never Never Land in the economy of nineteenth-century musical imagery." See also McClary, "Pitches, Expression, Ideology."

17. Frisch reads m. 56 as a codetta in which the descending melody signifies "embarrassed compensation" for the preponderance of rising sequences in the rest of the exposition; see *Brahms and the Principle of Developing Variation*, 38.

18. Dickensheets has noted S's *style hongrois*, although here, she says, it has "a tone more reminiscent of the dance hall than of actual Gypsies" ("The Topical Vocabulary of the Nineteenth Century," 134). On the *style hongrois* as a topic, see Bellman, *The Style Hongrois in the Music of Western Europe*.

19. Others have observed the Beethoven intertext in the C material, including Newman, *The Sonata since Beethoven*, 333, and Dickensheets, "The Topical Vocabulary of the Nineteenth Century," 135.

20. *Correspondence measures* are bar-for-bar restatements in the recapitulation of measures from the exposition, perhaps at a different tonal level. See Hepokoski and Darcy, *Elements of Sonata Theory*, 239–42.

21. As is well known, Brahms's relationship with Clara Schumann was complex, and I make no claim that this daytime television–style reduction of the story does it justice. For a helpful, more nuanced introduction to the topic, see Reich, "Clara Schumann and Johannes Brahms." Kramer's discussion of nineteenth-century perspectives on gender roles, especially the problems associated with achieving historical ideals of masculinity (problems that inform narratives such as the Brahms-Clara tale), also helps contextualize the issues; see his *Franz Schubert: Sexuality, Subjectivity, Song*, 129–51.

22. For the completion date of op. 2, see the chronology given in Bozarth, "Brahms's *Lieder ohne Worte*," 349. According to Newman (*The Sonata since Beethoven*, 331), the dedication to Clara was added after the sonata's completion and not conceived in advance, and Brahms apparently also considered dedicating the work to Joachim or Robert Schumann.

23. Hepokoski and Darcy, *Elements of Sonata Theory*, 169–70. See also Caplin, *Classical Form*, 101–7.

24. Jenkins, "Expositional Trajectories Gone Awry," is an example, as is Jones, "Cadence in Mahler."

25. The literature is extensive and growing. See, among others, Horton, *Bruckner's Symphonies*; Taruskin, "Speed Bumps"; Wingfield, "Beyond 'Norms and Deformations'"; Vande Moortele, *Two-Dimensional Sonata Form*; and Neuwirth, "Joseph Haydn's 'Witty' Play on Hepokoski and Darcy's *Elements of Sonata Theory*."

26. Hepokoski and Darcy, *Elements of Sonata Theory*, 11 ("customizing the norm").

27. As in, for example, Darcy, "Bruckner's Sonata Deformations."

28. I thank the anonymous reader of the manuscript for calling my attention to this issue.

29. Rabinowitz, "Truth in Fiction: A Reexamination of Audiences." See also Rabinowitz, *Before Reading: Narrative Conventions and the Politics of Interpretation*.

30. Rabinowitz, "Truth in Fiction," 126. See also Booth's commentary on Rabinowitz's work, in *The Rhetoric of Fiction*, 422-23.

31. Rabinowitz, "Truth in Fiction," 127 ("imitation audience"); Booth, *The Rhetoric of Fiction*, 423 ("inside the narrative").

32. Rabinowitz, "Truth in Fiction," 127.

33. Ibid., 129.

34. Ibid., 126–27.

35. Ibid., 128.

36. Ibid., 127–28n15.

37. Horton, "Bruckner's Symphonies and Sonata Deformation Theory," 17.

38. As in, for example, Jenkins, "Expositional Trajectories Gone Awry," and Jones, "Cadence in Mahler."

7 Treatment of the Development and Recapitulation

Romantic development sections engage in their own characteristic ways with the aesthetics of fragmentation. Perhaps the most important among several common strategies is that in which the development is treated as a privileged, idealized space in which to explore, or propose new solutions to, structural and expressive problems facing the exposition.

The development section in Brahms's op. 1 provides a good initial example. It contains two atemporal interpolations, as shown in figure 4.2. The first suggests a development section fragmented at its front end; the second splits open the center of the development to propose a new, idealized version of the exposition. Consider mm. 88–99 first: this module restates the cadence-denying $^6_4$ material from mm. 51 and 75, now over a G pedal and expanded with imitation between the left and right hands. These measures are expressively significant because they contravene basic principles of rotational ordering, in which development sections normatively open with P-based material and continue with S.[1] As such, they invite an interpretation in which they are understood as outside the first narrative, sequestered within a secondary, atemporal stream; and they suggest, moreover, that the development section, in true Romantic fragmentary fashion, opens with a nonopening—with the narrating agent diving directly into the story from the outside and breaking open the sonata's otherwise cohesive, Classical temporality. Various readings present themselves: the event may connote another crisis of continuation, in which the narrator intervenes because continuing with the story is too painful; it may constitute a structural pause (in Genette's sense) for the narrator to comment or reflect on what just happened in the expositional rotation; or it may be an instance of the narrator forcing the sonata open at a critical structural juncture in order to make space in which to continue to reminisce wishfully on "what might have been." The G pedal in the bass may be significant in this regard: if the G functions as dominant of C, one might wish to hear the narrator looking forward, proleptically, with barely concealed anticipation, toward the C-major material at m. 139; on the other hand, if G is a tonic (because the bass pedal was staged as, and eventually accepted as, a tonic in both of the previous $^6_4$ interpolations, at mm. 51 and 75), one might wish to hear the narrator looking backward, analeptically, with an air of gentle pleading or even a tone of regret (signified by the *piano* dynamic and the *con espressione* at m. 88), where G is the pitch that "might have been," or the pitch that one "wishes" had been, the tonic in the expositional S-theme. In any case, the sudden, *forte*, a *tempo* outburst at m. 100 signals a gateway out of the interpolation. The sonata gears reengage and the narrator awakens to reality, as if having found the will to move on with the rest of the tale.

The second interpolation spans mm. 139–72. It follows on the heels of a traditional sonata development that treats, mostly in rotational order, elements of the P-theme (mm. 100–10), then elements of the P- and S-themes together, as if P and S are locked in a frantic battle (beginning at m. 111). P yields completely to S-based material at m. 124, with S overtaking the narrative, *fortissimo*, precisely at the moment of an assertive PAC in none other than the extraordinarily distantly related, heavily marked key of B minor (vii!). Surely such a key should be understood as a gesture of futility: if S has entered here seeking a viable opportunity to correct the problems that have plagued it since the exposition, B minor will offer no hope. Into this environment steps the narrator, with deliberate abruptness, at m. 136. Here, the bass signifies a non sequitur by stepping chromatically down by step onto a low-register C♮: the register of the C♮, together with the tonal disjunction effected by its appearance within a passage (mm. 124–35) that sequentially composes out a B-minor triad, can be heard as a portentous warning—perhaps a "wait, go no further!" gesture, in the middle of a development section that at the largest level has lost its tonal way. The non sequitur initiates a gateway passage, mm. 136–38, based on the ascending-third motive from P (or perhaps a lingering echo of the head-motive from S) and in the key of C minor—thus discarding the key of B minor. The full rupture occurs at m. 139, shifting the level of discourse—mimesis shifts to diegesis—via expressively marked discontinuities in multiple parameters, including dynamic level (the shift to *pianissimo* contrasts markedly with the previous *fortissimo* that had been sustained from the pickup to m. 124, and the performer may even be well advised to add the *una corda*), expressive indication (*dolcissimo* replaces the earlier *ben marcato*, from m. 124), register (specifically a return to the very same high register as was heard earlier in the interpolated cadence denials, at mm. 51 and 75), and texture (a return to parallel thirds, also heard earlier, at mm. 51 and 75). The last two of these features are especially important in that the explicit, audible return here to the very same register and texture as in the two parenthetical interpolations from the expositional S-space explicitly and audibly signals a return to the very same diegetic, narrating voice.

The interpolated excursus that follows is expressively supercharged in the sense that it comprises nothing other than a new, idealized, perfected version of the very sonata exposition that did not occur earlier in the movement's real expositional space—complete, now, with a P in the home tonic, C major, and an S in the "correct" key of the major dominant, G major. Rhetorically, this should be regarded as a proposal for what the exposition was supposed to look like, a crystallized version of what could have happened there but was not permitted to happen. The narrator floats before us a longing, wishful, reminiscent reverie—perhaps a fleeting look backward toward an imagined vision of an unspoiled Arcadia that "might have been." Several features of the passage support such a reading. Measure 139 returns to the home key of C major and thus modally brightens the C minor of the gateway passage: the lights come on to reveal before us the image of paradise. The shimmering, high-register restatement that follows, in parallel thirds, of the rhythmic head motive from the P-theme can be understood as a substitute, ethereal, "heavenly" vision of the P-theme itself, the sweetness of which is underscored, literally, with the *dolcissimo* marking at m. 139 as well as with the *portamento* at m. 141—where the latter may connote a kind of ecstatic lingering, as if the narrator is awed by the sheer beauty of the image. The imitative texture that emerges in m. 140 musically signifies a certain spatial effect: an echo, as if to suggest that the narrator is speaking into a vast expanse of open space—perhaps from a mountaintop (picture a typical Romantic landscape painting), across a fertile valley, with the sound of the words echoing back from the distant mountains on the other side. And, consistent with its status as a dream, the new P-theme is not so much a pure, pristine P as it is a ghostly vision of a P haunted by the lingering effects of the trauma just endured. The composed-out E-G-B arpeggiation in mm. 139–45, for example, looks back analeptically onto the E-G-B-D arpeggiation from mm. 44–46; and the C-major at m. 139 is not a pure C major but rather a C major that at once reminisces on A minor and E minor from the troubled expositional S (note the A-minor and E-minor triads composed out in mm. 139–42 and 142–45, respectively) and finds itself undercut by its latent status as subdominant of the S-theme's G major (note the persistent $F_\sharp$s).

The interpolation also immanently asserts its status as a proposed exposition in certain features of its structure, which is well formed in ways that the actual exposition's structure is not. For example, mm. 139–49 function as a concise P-TR-MC complex: a sentential presentation in mm. 139–42 functions as a short P; a dissolving-continuation TR begins at m. 143 and modulates to the major dominant, G major; and m. 149 terminates the TR as a V:HC MC. Four bars of CF follow in mm. 149–52 before the dominant yields normatively to the tonic G at m. 153. This is the downbeat of a new, proposed S-theme, marked "S$^{\text{prop.}}$" in figure 4.2. Had this theme been present in the real expositional space, it might have qualified as one of Brahms's most longingly beautiful S-themes. Delivered *piano* and *con espressione*, it stands as a near-perfect realization of an idyllic, Arcadian world missing entirely from the movement's exposition proper. This is an S well-formed and rhetorically confident in ways that the expositional S was not: it comprises a neatly formatted sentence, with a pair of four-bar basic ideas, mm. 153–56 and 157–60 (S$^{\text{prop. (pres.)}}$), followed by a continuation in m. 161 (S$^{\text{prop. (cont.)}}$); and it is entirely secure in its tonality, self-confidently composing out the G-major tonic triad within each of its four-bar basic ideas and invoking none of the tonal consternation that characterized the expositional S.

But all good things must come to an end. What one wants one cannot have; the Romantic is destined for infinite longing. Ultimately, the proposed exposition, like the real exposition, is destined for failure in the sense that it will fail to secure a full PAC. The S$^{\text{prop. (cont.)}}$ module opens at m. 161 over a dominant chord in G major, in the destabilized $^6_4$ position, with A in the bass. This indicates a disturbance—a first sign, perhaps, that this is but an impossible, unsustainable delusion. A modal collapse follows in short order, when the B in mm. 167–68 decays to a B♭ in m. 169, producing a dominant-functioning, fully diminished-seventh chord on C♯. This proves to be the jolt that awakens the narrator from the dream and initiates the gateway out of the atemporal stream. The C♯°7 is best understood as tonicizing D, V/V in G major, and it appears momentarily that it might point toward a development-ending, retransitional bridge back to the tonic C major. But the reentry into present-tense reality is not so smooth: the S-theme, and with it the entire proposed exposition, abruptly collapses—ruptures, in fact—when the C♯°7 resolves elliptically at m. 173 onto a major-minor seventh chord with C in the bass. The expressive significance of this move belies the apparent smoothness and ease of the voice leading required to make it: this is the rhetorical gesture that shifts the discursive level—perhaps reluctantly and with an air of resignation—from the diegesis of the interpolation back to the mimesis of the sonata proper. Retrospectively, the C at m. 173 can be understood as the very C that intruded into the bass voice at m. 136. There the C was perhaps a proposal for a dominant that signaled an impending subdominant recapitulation; mm. 136–38 were then a darkened, minor-mode questioning of this C♮'s viability; and m. 139 descended into an atemporal interpolation that suspended, or wedged open, this C in favor of backing up and revisiting, and correcting, some of the sonata's more problematized features. The interpolation could be deleted without disturbing the movement's essential sonata-structural outlines.[2]

The proposed exposition thus remains but a fleeting fragment in the Romantic sense—open ended, with no cadential conclusion; self-contained and autonomous yet impossibly incomplete, no matter how beautiful or perfectly formed it may appear to be. The vision is not viable, furthermore, in a purely structural, formalistic sense: a sonata's developmental rotation is no place for a P-theme in the tonic and an S-theme in the dominant. And, similarly, it is a vision that finds itself framed by an imperfect exposition and an equally imperfect recapitulation—as if it were the centerpiece of the movement but also as if pressured on both sides, beginning and end. Thus, for all its imagined perfection, this vision of the perfect exposition ultimately has no power to rescue the sonata from its own deficiencies.

* * *

Similar situations appear in the development sections of each of the other sonata form movements from Brahms's piano sonatas. Each sets forth in its own way an interpolated vision of a more perfect, more ideal S-theme, or a more perfect vision of a full exposition, one that did not occur, or one that was suppressed, earlier in the movement's first rotation.

In op. 2/i, for example, the development as a whole comprises a subrotational structure in which one subrotation ("SUB¹" in figure 5.1) begins at m. 83 and another ("SUB²") at m. 108. The first subrotation modulates to A major by m. 90, where its forward-vectored motion appears to stall upon reaching a dominant in that key; the dominant repeats itself in m. 91, as if questioning whether A major can possibly be the right key. In retrospect, mm. 89–91 comprise a gateway to a rupture in m. 92, where the dominant yields, in striking fashion, to a tender, *piano dolce espressivo* reappearance in A major of none other than the idealized S$^{prop.}$ that originally appeared in m. 51. This is another expressively supercharged passage in which the S$^{prop.}$ appears out of rotational order and in the key of the relative major of the sonata's home tonic, F♯ minor—the very key that had been desired all along in this movement, ever since the expositional TR. A diegetic, interpolated reminiscence on the part of the lyric subject follows—another vision of "what might have been" had the exposition not lost its way and tragically rejected the relative major in favor of a minor-dominant S. As in op. 1, the vision is of a fantastical, Romanticized but subtly flawed paradise: a well-formed, eight-bar antecedent arrives unproblematically on a dominant in m. 99, thus compensating for the imperfect, truncated, seven-bar antecedent in the expositional S$^{prop.}$ (mm. 51–57), even while the accompaniment figure in the bass at m. 92 incorporates the opening triadic gesture from the actual S-theme at m. 40. Thus, the vision conflates the S$^{prop.}$ with the real S, absorbing real-world austerity into imaginary, relative-major bliss. Perhaps we should understand the vision as haunted, not as tranquil as it may seem, with the narrator unable to find complete comfort in this image of a flawless Arcadia. Ultimately, the dream is destined for collapse: an abrupt disintegration occurs via a dissolving continuation module in mm. 104–107, and first-narrative temporality—the development proper—resumes at m. 108. Measure 108 itself should be understood within the metaphor of resetting the clock: it backs up and restarts the same developmental rotation that began at m. 83, complete with another near-slippage into diegetic reminiscence at m. 116, where the S$^{prop.}$ tries again to break through. The module dissolves completely around m. 119, with any potential reappearance of the S$^{prop.}$ suppressed, perhaps, by the accumulated, unrelenting momentum of the mimetic developmental rotation. The recapitulation launches at m. 123.

The developments in both opp. 2/iv and 5/i include an interpolated excursus with a fully intact expositional trajectory, complete with a P, an MC, and an S; op. 5 even includes a full, unambiguous PAC that functions as a hypothetical, "false" EEC. In op. 2/iv (see figure 6.1), the development opens at m. 111 and immediately descends into a tonal and rhetorical stupor, passing in the next thirty bars through the tonic F♯ minor, the relative major, and the supertonic in mm. 134–42. The narrating agent, mired in confusion and in need of an exit strategy, intervenes abruptly in m. 143, opening up a fissure in the sonata and shifting the level of discourse. What follows can be regarded as a *fortissimo*, agitated shout, outside the first narrative and in an atemporal stream—indeed, the narrator's own revised retelling of the exposition's tale, idealized to such an extent that it can be nothing other than an impossible fantasy. The proposed revision tracks through a revised version of the P-TR complex beginning at m. 152; a well-formed and confident MC follows in m. 169; and m. 170 launches into what should be regarded as a highly idealized S-theme in the sense that it appears in a "corrected" major mode, one that the deformational, minor-mode expositional S had failed to procure. The proposed S is but an ironized impossibility: that is, it may be in the major mode, but its tonic is the hopelessly distant A♭—a chromatic half step away from the sought-after but forever-lost A major, so close, yet also so far away from the desired reality.

In op. 5/i, the rupture occurs at m. 78 (see figure 5.2), where the fate triplets from the original interpolation in the expositional P-space reappear and give way, in m. 79, to the interpolated material from mm. 7–16. Material from that interpolation follows, with some adjustments in its profile that reflect reconceived formal-rhetorical functions: that is, the pedal tones in mm. 79–83 and 84–88 (G♯ and D♯, respectively) function as local dominants instead of tonics; and the consequent module now cadences (m. 88) in its own key, G♯ minor, rather than in the key of the antecedent, C♯ minor. Measures 83–88 can thus be understood now as a TR, with the cadence in m. 88 functioning as a TR-ending MC-effect. There follows in m. 91 one of the most beautiful and most idealized of all of Brahms's hypothetical S-theme proposals ("S$^{\text{prop.}}$" in figure 5.2): a lyrical, *dolce, espressivo* whisper of a *Gesangsthema* S of which the exposition could only dream, sung forth now in a tenor register and in the same key, D♭, into which the exposition's S had slipped upon losing its grip on the idealized relative major.³ The theme comprises a well-formed sentence, with a yearning, upward-reaching, six-bar presentation and a proportional twelve-bar continuation that continues to reach ever higher, as if in search of the final triumph. The theme's most remarkable gesture occurs in m. 109, where it slides gently and contentedly onto a PAC in D♭ major, with the solo tenor achieving the closural $\hat{1}$ coincident with the tonic harmony and $\hat{1}$ in the bass. This moment should be understood in context as a reimagined, idealized, more perfect vision of an EEC-that-never-was—a stronger, secure, poignantly beautiful, and confident EEC that the actual exposition suppressed in m. 68. But again, the dream proves tenuous: a jarring, portentous F♭, appears at m. 110, signaling a darkened, threatening turn toward D♭ minor, and the dream comes crashing down completely at m. 117. Mimetic sonata-space reality returns here via stark disjunctions in tonality (the shift to A♭ minor), dynamic level (a sudden *fortissimo* abruptly silences the *piano* and *pianissimo* whispers of the foregoing S$^{\text{prop.}}$), register (a cascading tumble brings the ethereal upper voices back to registral reality), and thematic profile (a more generically normative P-based development rotation begins anew at m. 119). The paradisiacal vision has been left behind, forever lost to the vicissitudes of Romantic temporality.

These examples reveal much with regard to how one should expressively interpret the rhetorical and expressive functions of development sections in Romantic sonata form movements. Most important, perhaps, is the frequent appearance in that repertoire of a fragmentary yet highly idealized rhetorical excursion in the middle of the development, in the center of the movement. The strategy is surely related, for example, to Brahms's own often-noted penchant for saving some of his most beautiful, lyrical themes for his development sections—a feature of his music that has usually been thought of as arising from an interest in contravening established Classical norms, where the turn toward extended passages of tonal-rhetorical stability within the development subverts the Classical paradigm of reserving the development-space for a sonata's most neutral, "conventional" thematic working-out.[4] But in almost every case in which a new, development-space theme appears in Brahms's music, the new material can be understood as a proposition for an impossible, unattainable dream world—usually a proposition for a new S-theme, in sonata formal terms—not achievable within the confines of a less perfectly formed exposition or recapitulation. The same strategy probably also accounts, furthermore, for the introduction of what have been known as "development themes" in the sonatas of other Romantics, including Beethoven himself. Among many others, notable examples include the first movement of Beethoven's Symphony no. 3 in E♭ major, op. 55 (the interpolated theme at m. 284, in the middle of the development section and in the key of the Neapolitan, E [= F♭] minor); Chopin's Piano Sonata in B minor, op. 58 (the interpolated S² module in D♭ major, at m. 117, in the middle of the developmental-space in a Type 2 sonata); Liszt's Piano Sonata in B minor (the idealized S-theme in the major [!] dominant, F♯ major, m. 335); and Mahler's Symphony no. 7 in E minor (the new, similarly idealized S-theme, again in the major [!] dominant, B major, m. 317). All such situations can be productively interpreted in terms of the sonata's temporal-narrative processes: all of them can be understood as signifying various forms of deflections away from more normative developmental procedures, forcing open the sonata structure and interpolating within it a moment of diegetic commentary, reflection, reminiscence, or some other form of atemporal excursus, external to the first-narrative proper.

The development in op. 2/iv (refer to figure 6.1) is especially revealing with regard to an important aspect of Brahms's developmental strategies. Note that nearly the entire development section in that movement occupies a diegetic rather than a mimetic stream in the narrative. Thus, it goes further than the others, rhetorically speaking and relative to the function of the development within the rest of the sonata movement. That is, here Brahms has treated the development as a whole as a large, privileged space almost completely disengaged from the first-narrative stream; as such, it provides an opportunity to contemplate, ponder, or reminisce on the tale that surrounds it while remaining sequestered in the diegetic mode. In a sense, this means that the sonata proper—the mimetic space in which the first narrative unfolds—has been reduced from three rotations to two, namely the exposition and the recapitulation, with the development itself removed from the mimetic sonata-space. The first-narrative sonata form in such movements could thus be understood as something like what Sonata Theory would regard as a Type 1 sonata instead of the more obvious Type 3 that clearly governs the form at the surface level. Such expressive strategies might account well for many of Brahms's most unusual, idiosyncratic development sections, including those in the Violin Sonatas in A major, op. 100, and D minor, op. 108. I find the latter a particularly compelling example because the entire development section (mm. 84–129) is sounded over a pedal point on a dominant-functioning A. If the shift onto the dominant pedal at m. 84, the discontinuities brought about by the emergence of a learned-style topic, the dynamic shift to a *molto piano*, and the *sotto voce sempre* are all thought of as triggering ruptures in the first-narrative sonata fabric, then in this case the whole development—literally all of it—is best regarded as occupying an interpolated, atemporal stream. The sonata proper that surrounds it is thus in some sense a birotational form, comprising only the spaces traditionally thought of as the exposition and recapitulation.

* * *

Romantic sonata recapitulations typically manifest fragment aesthetics in two ways. One is the various forms of the strategy that I will refer to as the *fragmented recapitulation*: a recapitulation in which the P-theme, ostensibly a normative, stable point of initiation for the sonata's final rotation, becomes rhetorically undercut in a way that leaves a normatively closed formal unit syntactically open at its front end. In such situations, the statement of the P-theme comprises an initiatory event in one sense, but in another, it functions to continue a separate, ongoing, developmental rhetorical process, one that had its beginnings elsewhere in the sonata-space. The procedure has already been recognized as a hallmark of Brahms's compositional approach, in which it stems from an apparent propensity for extending developmental procedures past the point at which the rhetorical recapitulation begins— another aspect of the misalignment of parameters that Smith calls dimensional counterpoint.[5] The other is a "telescoping" of the P-TR complex such that it quickly and efficiently reaches its MC and, subsequently, the recapitulatory S-C block. On its surface, this procedure appears to stem from what is often understood as the characteristic nineteenth-century concern for compositional concision and avoidance of exact repetition—including even the repetition built into the sonata structure itself, in the exposition-recapitulation relationship. But again, commonality in the repertoire should not be equated with expressive neutrality: the procedure can almost always be construed as a rhetorical strategy that brings to light aspects of the sonata's narrative and overall expressive meaning.

The recapitulations in Brahms's opp. 1/i (figure 4.2) and 2/i (figure 5.1) provide straightforward examples of both procedures. In op. 1/i, the recapitulation launches in m. 173 on a destabilizing V7 of F (a form of the Classical "subdominant recapitulation"),[6] in essence extending a feature of the development section—the dominant-lock—across the recapitulatory downbeat. The key point here is that the presence of a terminal dominant-lock in this development is a more complex matter, one that requires accounting for the presence of multiple temporal levels in the narrative. That is, as mentioned, the dominant-functioning C in the bass at m. 173 recaptures the bass C from m. 136, one of the possible functions of which was that of an RT-initiating dominant-lock in anticipation of a subdominant recapitulation. The C from m. 136 thus can be understood as extending forward in time, across (or in the background, underneath) the atemporal stream interpolated into mm. 139–72, and all the way into the recapitulation itself. A telescoped P-TR complex then follows. The $P^{ant.}$ module corresponds structurally to its eight-bar expositional precedent (mm. 173–80 = mm. 1–8), while the ensuing P$^{cons.}$ opens on C minor instead of m. 9's B♭ major before promptly dissolving into TR-rhetoric—as if it cannot wait to get on with the obligatory sonata processes. The bass proceeds sequentially through a fifths-cycle C-F, D♭-G♭, D-G before moving elliptically onto E♭ at the end of m. 186; a brief augmented sixth at m. 186 b. 4 resolves onto a dominant in the key of G major at m. 187, and the sonata train is fully in motion. The crux appears at m. 187 (= m. 34), on a dominant-lock in the key of G major, and correspondence measures follow.[7]

This recapitulation's treatment of its crux and the music that follows it deserves additional comment, as it signifies multiple temporal values and cues a range of expressive meanings. The interpretation hinges on the dominant of G major present at the crux. In one sense, this is exactly where the recapitulation needs to be, tonally speaking. That is, in the exposition, the TR-ending dominant-lock and MC occurred in the key of E minor, while the expositional S opened on A minor, a fifth away; assuming the recapitulation will make a similar move, the recapitulatory MC needs to be in the key of G in order for the recapitulatory S to open in the tonic, C. But the tonicization of G major at m. 187 is also heavily marked. It musically embodies an impossibility, suggesting the prospect of an S-theme in the key of the major dominant (where such a tonal choice is untenable, here in the sonata's recapitulation) and, at the same time, cues a temporal look backward, constituting a final, reminiscent glance toward the development section's vision of an idealized, G-major S-that-might-have-been.

The latter reading accounts well for what happens next: seemingly aware that the G-major illusion cannot be sustained, the implied composer abandons the correspondence measures at the very moment the MC was due, in m. 189 (which should correspond to m. 36). This connotes another crisis of continuation; the dominant proceeds to dissolve in a *ben marcato e sempre fortissimo* peroration that invokes predominant-lock material from the exposition (compare mm. 191–93 with mm. 33–35), as if backing up (resetting the clock) in order to recover from a perceived error and revise the tonal course of events. The protest is necessarily brief: m. 194 arrives back on the dominant of G, as a "second crux," then yields, as expected, to an MC-CF complex that first refers obliquely to its expositional precedent before consenting to engage with it directly (mm. 194–95 ≈ m. 36, mm. 196–97 = mm. 37–38). The whole series of events supports multiple, but similar, readings: perhaps we have a settling into a familiar pattern (crux 1), followed by a crisis and an abandonment of that pattern in favor of a reevaluation, followed by a resumption of the familiar pattern again (crux 2), this time satisfied that the chosen pathway is correct. Alternatively, we have an early, disillusioned arrival of the dominant-lock in G major (crux 1), then a suppression of the expected MC and space for reassessment, then a recovery (crux 2) that leads to a more secure, confident MC-arrival. The recapitulation-coda complex follows, with S opening at m. 198 (= m. 39) in the negatively inflected C minor—the negativity of which may be understood as forecasting the impending nonresolving recapitulation, in which the very same rupture-producing, cadence-denying $^6_4$ gestures from the exposition appear in m. 210 (= m. 51) and m. 234 (= m. 75).

In Brahms's op. 2/i, the recapitulation also opens in fragmentary fashion before proceeding with another form of a telescoped P-TR block. The fragmentation is apparent at the recapitulatory downbeat, which occurs at m. 123 over an anxious, exclamatory, destabilizing fully diminished-seventh chord that conflates the keys of the tonic and the dominant. That is, the chord contains the root and third from the tonic triad, F♯ and A, and as such can be thought of as a form of the familiar common-tone diminished seventh (connected by common tones to the tonic triad); but at the same time, it also functions as a vii°7/V, tonicizing the dominant, with the ostensible root, B♯, in the bass. Eight bars of P-theme then gradually recover the tonic, in a procedure typical of many fragmented recapitulations. The presentation module (mm. 123–24) composes out the initiatory diminished seventh, while the continuation opens (m. 125) on a C♮ pedal, a half step away from the correct tonal level; the bass effects a partial correction in m. 127 by stepping up to C♯, but a restless fully diminished seventh (now C♯°7) persists in the upper voices; and a full correction occurs in m. 129, where the dominant (V9) in the key of F♯ minor appears just in time for the blustery crash landing onto the TR-downbeat at m. 131 (= m. 9). Recomposition begins immediately in the TR module, which arrives in m. 135 on a G♯—which itself functions, in mm. 136–37, as a leading tone in the key of A major.

This last move is remarkable. It can be heard as signifying a descent into tonal distress, in that the recapitulatory TR has modulated, surprisingly, to the key of the relative major, just as did the expositional TR. Perhaps this is best understood as an expressively marked, wishful, backward-looking gesture in which the sonata makes one last attempt to recover the Arcadian relative-major paradise that had been touched on in the expositional TR but then lost, never again to be recovered within the sonata-space proper. It also suggests a certain parallelism between op. 2's recapitulatory TR and that of op. 1, specifically the attempt in op. 1 to recover the major dominant, G major, that had been proposed and then lost in the development; the turbulence and signified angst of the recapitulation in op. 2 can also be thought of as a direct consequence of the loss of the A-major Arcadian vision in its development section. In any case, the same proposed MC as in the exposition arrives in m. 137 (= m. 14) before yielding, again as before, to a regression back to the key of the tonic and a i:HC MC (mm. 137–38 = mm. 14–15). Another crisis of continuation ensues: correspondence measures cease; the fermata that appeared over the original MC in m. 15 is written out in mm. 138–39; the next four bars comprise a ponderous, low-register repetition of the entire reconsideration gesture, including the MC itself; and mm. 140–43 comprise a varied repetition of mm. 137–39. S then launches, in the tonic, immediately in m. 144 (= m. 40), and the original atemporal digression from mm. 16–39 gets skipped over entirely—in effect confirming the status of mm. 16–39 as an extrastructural interpolation (in that the recapitulation treats the entire interpolation as expendable). Measure 144, furthermore, should be understood as the second crux in another double-crux situation, similar to what happened in op. 1.

The specific strategy in which, in a telescoped recapitulation, an atemporal interpolation from the exposition is deleted from a recapitulation is more than a reflection of Brahms's interest in compositional concision. The procedure invites a hermeneutic interpretation wherein recounting the original crisis is redundant, in a narrative sense, or perhaps wherein whatever crisis the original interpolation had served to address—whatever trouble the narrator was responding to by suspending mimetic sonata procedures and effecting a discursive shift to the diegetic mode—must now be less acute, or must now have passed entirely. In op. 2 specifically, perhaps the narrator is aware that the quick nod toward the relative major in the recapitulatory TR must be but an unrealizable fantasy; perhaps we might hear a certain confidence in the move directly from the MC to the S—a confidence that might arise from not having to stare, as in the exposition, into the darkness of a minor-dominant, S-theme abyss. The strategy appears to be common in Romantic sonatas more broadly: evidence suggests that interpolations appearing early in the first half of a sonata's expositional rotation (usually in the P-TR complex) may be removed, or at least significantly condensed, in cases in which the final rotation is in dialogue with the principle of the fragmented recapitulation. The procedure may have expressive as well as practical motivations. That is, if the aim is fragmentation, then an interpolation that functioned to break apart the expositional P-TR cycle may no longer be necessary in a recapitulation the temporal coherence of which has already been undermined other ways—by, for example, a developmental, off-tonic recapitulatory opening.

Consider in this context the recapitulation in the first movement of Brahms's op. 5 (see figure 5.2). This recapitulation reiterates the format of its corresponding exposition almost exactly, but without one of the exposition's interpolations. The P-module's terminal i:HC arrives in m. 137 (≈ m. 6), but then the recapitulation segues directly into its TR rather than into the interpolation that was originally present in mm. 7–16 (such that m. 138 ≈ m. 17, not m. 7). Measures 138–44 then correspond with mm. 17–22 (where, incidentally, the added m. 142 constitutes a good example of a durational atemporality that produces a lingering or hesitating effect—a momentary pause in which the narrator can be heard wondering aloud how the tale might proceed); and the MC arrives at m. 144 (≈ m. 22). Again, the ellipsis in this situation probably results from the fact that the recapitulation opens at m. 131 as another form of a fragmented recapitulation—this time fragmented not so much with respect to harmony, tonality, or phrase structure (all of which remain intact) but rather with respect to the rhetoric of recapitulation itself. That is, while m. 131 unambiguously marks the recapitulatory downbeat in the sense that the P-theme returns, it does not fully participate in the recapitulatory spirit: instead of confidently relaunching the first-narrative P TR ' S / C cycle, m. 131 is better thought of as gradually easing into the rotation—as initiating a process of "waking up," so to speak, in the sense that it functions as a gateway out of an ongoing atemporal interpolation that began in m. 123.[8] Thus, the recapitulatory opening provides the narrator an opportunity to reenter the story-space gradually, sliding gently from reminiscent fantasy to tangible reality. The awakening is complete by the *sempre più forte* at m. 135 (≈ m. 5), which is a moment staged as so startling that it bears repetition in m. 136—as if mm. 135–36 together comprise hammer blows over the still-delirious sonata's head.

The same strategy can appear in different forms. The recapitulation in the first movement of Chopin's B-minor Sonata, op. 58, for example, condenses its original ten-bar pre-MC interpolation from mm. 19–28 into just three bars, mm. 139–42, instead of deleting it altogether.[9] And movements in which the recapitulation opens in a more intact, unfragmented form seem inclined to retain their expositional interpolations. The first movements of Schumann's F♯-minor and G-minor Sonatas, opp. 11 and 22, for example, both retain pre-MC interpolations in the wake of recapitulatory openings that repeat their expositional precedents mostly without alteration. In op. 11, the interpolation originally inserted in mm. 107–34 reappears in mm. 358–81; in op. 22, the interpolation in mm. 44–56 reappears in mm. 237–49. Note that the way in which the procedure manifests in a given sonata form movement appears to be independent of any of the issues surrounding sonata types: both of the Brahms and Schumann movements mentioned here adhere to Sonata Theory's Type 3 format, while the Chopin is a Type 2.

Notes

1. I regard rotational ordering as a first-level default procedure in Classical development sections, which normatively treat their thematic material in the same order in which it appeared in the exposition. See Hepokoski and Darcy, *Elements of Sonata Theory*, 205–20. The principle is a useful starting point for interpreting the music of Brahms and other Romantics, although it is not without its controversy: see, for example, the critique in Wingfield, "Beyond 'Norms and Deformations,'" 149–53.

2. For a different, yet occasionally overlapping, reading of mm. 134–73, see Frisch, *Brahms and the Principle of Developing Variation*, 53–56.

3. For Frisch, m. 91 begins "the grandest variation of all" in a movement that comprises "a strange *Mischform* combining features of both variation and sonata" (ibid., 38). Frisch (ibid.) also notes the similarity, in a structural sense, of the G-major episode in the op. 1 development with this D♭-major episode in the middle of the op. 5 development.

4. "Conventional" is Caplin's term and is the opposite of "characteristic" (*Classical Form*, 37 and, for the glossary definition, 253–54). Brahms's development sections have received extensive attention in the literature: among many others, see Frisch, *Brahms and the Principle of Developing Variation*, 53–56; or, more recently, Horne, "The 'Still Center' in Brahms's Violin Concerto, op. 77."

5. For more on recapitulations within the context of dimensional counterpoint, see Smith, *Expressive Forms in Brahms's Instrumental Music*, 42–49 and 68–89. See also ibid., 99–107 (on recapitulatory strategies in the context of Brahms's predilection for motivic development) and 116–21 (on recapitulatory strategies as manifesting Brahms's concern for organic continuity).

6. Normative "subdominant recapitulations" comprise a recapitulatory P in the key of the subdominant rather than the tonic. Here, the recapitulation opens with P on the dominant seventh in the key of F major, with C in the bass, thus also providing a good example of what Walter Frisch calls *thematic transformation*, in which a theme "retains its original melodic outline"

(*Brahms and the Principle of Developing Variation*, 36) but changes its "mode, harmony, tempo, rhythm, or meter" so as to effect "a radical change in mood or character" (ibid., 42).

7. The crux is the point at which the recapitulation rejoins the events of the exposition. See Hepokoski and Darcy, *Elements of Sonata Theory*, 239–42.

8. Bozarth ("Brahms's *Lieder ohne Worte*," 373) has noticed this feature, observing that the recapitulation begins *pianissimo, misterioso*, and "still under the influence" of the "quiet, pulsating accompaniment" from mm. 91–116 and 123–30.

9. For more, see Davis, "Chopin and the Romantic Sonata."

8 Treatment of the Slow Introduction and Coda

Slow introductions and codas, because they can be understood as outside the boundaries of the rotational sonata form proper, present obvious opportunities in which to disengage from first-narrative temporality and shift to the diegetic mode, within the context of a fragmented, Romantic sonata-aesthetic environment.[1] The finale of Brahms's op. 2 provides a good initial example.

The movement's first eight bars declare their status as outside the first-narrative stream almost immediately. They open in a rhetorically conspicuous, declamatory fashion, with a monophonic F♯ giving way immediately to an E: thus the movement opens on its tonic but then immediately falls away from it, as if pulled downward by the force of gravity. An eight-bar sentence then proceeds to explore the implications of this opening gesture. A presentation module (INT$^{1.1\ (\text{pres.})}$ in figure 6.1) accepts these opening two notes as—or perhaps forces them to become—$\hat{6}$ and $\hat{5}$ in the key of A, and the sonata has shifted remarkably early to the expressively charged key of its relative major. Such a shift connotes an underlying expressive concern with desire: that is, right at its outset, the movement rejects, or seeks to escape, present-day reality (the minor tonic) in favor of wishing for or reminiscing on the paradise world of the relative major—a world that the sonata's first movement had staged as, first, lost and unattainable, then violently suppressed. The continuation proceeds by standing the presentation on its head, inverting its contour with a series of rising arpeggiations that culminate, in m. 6, with a minor-seventh leap—B up to A—that resolves onto E–G♯, the major third of the dominant triad in A major. The high A in this gesture is conspicuously rhetorical as well: this is the highest note sounded thus far; it appears at the end of a *crescendo* in mm. 4–6; the G♯ onto which it resolves arrives with a *sforzando* that marks it as the culmination of the entire opening phrase; and the minor seventh is the inversion of the movement's opening major second—as if it constitutes a response to a proposed statement or an answer to a proposed question. In fact, the minor seventh can be thought of as rhetorically foregrounded specifically because it bears another expressively rich intertext with Beethoven, this time an allusion to the distinctive minor-seventh leap from the E-major slow movement of the Piano Concerto No. 5 in E♭ major, op. 73 ("Emperor").[2] There, the gesture comprises the initiatory motive in the principal theme's continuation module, as in mm. 5–6 (shown in example 8.1), as well as the source of that movement's ubiquitous upper-neighbor motives (as in mm. 13–14 in example 8.1).

Treatment of the Slow Introduction and Coda | 169

Example 8.1. Beethoven, Piano Concerto no. 5 in E♭ major, op. 73, ii, mm. 1–17.

All of these events—the declamatory opening, the immediate shift to the relative-major fantasy world, and the Beethoven intertext—together suggest that the entire introduction should be understood as an atemporal, diegetic peroration of the narrating agent. This is an initiatory address to the implied listener that lies outside the sonata's first-narrative stream; a musical analog for a "once upon a time" gesture, delivered diegetically in the voice of the narrating agent;[3] an oration that opens up space for the tale that is about to be told. Janice Dickensheets reads this music similarly, suggesting that these eight bars contain a topical reference to the *bardic style*: a projection in music of "the bard of ancient times," complete with introductory fanfare motives (mm. 1–4) followed by the sound of the poet strumming a harp (mm. 5–8).[4] And Hepokoski and Darcy have noticed these kinds of expressive strategies in nineteenth-century symphonic poems or programmatic symphonies in general, in which, they write, one of the generically normative rhetorical functions of slow introductions is to serve as the "representation of the 'narrator' . . . of the tale told in the sonata," or, in some cases, "the strumming of the harp" that "characteristically calls up images of a bard singing an age-old tale."[5] Such views dovetail nicely with one in which the Romantic sonata's narrative discourse is understood as comprising multiple temporal streams, where, as a rule, slow introductions can be understood discursively as divorced from the sonata's first narrative proper and as comprising content that remains separate from the content of the actual story itself, which has not yet begun. Mendelssohn's Overture to *A Midsummer Night's Dream* is definitive in this regard, but even pieces not usually regarded as programmatic in the narrowest sense invite similar interpretations. Examples include, among many others, Chopin's Ballade no. 1 in G minor, op. 23 (mm. 1–7; Klein: "once upon a time, there was a waltz"). Mahler's Symphony no. 7 in E minor (mm. 1–7; again, a "once upon a time" prelude to the thirty-one-bar slow introduction), and Tchaikovsky's Piano Concerto no. 1 in B♭ minor, op. 23 (mm. 1–6; a "once upon a time" prelude to the strikingly deformational, D♭-major, extrarotational vision of paradise that follows).[6]

In the specific case of Brahms's op. 2/iv, the narrator can be heard making a retrospective look back to the past within what should be regarded as a highly Romanticized expressive trajectory informed by aspects of the pastoral narrative. First, the rejection of F♯ minor in favor of A major, as mentioned, constitutes an escape from flawed, present-tense reality in favor of gazing into an idealized, nonpresent (in this case probably past-tense) fantasy; mm. 5–8 then crystallize that fantasy in the form of an A-major vision of Beethoven. Such a reading, including the signification of the past tense, is invited by the fact that the rising arpeggiated figures beginning at the pickup to m. 5 have a certain antiquating effect that stems directly from their basis in a compositional model dating from the early-seventeenth-century *partimento* tradition. The model is known today as the "ascending 8ˆ7-6" and comprises a series of falling suspension figures within a parallel linear ascent over a scalar bass. Example 8.2a shows the pattern as it appears in an eighteenth-century treatise of Fedele Fenaroli, while example 8.2b shows Brahms's mm. 4–6.[7] Thus, the gesture looks backward to a compositional technique that in the nineteenth century was dated and archaic; it therefore can be understood as a musical synecdoche for an idealized Classical past—literally a musical gaze into a beautiful, lost era no longer available in a present-day, imperfect world. Going further, the intertextual allusion to the Emperor Concerto in mm. 7–8 might even be regarded as proposing Beethoven himself as the inhabitant of the Romanticized golden age thus summoned up, as if to suggest that Beethoven himself is the lonely shepherd wandering through the unspoiled Arcadian wilderness. "Once upon a time, there was a more perfect world in which Beethoven lived."

The movement's coda can be interpreted using similar correlations. The key feature of the coda—which opens with the deflection away from the first-narrative stream at m. 258—is the reappearance of material from the slow introduction at m. 270 (compare m. 5). This invokes a form of the strategy known as the "introduction-coda frame," which in this instance signifies that the voice of the narrator returns at the end of the movement to punctuate the tale that was

Example 8.2. a) Ascending 8̂-7-6 schema, as shown in Fedele Fenaroli, *Partimenti ossia basso numerato*, III:1 (transcribed in Sanguinetti, "La scala come modelo per la composizione," 85). b) Brahms, Piano Sonata in F♯ minor, op. 2, iv, mm. 1-6.

just completed.[8] As such, the coda comprises another diegetic oration delivered in the narrator's own voice—not so much a "once upon a time" gesture this time but perhaps a complementary "thus went the story of. . . ."[9] The gesture's expressive meaning is particularly rich, moreover, due to the presence of certain subtle differences between the material at m. 270 and the original material at m. 5. First, in the coda this material appears within the context of a deflection to the subdominant B major in m. 268: mm. 268–69 imply a preparatory V of V in B, while the tonic triad arrives in m. 270 in the form of an arrival $^6_4$ chord over $\hat5$, F♯. Others have regarded such subdominant-side shifts as marking shifts of tense, and it can probably be understood in similar fashion here—as signifying, that is, a shift either from present to past or, better in this instance, from the past tense of mimetic story time to the present tense of diegetic narrative time.[10] Second, there follows two bars of the same ascending 8̂-7-6 schema that appeared in mm. 4–6, as shown in example 8.3, but this time the pattern is not rendered in precisely the same way. Now it suggests an audibly intensified sense of longing for the past. Compare the details of m. 270 with the details of m. 5: in m. 270, extra motion in an inner voice means that every eighth note receives its own articulation and that the pattern sounds very much like the prototype shown in example 8.2a; in m. 5, on the other hand, upper voices sounded on both halves of beats 2 and 4 and inner voices sounded on beats 1 and 3, but there was no articulation at all on the second eighth of beats 1 and 3.

Example 8.3. Brahms, Piano Sonata in F♯ minor, op. 2, iv, mm. 268–72 (compare example 8.2).

This more fully rendered version, in mm. 270–71, of the ascending 8̂-7-6 schema bears another rhetorically charged intertext, not with Beethoven this time but with Bach—specifically with the Prelude no. 12 in F minor, BWV 857, from the *Well-Tempered Clavier* Book I, a piece that contains one of the best known and most expressive eighteenth-century uses of the same *partimento* model. As shown in example 8.4, the pattern first appears in that piece, briefly, in a poignant F minor in m. 1, then appears again shortly after, in mm. 6–7, in a sweetly *cantabile* A♭ major. In the second instance, the pattern is replicated in two voices: the bass voice deploys the ascending 8̂-7-6 schema, while the upper voice deploys the related form known as the "ascending 10̂-9-8," which is shown in example 8.5 and which Giorgio Sanguinetti has described as imbued with even more "intense and pregnant expressivity" than its 8̂-7-6 relative.[11] Brahms's mm. 270–71 resonate specifically with the bass from Bach's mm. 6–7, in large part because the rhythmic and melodic profiles in the two passages are nearly identical; both deploy the arpeggiated triads in the same ($^6_3$) position, and their rhythmic surfaces are the same (Brahms's sonata articulates every eighth, Bach's prelude every sixteenth). As such, the intertext can be brought to bear on the narrative in the Brahms, the slow introduction and the coda of which together suggest the remembrance of a Classical past in which Beethoven is the resident. The memory remains partial and obscure in the introduction, becoming fuller and clearer only later, in the coda—where the newfound lucidity may be brought about by the lessons learned in the tragic story that transpired in the sonata proper.

* * *

The coda in the first movement of Brahms's op. 5 (refer to figure 5.2) provides an example of another of the potential expressive functions of codas in Romantic sonatas: as a space in which to explore problematic moments from earlier in the movement and to imagine a different, often better or more idealized, solution. In this movement specifically, the coda composes out an idealized version of what might have happened in the development section, at m. 123—very much in the way that the development section itself composes out an idealized version of what might have happened in the exposition.

To make complete sense of the op. 5 coda, first consider the music leading up to it, in the movement's recapitulatory S-space. S launches in m. 161 (= m. 39),

Example 8.4. Bach, Prelude no. 12 in F minor, BWV 857, from the *Well-Tempered Clavier*, Book I, mm. 1–8.

Example 8.5. Ascending 10ˆ9–8 schema, as shown in Sanguinetti, "La scala come modelo per la composizione," 87.

following the same post-MC interpolation that appeared in the exposition (mm. 145–60 = mm. 23–38). The central formal and expressive questions in the recapitulatory S are, first, whether or not the S-theme will appear in the major mode and thus emancipate the music from the grip of F minor, and, second, whether S will be able to hold on to its original tonic and produce a satisfactory ESC in the form of a cadence in the same key in which it began. The first issue is quickly put to rest: S: S does indeed appear in the positively inflected, Arcadian key of the major, not the minor, tonic. The second issue is more problematic. At first, it seems that the S, and with it the very sonata itself, is destined for fragmentation via another tonal failure. It proceeds initially as a bar-for-bar replica of its expositional precedent, complete with the same modulation up a fourth, this time from F major to B♭ major: the modulation begins around m. 165 (= m. 43); the first cadential module, in B♭ major, materializes on schedule in mm. 176–77 (= mm. 54–55); and the same blocked cadence appears, as before, at m. 178 (= m. 56). There follows exactly the same cadence-suppressing interpolation in mm. 178–89 (= mm. 56–67), such that the recapitulation appears headed for an impossible situation parallel to that of the exposition: an ESC in the wrong key, this time in B♭ major.

But there are signs that such a trajectory will not simply be accepted without resistance. Observe, for example, the difference in the expressive markings at parallel moments in the exposition and recapitulation. In the exposition, the interpolation in mm. 56–67 comprised a nervous delay or postponement of the inevitable—a passage in which the narrator intervened to hurriedly and anxiously consider the problem of the forthcoming cadence in the D♭-major fantasy land: the *un poco accelerando* markings at mm. 56 and 62 underscore this effect. But in the recapitulation, the interpolation, instead of accelerating toward the cadence, alternatively speeds up and slows down, as if the narrator is confused or simply unable to commit to continuing the ironic tale all the way to its predicted, tragic outcome. A *poco ritardando* at m. 182 gives way almost immediately to an *accelerando* at m. 184 and then, shortly thereafter, to another *poco ritardando* at m. 188. The latter leads, in most astonishing fashion, to a suppression—a miraculous avoidance, in fact—of the unthinkable, the wrong-key ESC: at m. 190 (= m. 68), at the last possible second and at the very moment at which the cadence was due to materialize, the narrator abruptly jettisons the expositional trajectory and stunningly reverses course. The bass reneges, shifting up chromatically by half step to F♯ instead of down by fifth to B♭, and the upper voices likewise sustain the A-E♭ tritone and refuse to resolve normatively onto B♭-D. The F♯ in the bass then gives way to a pedal G (mm. 192–98), which is in turn reinterpreted as a V of V in F major that yields, in mm. 198–99, to the much-delayed, long-awaited cadential progression in the key of F major.

Thus, the sonata has apparently been rescued from tonal failure. But the rescue takes place only on the surface; lurking beneath is evidence of an ironic failure of will. The moment of the cadence itself, m. 200, is staged as extremely problematic: just as in the parallel moment in the exposition, again the cadence immanently calls into question its status as a fully closural PAC. This time, all the voices except the bass drop out, undercutting the cadence at the expected moment of completion.[12] This is a signal that S-space has been abandoned at this moment in favor of a launch of P-based material—in favor of, that is, an extrastructural coda. Thus, rather than having been deferred, the ESC has been suppressed entirely; the narrator has discarded the S altogether and left behind a fragmented sonata, a sonata in ruins. This may be a form of the pastoral narrative's characteristic retreat and return: the dream of the Arcadian paradise has been lost forever amid a shattering return to an imperfect present.

There commences at this point the coda's recomposition, or reimagination, of the development's trajectory. The coda immediately signals its purpose by opening not with an exact restatement of the expositional P-theme but rather with a restatement of P in the form in which it appeared in the development, at m. 119 ("P$^{\text{dev.b}}$" in figure 5.2).[13] A four-bar presentation module ensues, such that mm. 200–3 ≈ mm. 119–22. In the development, this sentence ruptured at m. 123, with sharp discontinuities at that moment in dynamic level (*fortissimo* collapses to *pianissimo*) and texture (gone is the contrapuntal upper voice, and even the lower voice becomes fragmented with regard to its motivic and thematic continuity) signaling that m. 123 was not the continuation module that was supposed to have occurred but instead new material that functioned to overwrite that which was expected in its place.[14] In the coda, however, rather than rupturing at the moment of the anticipated continuation, the sentence instead produces a normative continuation module at m. 204. In this sense, m. 204—and in fact the coda as a whole—comprises a solution (perhaps only hypothetical or imagined) to an earlier problem: m. 204 initiates the continuation module that was overwritten by the interpolation at m. 123 and thus enters into an idealized form of "what might have been," had the development proceeded in a more normative fashion in its drive toward the recapitulation.

This proposed continuation proceeds in grand fashion toward a cadence that can be interpreted as an attempt—a futile one, in that it comes too late and after the fact, after sonata-space has already been closed—to salvage some semblance of tonal closure following the ruined recapitulation. Measures 204–16 comprise a grandiose, glorified staging of, finally, a genuine perfect authentic cadence in F major, which materializes in m. 217. But again, the cadence is one that superimposes $\hat{3}$ (A) on top of the PAC's requisite $\hat{1}$ (F), just as in the earlier attenuated EEC, in m. 68. As such, again it invites multiple readings. Some may wish to hear the entire event, whether a PAC or an IAC, as an ironic gesture of pure pomposity—a blustery, after-the-fact corrective action that feebly covers up for the earlier sonata failure.[15] Others may wish to foreground the $\hat{3}$, either as another attenuating gesture or perhaps even, in its local context, as an upward-reaching gesture that accepts the latent potential for salvation in the exposition's EEC. The latter reading in particular may be appropriate because the movement concludes by reiterating its tonic triad no fewer than four times (in mm. 217, 219, 220, and 221), always with $\hat{3}$ in the highest voice, as if reaching as high as possible—to the heavens, as it were—in an effort to lift up the remnants of the ruined sonata that lies before it. Either way, the point is that the coda, in the wake of fragmented sonata that precedes it and especially the cadence failure in m. 200, can be understood as an idealized "alternative ending"—one that looks back over the sonata as a whole and proposes a better solution, complete with the obligatory tonal closure that the sonata itself failed to achieve.

Notes

1. On slow introductions and codas as "parageneric," see Hepokoski and Darcy, *Elements of Sonata Theory*, 281–305.

2. Janice Dickensheets ("The Topical Vocabulary of the Nineteenth Century," 133) hears a different, though equally plausible, intertextual reference to Beethoven in this movement's opening measures: the initial basic idea (mm. 1–2) alludes to the S-theme from Beethoven's Fifth Symphony, mm. 59–62.

3. "Once upon a time" is from Klein, "Chopin's Fourth Ballade as Musical Narrative," 37. Klein takes it from Adorno's interpretation of Mahler's Fourth Symphony, in *Mahler: A Musical Physiognomy*, 96.

4. Dickensheets, "The Topical Vocabulary of the Nineteenth Century," 133–36. The bardic style—closely related to what Jonathan Bellman calls the *chivalric style* (see Bellman, "*Aus alten Märchen*")—grows out of the nineteenth-century fascination with the fictional bard Ossian, created in the work of poet James Macpherson. Daverio links the nineteenth-century interest in Ossian to the collective glance backward in Romanticism "to a glorious but now extinct past," in Daverio, "Schumann's Ossianic Manner."

5. Hepokoski and Darcy, *Elements of Sonata Theory*, 304.

6. On the Mendelssohn, see Hatten, "Music and Tense"; and Hepokoski and Darcy, *Elements of Sonata Theory*, 304–5. On the Chopin, see Klein, "Chopin's Fourth Ballade as Musical Narrative," 37.

7. For the Fenaroli, see Sanguinetti, "La scala come modelo per la composizione," esp. 84–88. I thank Professor Sanguinetti for calling my attention to the *partimento* origins of the pattern in the Brahms and for directing me to his article.

8. On the "introduction-coda frame," see Hepokoski, "Framing *Till Eulenspiegel*." See also Hepokoski, "Beethoven Reception," 451; and Hepokoski and Darcy, *Elements of Sonata Theory*, 304–5.

9. Newcomb ("The Polonaise-Fantasy and Issues of Musical Narrative," 101) hears a return of the bard (singing "thus went the story of . . .") at the end of Chopin's Polonaise-Fantasy.

10. On the subdominant as a signifier for the past tense, see Klein, "Chopin's Fourth Ballade as Musical Narrative," 34–44. See also Newcomb, ibid. For more on issues of music and tense, see Hatten, "Music and Tense."

11. Sanguinetti, "La scala come modelo per la composizione," 87: "L'effetto del 9-8 ascendente è simile a quello del 7-6 ascendente, ma con una più intensa e pregnante espressività." Sanguinetti also points to the Bach F-minor Prelude as an example of the pattern.

12. This is a classic, albeit extreme, example of what Hepokoski and Darcy (*Elements of Sonata Theory*, 169–70) call an *evaded cadence*: a noncadence in which "one structural voice drops out at the tonic-moment of the otherwise normative PAC, creating a momentary blank or absence on the downbeat of the measure in either the treble or the bass."

13. Bozarth ("Brahms's *Lieder ohne Worte*," 373) also observes that this material is taken from the development section and not from the expositional P-theme.

14. Bozarth (ibid.) also hears a sense of rupture at m. 123: the *maestoso* material at m. 119, he says, "seems to be leading back to the opening episode [that is, the opening module in the development, from m. 75] when suddenly the quiet, pulsating accompaniment of the central theme [the D♭-major development theme, m. 91] is recalled (bars 123 ff.)."

15. Hepokoski and Darcy hear an ostentatious display of "bluff and bravado" in similar moments in the Classical repertoire; see *Elements of Sonata Theory*, 246.

Conclusion

ONE OF THE most important points in the foregoing analyses is that nineteenth-century Romantic sonatas (and Romantic sonata forms more broadly) are governed in both structure and content by a central conflict—an essential expressive opposition that can be construed in a variety of ways: perfect versus imperfect, present versus nonpresent, real versus unreal, and so on. The conflict is best understood as stemming from the Romantic compulsion for creating, or re-creating, something better than what is currently available in one's present situation—looking toward a better future, for example, or reminiscing on a better past. The most common narrative paradigm in which such conflicts manifest in music is the pastoral narrative, with its (usually tragic) stories of unsatisfied longing or imagined wish fulfillment unfolding within plots involving metaphorical retreats and returns. In Romantic sonatas, such plots should be understood as being narrated by an agent—the lyric subject or the "narrating survivor"—who, while grappling or otherwise coming to terms with the tragic tale, often steps in to comment diegetically, thus fragmenting or breaking apart the sonata's Classical unity and coherence and, in so doing, opening up opportunities to explore an inner realm of subjective consciousness and the unknowable depths of the soul.

In the Romantic sonata form, this central opposition is often situated as a conflict specifically between a P-theme signifying the present, or reality, and an S-theme signifying something nonpresent, unreal, or unattainable. This explains the common (though not universal) contrast in such forms between a restless, agitated, angular, and often minor-mode P and a maximally contrasting, expansively lyrical, relative-major, *Gesangsthema* S. Often, however, the conflict is not as simple as such a straightforward formulation might suggest. While many sonatas stage their S-spaces as conflicted, troubled, or otherwise highly problematized searches for the ideal, paradisiacal S-theme itself, others may stage S, for example, in a minor mode (the minor dominant or some other), with the idealized world of the relative major saved for later (later in the S-space, perhaps, as in Brahms's op. 2, or later in the sonata—in the development, perhaps, as in Brahms's opp. 1 and 5).

Such conflicts can, furthermore, play out in many other ways, some of which do not involve P- or S-themes at all and some of which can complicate the sonata structure considerably. Cases exist of situations—some of them highly deformational, some of them in music of the Romantic generation, and some of them in music from after or even before that period—for which an awareness of the central expressive conflict of Romanticism itself, together with an interpretive apparatus that allows for multiple signified temporal levels and streams in the narrative, can—with appropriate modifications sensitive to the historical context of any given piece—aid in forming text-appropriate readings and reveal remarkable consistencies in the structural, rhetorical, and expressive strategies in large swaths of the common practice. I have in mind situations that appear in music of Tchaikovsky, Mahler, Bruckner, Strauss, Prokofiev, Rachmaninoff, and Ravel; or—perhaps with different aesthetic impetuses and different expressive meanings—in Beethoven (consider the "Eroica" Symphony), Mozart (consider the Piano Sonata in F major, K. 332), or even other Classicists.

However one construes expressive content in such complex situations and whatever the aesthetic motivations for them might be at any given music-historical moment, they have in common a discourse that depends essentially on a breaking apart, or a fragmenting, of an underlying, Classical, formal perfection; on an introducing into the quintessential Classical form and its coherent, linearly directed temporality a self-conscious, self-critical, and in many cases *Romantic* discontinuity; and on an intentional incoherence or disjointedness that subjects the very history of the Classical sonata form to a probing, inquiring, skeptical reexamination. These situations thus realize in music, as in other of the nineteenth-century literary and visual art forms, the impulse toward a subjective, self-conscious assessment of one's historical situation and one's artwork—indeed, an assessment of the very place of humankind in an unstable, imperfect world—that is the fundamental question posed by Romanticism itself.

Selected Bibliography

Abbate, Carolyn. "What the Sorcerer Said." *19th-Century Music* 12, no. 3 (1989): 221–30.
———. *Unsung Voices: Opera and Musical Narrative in the Nineteenth Century*. Princeton, NJ: Princeton University Press, 1991.
———. "Immortal Voices, Mortal Forms." In *Analytical Strategies and Musical Interpretation*, edited by Craig Ayrey and Mark Everist, 288–300. Cambridge, UK: Cambridge University Press, 1996.
Abrams, M. H. "Structure and Style in the Greater Romantic Lyric." Reprinted in *Romanticism and Consciousness: Essays in Criticism*, edited by Harold Bloom, 201–29. New York: Norton, 1970.
Abrams, M. H., and Geoffrey Galt Harpham. *A Glossary of Literary Terms*. 9th ed. Boston: Wadsworth Cengage, 2009.
Adorno, Theodor W. *Mahler: A Musical Physiognomy*. Translated by Edmund Jephcott. Chicago: University of Chicago Press, 1992. Originally Adorno, Theodor W. *Mahler: Eine musikalische Physiognomik*. Frankfurt: Suhrkamp, 1971.
Adrian, Jack. "The Ternary-Sonata Form." *Journal of Music Theory* 34, no. 1 (1990): 57–80.
Agawu, V. Kofi. *Playing with Signs: A Semiotic Interpretation of Classic Music*. Princeton, NJ: Princeton University Press, 1991.
———. "The Narrative Impulse in the Second *Nachtmusik* from Mahler's Seventh Symphony." In *Analytical Strategies and Musical Interpretation*, edited by Craig Ayrey and Mark Everist, 226–41. Cambridge, UK: Cambridge University Press, 1996.
———. *Music as Discourse: Semiotic Adventures in Romantic Music*. Oxford, UK: Oxford University Press, 2009.
Almén, Byron. "Narrative Archetypes: A Critique, Theory, and Method of Narrative Analysis." *Journal of Music Theory* 47, no. 1 (2003): 1–39.
———. *A Theory of Musical Narrative*. Bloomington: Indiana University Press, 2008.
Almén, Byron, and Robert S. Hatten. "Narrative Engagement with Twentieth-Century Music: Possibilities and Limits." In *Music and Narrative since 1900*, edited by Michael Klein and Nicholas Reyland, 59–85. Bloomington: Indiana University Press, 2013.
Arnold, Janice Margaret. "The Role of Chromaticism in Chopin's Sonata Forms: A Schenkerian View." PhD diss., Northwestern University, 1992.
BaileyShea, Matthew. "Wagner's Loosely Knit Sentences and the Drama of Musical Form." *Intégral* 16–17 (2002): 1–34.
———. "The Wagnerian *Satz*: The Rhetoric of the Sentence in Wagner's Post-Lohengrin Operas." PhD diss., Yale University, 2003.
———. "Beyond the Beethoven Model: Sentence Types and Limits." *Current Musicology* 77 (2004): 5–33.
Bakhtin, M. M. "Discourse in the Novel." In *The Dialogic Imagination: Four Essays*, edited by Michael Holquist, translated by Caryl Emerson, 259–422. Austin: University of Texas Press, 1981.
———. "Forms of Time and of the Chronotope in the Novel: Notes toward a Historical Poetics." In *The Dialogic Imagination: Four Essays*, edited by Michael Holquist, translated by Caryl Emerson, 84–258. Austin: University of Texas Press, 1981.

Barthes, Roland. "The Death of the Author (1968)." In *Image-Music-Text*, translated by Stephen Heath, 142–48. New York: Hill & Wang, 1977.
———. *S/Z*. Translated by Richard Miller, preface by Richard Howard. New York: Hill & Wang, 1974. First edition New York: Hill & Wang, 1970.
———. "Textual Analysis: Poe's Valdemar (1973)." Reprinted in *Untying the Text: A Post-Structuralist Reader*, edited by Robert Young, 133–61. London: Routledge and Kegan Paul, 1981.
Behler, Ernst. "The German Romantic Revolution." In *English and German Romanticism: Cross-Currents and Controversies*, edited by James Pipkin, 61–77. Heidelberg, Germany: Carl Winter, 1985.
Bellman, Jonathan. *The Style Hongrois in the Music of Western Europe*. Boston: Northeastern University Press, 1993.
———. "*Aus alten Märchen*: The Chivalric Style of Schumann and Brahms." *The Journal of Musicology* 13, no. 1 (1995): 117–35.
Berger, Karol. "Narrative and Lyric: Fundamental Poetic Forms of Composition." In *Musical Humanism and Its Legacy: Essays in Honor of Claude Palisca*, edited by Nancy Kovaleff Baker and Barbara Russano Hanning, 451–70. Stuyvesant, NY: Pendragon, 1992.
———. "Chopin's Ballade Op. 23 and the Revolution of the Intellectuals." In *Chopin Studies 2*, edited by John Rink and Jim Samson, 72–83. Cambridge, UK: Cambridge University Press, 1994.
———. "The Form of Chopin's *Ballade*, Op. 23." *19th-Century Music* 20, no. 1 (1996): 46–71.
———. *Bach's Cycle, Mozart's Arrow: An Essay on the Origins of Musical Modernity*. Berkeley: University of California Press, 2007.
Beveridge, David. "Non-Traditional Functions of the Development Sections in Sonata Forms by Brahms." *The Music Review* 51, no. 1 (1990): 25–35.
Bickley, Nora, ed. and trans. *Letters to and from Joseph Joachim*. Preface by J. A. Fuller-Maitland. London: Macmillan, 1914.
Blackall, Eric A. *The Novels of the German Romantics*. Ithaca, NY: Cornell University Press, 1983.
Bloom, Harold. "The Internalization of Quest-Romance (1969)." Reprinted in *Romanticism and Consciousness: Essays in Criticism*, edited by Harold Bloom, 3–24. New York: Norton, 1970.
———. *The Anxiety of Influence: A Theory of Poetry*. 2nd ed. New York: Oxford University Press, 1997. First edition New York: Oxford University Press, 1973.
———. *A Map of Misreading*. 2nd ed. New York: Oxford University Press, 2003. First edition New York: Oxford University Press, 1975.
———. *Kabbalah and Criticism*. New York: Seabury, 1975.
———. *Poetry and Repression: Revisionism from Blake to Stevens*. New Haven, CT: Yale University Press, 1976.
———. *Agon: Towards a Theory of Revisionism*. New York: Oxford University Press, 1982.
———. *The Breaking of the Vessels*. Chicago: University of Chicago Press, 1982.
Booth, Wayne C. *The Rhetoric of Fiction*. 2nd ed. Chicago: University of Chicago Press, 1983. First edition Chicago: University of Chicago Press, 1961.
———. *A Rhetoric of Irony*. Chicago: University of Chicago Press, 1974.
———. "'The Way I Loved George Eliot': Friendship with Books as a Neglected Critical Metaphor." *The Kenyon Review* 2, no. 2 (1980): 4–27.
Bozarth, George S. "Brahms's Lieder Inventory of 1859–60 and Other Documents of His Life and Work." *Fontes Artis Musicae* 30, no. 3 (1983): 98–117.

———. "Brahms's *Lieder ohne Worte*: The 'Poetic' Andantes of the Piano Sonatas." In *Brahms Studies*: *Analytical and Historical Perspectives*, edited by George S. Bozarth, 344–78. Oxford, UK: Clarendon, 1990.
———. "Johannes Brahms's Collection of *Deutsche Sprichworte* (German Proverbs)." In *Brahms Studies* 1, edited by David Brodbeck, 1–29. Lincoln: University of Nebraska Press, 1994.
Brett, R. L., and A. R. Jones, eds. *Wordsworth and Coleridge*: *Lyrical Ballads*. London: Routledge, 2005.
Brodbeck, David. "Brahms, The Third Symphony, and the New German School." In *Brahms and His World*, rev. ed., edited by Walter Frisch and Kevin C. Karnes, 95–116. Princeton, NJ: Princeton University Press, 2009.
Brooks, Peter. *Reading for the Plot*: *Design and Intention in Narrative*. New York: Knopf, 1984.
Brown, A. Peter. "Brahms' Third Symphony and the New German School." *The Journal of Musicology* 2, no. 4 (1983): 434–52.
Brown, David. "Deciphering Liszt: The B-Minor Sonata Revisited." *The Musical Times* 144, no. 1882 (2003): 6–15.
Browne, Richmond. "Review of *The Structure of Atonal Music*, by Allen Forte." *Journal of Music Theory* 18, no. 2 (1974): 390–415.
Burkholder, Peter. "Brahms and Twentieth-Century Classical Music." *19th-Century Music* 8, no. 1 (1984): 75–83.
———. "Rule-Breaking as a Rhetorical Sign." In *Festa Musicologica*: *Essays in Honor of George J. Buelow*, edited by Thomas J. Mathiesen and Benito V. Rivera, 369–89. Stuyvesant, NY: Pendragon, 1995.
———. "A Simple Model for Associative Meaning in Music." In *Approaches to Meaning in Music*, edited by Bryon Almén and Edward R. Pearsall, 76–106. Bloomington: Indiana University Press, 2006.
Butler, Christopher. "Music and Narrative in Recent Theory." In *Musicology and Sister Disciplines*: *Past*, *Present*, *Future*, edited by David Greer, with Ian Rumbold and Jonathan King, 118–28. Oxford, UK: Oxford University Press, 2000.
Butler, Marilyn. *Romantics, Rebels, and Reactionaries*: *English Literature and Its Background, 1760–1830*. New York: Oxford University Press, 1982.
Caplin, William E. "The 'Expanded Cadential Progression': A Category for the Analysis of Classical Form." *The Journal of Musicological Research* 7 (1987): 215–57.
———. *Classical Form*: *A Theory of Formal Functions for the Instrumental Music of Haydn, Mozart, and Beethoven*. New York: Oxford University Press, 1998.
———. "The Classical Cadence: Conceptions and Misconceptions." *Journal of the American Musicological Society* 57, no. 1 (2004): 51–117.
———. "Beethoven's 'Tempest' Exposition: A Springboard for Form-Functional Considerations." In *Beethoven's "Tempest" Sonata*: *Perspectives of Analysis and Performance*, edited by Pieter Bergé, coedited by Jeroen D'hoe and William E. Caplin, 87–125. Leuven, Belgium: Peeters, 2009.
———. "Comments on James Hepokoski's Essay 'Sonata Theory and Dialogic Form.'" In *Musical Forms, Form, and Formenlehre*, edited by Pieter Bergé, 90–95. Leuven, Belgium: Leuven University Press, 2009.
———. "What Are Formal Functions?" In *Musical Forms, Form, and Formenlehre*, edited by Pieter Bergé, 21–40. Leuven, Belgium: Leuven University Press, 2009.
de Castro, Paulo F. "Topic, Paratext, and Intertext in the *Prélude d'Après-midi d'un Faune* and Other Works of Debussy." Paper presented at the International Conference

on Music Semiotics in Memory of Raymond Monelle, Edinburgh, UK, October 26–28, 2012.

Chatman, Seymour. *Story and Discourse: Narrative Structure in Fiction and Film*. Ithaca, NY: Cornell University Press, 1978.

———. *Coming to Terms: The Rhetoric of Narrative in Fiction and Film*. Ithaca, NY: Cornell University Press, 1990.

Chua, Daniel K. L. "Beethoven's Other Humanism." *Journal of the American Musicological Society* 62, no. 3 (2009): 571–645.

Cinnamon, Howard. "Classical Models, Sonata Theory, and the First Movement of Liszt's *Faust Symphony*." *Gamut* 4, no. 1 (2011). Retrieved January 3, 2014 (http://trace.tennessee.edu/gamut/vol4/iss1/4/).

———. "Classical Models, Sonata Theory, Equal Division of the Octave and Two Nineteenth-Century Sonata Movements: Comparing Analytical Approaches." *Gamut* 6, no. 1 (2013). Retrieved January 3, 2014 (http://trace.tennessee.edu/gamut/vol6/iss1/3/).

Colebrook, Claire. *Irony*. London: Routledge, 2004.

Cone, Edward T. *The Composer's Voice*. Berkley: University of California Press, 1974.

———. "Three Ways of Reading a Detective Story—Or a Brahms Intermezzo." In *Music: A View from Delft*, by Edward T. Cone, edited by Robert P. Morgan, 77–93. Chicago: University of Chicago Press, 1989. Originally published in *The Georgia Review* 31, no. 3 (1977): 554–74.

———. "Schubert's Promissory Note: An Exercise in Musical Hermeneutics." *19th-Century Music* 5, no. 3 (1982): 233–41.

———. "Responses." *College Music Symposium* 29 (1989): 75–80.

———. "Poet's Love or Composer's Love?" In *Music and Text: Critical Inquiries*, edited by Steven Paul Sher, 177–92. New York: Cambridge University Press, 1992.

Culler, Jonathan. *The Pursuit of Signs: Semiotics, Literature, Deconstruction*. Ithaca, NY: Cornell University Press, 1981.

———. Foreword to *Narrative Discourse*, by Gérard Genette, 7–13. Ithaca, NY: Cornell University Press, 1988.

Cumming, Naomi. "The Subjectivities of 'Erbarme Dich.'" *Music Analysis* 16, no. 1 (1997): 5–44.

———. *The Sonic Self: Musical Subjectivity and Signification*. Foreword by David Lidov. Afterword by Robert S. Hatten. Bloomington: Indiana University Press, 2000.

Dahlhaus, Carl. "Brahms und die Idee der Kammermusik." *Neue Zeitschrift für Musik* 134, no. 9 (1973): 559–63. Reprinted in *Brahms-Studien* 1 (1974): 45–57.

———. *Between Romanticism and Modernism: Four Studies in the Music of the Later Nineteenth Century*. Translated by Mary Whittall. Berkeley: University of California Press, 1980. Originally *Zwischen Romantik und Moderne: Vier Studien zur Musikgeschichte des späteren 19. Jahrhunderts*, by Carl Dahlhaus. Munich, Germany: Katzbichler, 1974.

———. *Nineteenth-Century Music*. Translated by J. Bradford Robinson. Berkeley: University of California Press, 1989. Originally *Die Musik des 19. Jahrhunderts*, by Carl Dahlhaus. Neues Handbuch der Musikwissenschaft, vol. 6. Wiesbaden, Germany: Akademische Verlagsgesellschaft Athenaion, 1980.

———. "Brahms and the Chamber Music Traditions." *The American Brahms Society Newsletter* 7, no. 2 (1989): 1–5.

Darcy, Warren. "Bruckner's Sonata Deformations." In *Bruckner Studies*, edited by Paul Hawkshaw and Timothy L. Jackson, 256–77. Cambridge, UK: Cambridge University Press, 1997.
Daverio, John. *Nineteenth-Century Music and the German Romantic Ideology*. New York: Schirmer, 1993.
———. "Brahms's *Academic Festival Overture* and the Comic Modes." *The American Brahms Society Newsletter* 12, no. 1 (1994): 1–3.
———. "From 'Concertante Rondo' to 'Lyric Sonata': A Commentary on Brahms's Reception of Mozart." In *Brahms Studies* 1, edited by David Brodbeck, 111–38. Lincoln: University of Nebraska Press, 1994.
———. "Schumann's Ossianic Manner." *19th-Century Music* 21, no. 3 (1998): 247–73.
———. *Crossing Paths: Schubert, Schumann, and Brahms*. New York: Oxford University Press, 2002.
Davis, Andrew. "Chopin and the Romantic Sonata: The First Movement of Op. 58." *Music Theory Spectrum* 36, no. 2 (2014): 270–94.
Davis, Nathan Kroms. "Stasis in the Development Sections of Two Sonata Forms by Brahms." PhD diss., University of California Davis, 2007.
Day, Aidan. *Romanticism*. 2nd ed. London: Routledge, 2012.
Derrida, Jacques. "The Law of Genre." Translated by Avital Ronell. *Critical Inquiry* 7, no. 1 (1980): 55–81. Originally published in *Glyph: Textual Studies* 7 (1980): 202–29. Reprinted in *On Narrative*, edited by W. J. T. Mitchell, 51–77. Chicago: University of Chicago Press, 1980.
Dickensheets, Janice. "The Nineteenth-Century Sonata Cycle as Novel: A Topical and Literary Analysis of the Second Piano Sonata of Johannes Brahms." PhD diss., University of Northern Colorado, 2004.
———. "The Topical Vocabulary of the Nineteenth Century." *The Journal of Musicological Research* 31, nos. 2–3 (2012): 97–137.
Dietrich, Albert, and J. V. Widman. *Recollections of Johannes Brahms*. Translated by Dora E. Hecht. London: Seeley, 1899. Portions originally printed as *Erinnerungen an Johannes Brahms in Briefe besonders aus seiner Jugendzeit*, by Albert Dietrich. Leipzig, Germany: Otto Wigand, 1898.
Dziadek, Magdalena. "Aesthetic, Ideological, and World-Outlook Foundations of the 'Young-Poland' Discourse on Chopin." Translated by Czesław Boniakowski. In *Chopin and His Work in the Context of Culture*, edited by Irena Poniatowska, 292–97. Krakow, Poland: Musica Iagellonica, 2003.
Ellis, John S. "A Narrative Analysis of Schumann's *Kinderszenen*." In *Musical Semiotics Revisited*, edited by Eero Tarasti, Paul Forsell, and Richard Littlefield, 303–19. Helsinki: International Semiotics Institute, 2003.
Fellinger, Imogen. "Brahms's View of Mozart." In *Brahms: Biographical, Documentary, and Analytical Studies*, edited by Robert Pascall, 41–57. Cambridge, UK: Cambridge University Press, 1983.
Fenaroli, Fedele. *Partimenti ossia basso numerato*. Volume III. Facsimile: Bologna, Italy: Forni.
Fink, Robert. "Desire, Repression, and Brahms's First Symphony." *Repercussions* 2, no. 2 (1993): 75–103.
Floros, Constantin. *Brahms und Bruckner: Studien zur Musikalischen Exegetik*. Wiesbaden, Germany: Breitkopf und Härtel, 1980.

Forte, Allen. "Motivic Design and Structural Levels in the First Movement of Brahms's String Quartet in C Minor." *The Musical Quarterly* 69, no. 4 (1983): 471–502.
Foucault, Michel. *The Order of Things: An Archaeology of the Human Sciences.* New York: Vintage, 1970. Originally *Les Mots et les choses.* Paris: Editions Gallimard, 1966.
———. "What Is an Author?" In *The Foucault Reader,* edited by Paul Rainbow, 101–20. New York: Pantheon, 1984.
Frisch, Walter. "Brahms and Schubring: Musical Criticism and Politics at Mid-Century." *19th-Century Music* 7, no. 3 (1984): 271–81.
———. *Brahms and the Principle of Developing Variation.* Berkeley: University of California Press, 1984.
Frye, Northrop. "The Drunken Boat: The Revolutionary Elements in Romanticism (1963)." Reprinted in *Northrop Frye's Writings on the Eighteenth and Nineteenth Centuries: Collected Works of Northrop Frye,* vol. 17, edited by Imre Salusinszky, 75–91. Toronto, ON: University of Toronto Press, 2005.
Furst, Lilian R. *European Romanticism: Self-Definition: An Anthology Compiled by Lilian R. Furst.* London: Methuen, 1980.
———. "Romanticism: Revolution *and* Evolution." In *English and German Romanticism: Cross-Currents and Controversies,* edited by James Pipkin, 79–87. Heidelberg, Germany: Carl Winter, 1985.
Galand, Joel. "Form, Genre, and Style in the Eighteenth-Century Rondo." *Music Theory Spectrum* 17, no. 1 (1995): 27–52.
———. "Formenlehre Revived." Review of *Classical Form: A Theory of Formal Functions for the Instrumental Music of Haydn, Mozart, and Beethoven,* by William E. Caplin. *Integral: The Journal of Applied Musical Thought* 13 (1999): 143–200.
———. "Some Eighteenth-Century Ritornello Scripts and Their Nineteenth-Century Revivals." *Music Theory Spectrum* 30, no. 2 (2008): 239–82.
Gauldin, Robert. "The Theory and Practice of Chromatic Wedge Progressions in Romantic Music." *Music Theory Spectrum* 26, no. 1 (2004): 1–22.
Gay, Peter. *The Rise of Modern Paganism.* Volume 1 of *The Enlightenment: An Interpretation.* New York: Norton: 1966.
———. *The Science of Freedom.* Volume 2 of *The Enlightenment: An Interpretation.* New York: Norton: 1969.
Geiringer, Karl. "Brahms' zweites Schatzkästlein des Jungen Kreisler." *Neue Zeutschrift für Musik* 100, no. 5 (1933): 443–46. Reprinted as Geiringer, Karl. "Brahms the Reader of Literature, History, and Philosophy." In *On Brahms and His Circle: Essays and Documentary Studies,* by Karl Geiringer, edited by George S. Bozarth, 30–46. Sterling Heights, MI: Harmonie Park, 2006.
———. *Brahms: His Life and Work.* 2nd ed. New York: Oxford University Press, 1947. Originally Geiringer, Karl. *Johannes Brahms: Leben und Schaffen eines Deutsches Meisters.* Vienna: Rohrer, 1935. First English edition Boston: Houghton Mifflin, 1936.
Genette, Gérard. *Narrative Discourse: An Essay in Method.* Translated by Jane E. Lewin. Foreword by Jonathan Culler. Ithaca, NY: Cornell University Press, 1980. Originally Genette, Gérard. *Discours du récit: essai de method.* In *Figures III,* 65–282. Paris: Éditions du Seuil, 1972.
———. *Narrative Discourse Revisited.* Translated by Jane E. Lewin. Ithaca, NY: Cornell University Press, 1988. Originally Genette, Gérard. *Nouveau discours du récit.* Paris: Éditions du Seuil, 1983.
Gifford, Terry. *Pastoral.* London: Routledge, 1999.

Gjerdingen, Robert O. *Music in the Galant Style*. Oxford, UK: Oxford University Press, 2007.
Gossett, Philip. "Carl Dahlhaus and the 'Ideal Type.'" *19th-Century Music* 13, no. 1 (1989): 49–56.
Graybill, Roger. "Brahms's Three-Key Expositions: Their Place within the Classical Tradition." PhD diss., Yale University, 1983.
———. "Brahms' Integration of Traditional and Progressive Tendencies: A Look at Three Sonata Expositions." *The Journal of Musicological Research* 8, nos. 1–2 (1988): 141–68.
Grimalt, Joan. "The Musical Topic of the Laugh: Analyzing Some Classical Examples." Paper presented at the 9th World Congress of the International Association for Semiotic Studies, Helsinki and Imatra, June 11–17, 2007.
Grimes, Nicole. "The Schoenberg/Brahms Critical Tradition Reconsidered." *Music Analysis* 31, no. 2 (2012): 127–75.
Hanslick, Eduard. *Geschichte des Concertwesens in Wien*. 2 vols. Vienna: Wilhelm Braumüller, 1869–70.
Hardt, Michael, and Kathi Weeks. Introduction to *The Jameson Reader*, edited by Michael Hardt and Kathi Weeks, 1–29. Oxford, UK: Blackwell, 2000.
Harrison, Daniel. *Harmonic Function in Chromatic Music: A Renewed Dualist Theory and an Account of Its Precedents*. Chicago: University of Chicago Press, 1994.
Hatten, Robert S. "Toward a Semiotic Model of Style in Music: Epistemological and Methodological Bases." PhD diss., Indiana University, 1982.
———. "On Narrativity in Music: Expressive Genres and Levels of Discourse in Beethoven." *Indiana Theory Review* 12 (1991): 75–98.
———. *Musical Meaning in Beethoven: Markedness, Correlation, and Interpretation*. Foreword by David Lidov. Bloomington: Indiana University Press, 1994.
———. "Grounding Interpretation: A Semiotic Framework for Musical Hermeneutics." *American Journal of Semiotics* 13, nos. 1–4 (1996): 25–42.
———. "Gestural Troping in Music and Its Consequences for Semiotic Theory." In *Musical Signification: Between Rhetoric and Pragmatics*, edited by Gino Stefani, Eero Tarasti, and Luca Marconi, 193–99. Bologna, Italy: CLUEB, 1998.
———. "The Expressive Role of Disjunction: A Semiotic Approach to Form and Meaning in the Fourth and Fifth Symphony." In *Perspectives on Anton Bruckner*, edited by Crawford Howie, Paul Hawkshaw, and Timothy L. Jackson, 145–84. Aldershot, UK: Ashgate, 2001.
———. *Interpreting Musical Gestures, Topics, and Tropes: Mozart, Beethoven, Schubert*. Bloomington: Indiana University Press, 2004.
———. "Expressive Doubling, Topics, Tropes, and Shifts in Level of Discourse: Interpreting the Third Movement of Beethoven's String Quartet in B-Flat, Op. 130." In *Beethoven: III: Studien und Interpretationen*, edited by Mieczysław Tomaszewski and Magdalena Chrenkoff, 125–44. Krakow, Poland: Akademia Muzyczna w Krakowie, 2006.
———. "The Troping of Temporality in Music." In *Approaches to Meaning in Music*, edited by Bryon Almén and Edward R. Pearsall, 62–75. Bloomington: Indiana University Press, 2006.
———. "Interpreting Beethoven's 'Tempest' Sonata through Topics, Gestures, and Agency." In *Beethoven's "Tempest" Sonata: Perspectives of Analysis and Performance*, edited by Pieter Bergé, coedited by Jeroen D'hoe and William E. Caplin, 163–80. Leuven, Belgium: Peeters, 2009.

———. "Aesthetically Warranted Emotion and Composed Expressive Trajectories in Music." *Music Analysis* 29, nos. 1–3 (2010): 83–101.
———. "Performance and Analysis—Or *Synthesis*: Theorizing Gesture, Topics, and Tropes in Chopin's F-Minor Ballade." *Indiana Theory Review* 28, nos. 1–2 (2010): 45–66.
———. "Musical Forces and Agential Energies: An Expansion of Steve Larson's Model." *Music Theory Online* 18, no. 3 (2012). Retrieved December 31, 2012 (http://mtosmt.org/issues/mto.12.18.3/mto.12.18.3.hatten.php).
———. "On Metaphor and Syntactic Troping in Music." In *Music Semiotics: A Network of Significations in Honour and Memory of Raymond Monelle*, edited by Esti Sheinberg, foreword by Eero Tarasti, 87–104. Burlington, VT: Ashgate, 2012.
———. "Melodic Forces and Agential Energies: An Integrative Approach to the Analysis and Expressive Interpretation of Tonal Melodies." In *Music, Analysis, Experience: New Perspectives in Musical Semiotics*, edited by Costantino Maeder and Mark Reybrouck, 315–30. Leuven, Belgium: Leuven University Press, 2015.
Helman, Zofia. "Norms and Individuation in Chopin's Sonatas." Translated by Radosław Materka and Maja Trochimczyk. *Polish Music Journal* 3, no. 1 (2000). Retrieved February 11, 2011 (http://www.usc.edu/dept/polish_music/PMJ/issue/3.1.00/helman.html).
Hepokoski, James. "Genre and Content in Mid-Century Verdi: 'Addio, del passato' (*La Traviata*, Act III)." *Cambridge Opera Journal* 1, no. 3 (1989): 249–76.
———. "The Dahlhaus Project and Its Extra-Musicological Sources." *19th-Century Music* 14, no. 3 (1991): 221–46.
———. "Fiery-Pulsed Libertine or Domestic Hero? Strauss's *Don Juan* Reinvestigated." In *Richard Strauss: New Perspectives on the Composer and His Work*, edited by Bryan Gilliam, 135–75. Durham, NC: Duke University Press, 1992.
———. *Sibelius: Symphony No. 5*. Cambridge, UK: Cambridge University Press, 1993.
———. "Masculine-Feminine." *The Musical Times* 135, no. 1818 (1994): 494–99.
———. "The Medial Caesura and Its Role in the Eighteenth-Century Sonata Exposition." *Music Theory Spectrum* 19, no. 2 (1997): 115–54.
———. "Back and Forth from *Egmont*: Mozart, Beethoven, and the Nonresolving Recapitulation." *19th-Century Music* 25, nos. 2–3 (2001–2002): 127–54.
———. "Beethoven Reception: The Symphonic Tradition." In *The Cambridge History of Nineteenth-Century Music*, ed. Jim Samson, 424–59. Cambridge, UK: Cambridge University Press, 2001.
———. "Rotations, Sketches, and the Sixth Symphony." In *Sibelius Studies*, edited by Timothy L. Jackson and Veijo Murtomäki, 322–51. Cambridge, UK: Cambridge University Press, 2001.
———. "Beyond the Sonata Principle." *Journal of the American Musicological Society* 55, no. 1 (2002): 91–154.
———. "Structure, Implication, and the End of *Suor Angelica*." *Studi Pucciniani* 3: *"L'insolita forma": Strutture e processi analitici per l'opera italiana mell'epoca di Puccini: Atti del Convegno internazionale di studi Lucca, 20–21 settembre 2001*, 241–64. Edited by Virgilio Bernardoni, Michele Girardi, and Arthur Groos. Lucca, Italy: Centro studi Giacomo Puccini, 2004.
———. "Framing *Till Eulenspiegel*." *19th-Century Music* 30, no. 1 (2006): 4–43.
Hepokoski, James, and Warren Darcy. *Elements of Sonata Theory: Norms, Types, and Deformations in the Late-Eighteenth-Century Sonata*. New York: Oxford University Press, 2006.
Hepokoski, James. "Approaching the First Movement of Beethoven's 'Tempest' Sonata through Sonata Theory." In *Beethoven's "Tempest" Sonata: Perspectives of Analysis*

and Performance, edited by Pieter Bergé, coedited by Jeroen D'hoe and William E. Caplin, 181–212. Leuven, Belgium: Peeters, 2009.

———. "Sonata Theory and Dialogic Form." In *Musical Forms, Form, and Formenlehre*, edited by Pieter Bergé, 71–89. Leuven, Belgium: Leuven University Press, 2009.

———. "Formal Process, Sonata Theory, and the First Movement of Beethoven's 'Tempest' Sonata." *Music Theory Online* 16, no. 2 (2010). Retrieved December 31, 2013 (http://www.mtosmt.org/issues/mto.10.16.2/mto.10.16.2.hepokoski.ht).

———. "Ineffable Immersion: Contextualizing the Call for Silence." *Journal of the American Musicological Society* 65, no. 1 (2012): 223–30.

———. "Monumentality and Formal Processes in the First Movement of Brahms's Piano Concerto No. 1 in D Minor, Op. 15." In *Expressive Intersections in Brahms: Essays in Analysis and Meaning*, edited by Heather Platt and Peter H. Smith, 217–51. Bloomington: Indiana University Press, 2012.

Hofmann, Kurt. "Brahms the Hamburg Musician: 1833–1862." Translated by Michael Musgrave. In *The Cambridge Companion to Brahms*, edited by Michael Musgrave, 3–30. Cambridge, UK: Cambridge University Press, 1999.

Holquist, Michael. Introduction to *The Dialogic Imagination: Four Essays*, by M. M. Bakhtin, xv–xxxiii. Austin: University of Texas Press, 1981.

Horne, William. "The 'Still Center' in Brahms's Violin Concerto, Op. 77." *The American Brahms Society Newsletter* 29, no. 1 (2011): 1–5.

Horton, Julian. "Postmodernism and the Critique of Musical Analysis." *The Musical Quarterly* 85, no. 2 (2001): 342–66.

———. *Bruckner's Symphonies: Analysis, Reception, and Cultural Politics*. Cambridge, UK: Cambridge University Press, 2004.

———. "Bruckner's Symphonies and Sonata Deformation Theory." *Journal of the Society for Musicology in Ireland* 1 (2005): 5–17.

Horton, Julian, and Paul Wingfield. "Norm and Deformation in Mendelssohn's Sonata Forms." In *Mendelssohn Perspectives*, edited by Nicole Grimes and Angela R. Mace, 83–112. Farnham, UK: Ashgate, 2012.

Hull, Kenneth. "Allusive Irony in Brahms's Fourth Symphony." In *Brahms Studies* 2, edited by David Brodbeck, 135–68. Lincoln: University of Nebraska Press, 1998.

———. "Brahms the Allusive: Extra-Compositional Reference in the Instrumental Music of Johannes Brahms." PhD diss., Princeton University, 1998.

Hunt, Graham G. "The Three-Key Trimodular Block and Its Classical Precedents: Sonata Expositions of Schubert and Brahms." *Integral: The Journal of Applied Musical Thought* 23 (2009): 65–119.

Iser, Wolfgang. *The Act of Reading: A Theory of Aesthetic Response*. Baltimore: Johns Hopkins University Press, 1978. Originally Iser, Wolfgang. *Der Akt des Lesens: Theorie ästhetischer Wirkung*. Munich, Germany: Fink, 1976.

———. "Interview." Introduction by Rudolf E. Kuenzli. Questions by Norman Holland and Wayne C. Booth. *Diacritics* 10, no. 2 (1980): 57–74.

———. *Prospecting: From Reader Response to Literary Anthropology*. Baltimore: Johns Hopkins University Press, 1989.

Jackson, Timothy L. "The Adagio of the Sixth Symphony and the Anticipatory Tonic Recapitulation in Bruckner, Brahms, and Dvořák." In *Perspectives on Anton Bruckner*, edited by Crawford Howie, Paul Hawkshaw, and Timothy L. Jackson, 206–27. Aldershot, UK: Ashgate, 2001.

Jaffe, Jane Vial. "Eduard Marxsen and Johannes Brahms." PhD diss., University of Chicago, 2009.

———. "Brahms as an Editor of Marxsen," *The American Brahms Society Newsletter* 28, no. 1 (2010): 1–5.

———. "The Symphonic Side of Eduard Marxsen." *The American Brahms Society Newsletter* 28, no. 2 (2010): 1–7.

Jameson, Fredric R. "Beyond the Cave: Demystifying the Ideology of Modernism." *The Bulletin of the Midwest Modern Language Association* 8, no. 1 (1975): 1–20.

Janowitz, Anne. "The Romantic Fragment." In *A Companion to Romanticism*, edited by Duncan Wu, 442–51. Oxford, UK: Blackwell, 1998.

Jauss, Hans Robert. *Question and Answer: Forms of Dialogic Understanding*. Edited, translated, and with a foreword by Michael Hays. Minneapolis: University of Minnesota Press, 1989. Reprinted from Jauss, Hans Robert. *Ästhetische Erfahrung und literarische Hermeneutik*. Frankfurt: Suhrkamp, 1982.

Jenkins, Kyle. "Expositional Trajectories Gone Awry: S-C Complications in Brahms's Sonata Movements." Paper presented at the annual meeting of the Society for Music Theory, New Orleans, LA, November 1–4, 2012.

Jones, Ryan C. "Cadence in Mahler: Principles, Types, and Transformations." Paper presented at the annual meeting of the Society for Music Theory, New Orleans, LA, November 1–4, 2012.

Kalbeck, Max. *Johannes Brahms*. 4 vols. Rev. ed. Tutzing, Germany: Hans Schneider, 1976. First edition Vienna and Leipzig: Wiener Verlag, 1904–14.

Kallberg, Jeffrey. "Chopin's Last Style." *Journal of the American Musicological Society* 38, no. 2 (1985): 264–315.

———. "The Rhetoric of Genre: Chopin's Nocturne in G Minor." *19th-Century Music* 11, no. 3 (1988): 238–61.

———. *Chopin at the Boundaries: Sex, History, and Musical Genre*. Cambridge, MA: Harvard University Press, 1996.

Kaplan, Richard. "Sonata Form in the Orchestral Works of Liszt: The Revolutionary Reconsidered." *19th-Century Music* 8, no. 2 (1984): 142–52.

Karl, Gregory. "The Temporal Life of the Musical Persona: Implications for Narrative and Dramatic Interpretation." *Music Research Forum* 6 (1991): 42–72.

———. "Structuralism and Musical Plot." *Music Theory Spectrum* 19, no. 1 (1997): 13–34.

Kayser, Wolfgang. *The Grotesque in Art and Literature*. Translated by Ulrich Weisstein. New York: Columbia University Press, 1981.

Kerman, Joseph. "Counsel for the Defense." Review of *The Main Stream of Music and Other Essays*, by Donald Francis Tovey. *The Hudson Review* 3, no. 3 (1950): 438–46.

———. "How We Got into Analysis, and How to Get Out." *Critical Inquiry* 7, no. 2 (1980): 311–31.

———. "Notes on Beethoven's Codas." In *Beethoven Studies* 3, edited by Alan Tyson, 141–59. Cambridge, UK: Cambridge University Press, 1982.

Kermode, Frank. "Secrets and Narrative Sequence." In *On Narrative*, edited by W. J. T. Mitchell, 79–97. Chicago: University of Chicago Press, 1980.

Keys, Ivor. *Brahms: Chamber Music*. Seattle: University of Washington Press, 1974.

Kinderman, William. *Beethoven*. 2nd ed. Oxford, UK: Oxford University Press, 2009.

———. "The First Movement of Beethoven's 'Tempest' Sonata: Genesis, Form, and Dramatic Meaning." In *Beethoven's "Tempest" Sonata: Perspectives of Analysis and Performance*, edited by Pieter Bergé, coedited by Jeroen D'hoe and William E. Caplin, 213–34. Leuven, Belgium: Peeters, 2009.

Klein, Michael. "Liszt and the Idea of Transcendence." *Journal of the American Liszt Society* 54–56 (2003–2005): 102–24.

———. "Chopin's Fourth Ballade as Musical Narrative." *Music Theory Spectrum* 26, no. 1 (2004): 23–55.
———. *Intertextuality in Western Art Music*. Bloomington: Indiana University Press, 2005.
———. "The Limits of Interpretation?" *Interdisciplinary Studies in Musicology* 5 (2005): 121–38.
———. "Ironic Narrative, Ironic Reading." *Journal of Music Theory* 53, no. 1 (2009): 95–136.
———. "Chopin Dreams: The Mazurka in C♯ Minor, Op. 30, No. 4." *19th-Century Music* 35, no. 3 (2012): 238–60.
Knapp, Raymond. *Brahms and the Challenge of the Symphony*. Stuyvesant, NY: Pendragon, 1997.
Korsyn, Kevin. "Towards a New Poetics of Musical Influence." *Music Analysis* 10, nos. 1–2 (1991): 3–72.
———. "Brahms Research and Aesthetic Ideology." *Music Analysis* 12, no. 1 (1993): 89–103.
Koselleck, Reinhart. *Futures Past: On the Semantics of Historical Time*. Translated and with an introduction by Keith Tribe. New York: Columbia University Press, 2004. Originally *Vergangene Zukunft: Zur Semantik geschichtlicher Zeiten*. Frankfurt am Main: Suhrkamp Verlag, 1979.
Kramer, Lawrence. "Romantic Meaning in Chopin's Prelude in A Minor." *19th-Century Music* 9, no. 2 (1985): 145–55.
———. *Music as Cultural Practice*. Berkeley: University of California Press, 1990.
———. "Haydn's Chaos, Schenker's Order; Or, Hermeneutics and Musical Analysis: Can They Mix?" *19th-Century Music* 16, no. 1 (1992): 3–17.
———. "Narrative Archetypes and Mahler's Ninth Symphony." In *Music and Text: Critical Inquiries*, edited by Steven Paul Sher, 118–36. New York: Cambridge University Press, 1992.
———. *Classical Music and Postmodern Knowledge*. Berkeley: University of California Press, 1995.
———. "The Strange Case of Beethoven's *Coriolan*: Romantic Aesthetics, Modern Subjectivity, and the Cult of Shakespeare." *The Musical Quarterly* 79, no. 2 (1995): 256–80.
———. *Franz Schubert: Sexuality, Subjectivity, Song*. Cambridge, UK: Cambridge University Press, 1998.
———. "Primitive Encounters: Beethoven's 'Tempest' Sonata, Musical Meaning, and Enlightenment Anthropology." *Beethoven Forum* 6 (1998): 31–65.
———. "Musicology and Meaning." *The Musical Times* 144, no. 1883 (2003): 6–12.
———. "Subjectivity Rampant! Music, Hermeneutics, and History." In *The Cultural Study of Music: A Critical Introduction*, edited by Martin Clayton, Trevor Herbert, and Richard Middleton, 124–35. New York: Routledge, 2003.
———. "Saving the Ordinary: Beethoven's 'Ghost' Trio and the Wheel of History." In *Phrase and Subject: Studies in Literature and Music*, edited by Delia de Soussa Correa, 73–86. Oxford, UK: Legenda, 2006.
———. "Subjectivity Unbound: Music, Language, Culture." In *The Cultural Study of Music: A Critical Introduction*, 2nd ed., edited by Martin Clayton, Trevor Herbert, and Richard Middleton, 395–406. New York: Routledge, 2012.
Kraus, Detlef. "Das Andante aus der Sonate Op. 5 von Brahms: Versuch Einer Interpretation." *Brahms-Studien* 3 (1979): 47–51.
Krebs, Carl, ed. *Des jungen Kreislers Schatzkästlein*. Berlin: Verlag der Deutschen Brahmsgesellschaft, 1909. In English as Krebs, Carl, ed. *The Brahms Notebooks: The Little Treasure Chest of the Young Kreisler: Quotations from Poets, Philosophers,*

and Artists. Translated by Agnes Eisenberger, annotations by Siegmund Levarie. Hillsdale, NJ: Pendragon, 2003.

Kretzschmer, August, and Anton Wilhelm von Zuccalmaglio. *Deutsche Volkslieder mit ihren Original-Weisen*. 2 vols. Berlin: Vereinsbuchhandlung, 1838, 1840. Reprint Hildesheim: G. Olms, 1969.

Kross, Siegfried. "Brahms and E. T. A. Hoffmann." *19th-Century Music* 5, no. 3 (1982): 193–200.

———. "The Establishment of a Brahms Repertoire, 1890–1902." In *Brahms 2: Biographical, Documentary and Analytical Studies*, edited by Michael Musgrave, 21–38. Cambridge, UK: Cambridge University Press, 1987.

———. "Thematic Structure and Formal Processes in Brahms's Sonata Movements." In *Brahms Studies: Analytical and Historical Perspectives*, edited by George S. Bozarth, 423–43. Oxford, UK: Clarendon, 1990.

Langer, Susanne. *Philosophy in a New Key*. 2nd ed. Cambridge, MA: Harvard University Press, 1951.

Larson, Steve. *Musical Forces: Motion, Metaphor, and Meaning in Music*. Bloomington: Indiana University Press, 2012.

Leikin, Anatoly. "The Dissolution of Sonata Structure in Romantic Piano Music (1820–1850)." PhD diss., University of California Los Angeles, 1986.

Levinson, Marjorie. *The Romantic Fragment Poem: A Critique of a Form*. Chapel Hill: University of North Carolina Press, 1986.

Lewin, David. "Brahms, His Past, and Modes of Music Theory." In *Brahms Studies: Analytical and Historical Perspectives*, edited by George S. Bozarth, 13–27. Oxford, UK: Clarendon, 1990.

Longyear, Rey M. *Nineteenth-Century Romanticism in Music*. Englewood Cliffs, NJ: Prentice Hall, 1988. First edition Englewood Cliffs, NJ: Prentice Hall, 1969.

———. "Beethoven and Romantic Irony." *The Musical Quarterly* 56, no. 4 (1970): 647–64.

———. "Tonic Major, Mediant Major: A Variant Tonal Relationship in 19th-Century Sonata Form." *Studies in Music from the University of Western Ontario* 10 (1985): 105–39.

Longyear, Rey M., and Kate R. Covington. "Liszt, Mahler, and a Remote Tonal Relationship in Sonata Form." In *Studien zur Instrumentalmusik: Lothar Hoffmann-Ebrecht zum 60. Geburstag*, edited by Anke Bingmann, Klaus Hortschansky, and Winfried Kirsch, 457–68. Tutzing, Germany: Hans Schneider, 1988.

Lovejoy, Arthur O. "On the Discrimination of Romanticisms." *Publications of the Modern Language Association of America* 39, no. 2 (1924): 229–53.

Lubin, Steven. "Transforming Reheard Themes: Brahms and the Legacy of Beethoven's Ninth." *The American Brahms Society Newsletter* 17, no. 1 (1999): 1–4.

Macdonald, Malcolm. *Brahms*. New York: Schirmer, 1990.

Mahrt, William P. "Brahms and Reminiscence: A Special Use of Classic Conventions." In *Convention in Eighteenth- and Nineteenth-Century Music: Essays in Honor of Leonard G. Ratner*, edited by Wye Jamison Allanbrook, Janet M. Levy, and William P. Mahrt, 75–112. Stuyvesant, NY: Pendragon, 1992.

de Man, Paul. *Allegories of Reading: Figural Language in Rousseau, Nietzsche, Rilke, and Proust*. New Haven, CT: Yale University Press, 1979.

Marx, Adolph Bernhard. *Die lehre von der musikalischen Komposition: praktisch theoretisch*. 4 vol. 4th ed. Leipzig, Germany: Breitkopf und Härtel, 1868.

Mason, Daniel Gregory. *The Chamber Music of Brahms*. Freeport, NY: Books for Libraries, 1970. First edition New York: Macmillan, 1933.

Matthews, Denis. *Brahms: Piano Music*. Seattle: University of Washington Press, 1978.
May, Florence. *The Life of Johannes Brahms*. 2 vol. 2nd ed. London: William Reeves, 1948. First edition London: E. Arnold, 1905.
McClary, Susan. "Pitches, Expression, Ideology: An Exercise in Mediation." *Enclitic* 7 (1983): 76–86.
———. *Feminine Endings: Music, Gender, and Sexuality*. Minneapolis: University of Minnesota Press, 1991.
———. *Conventional Wisdom: The Content of Musical Form*. Berkeley: University of California Press, 2000.
McClatchie, Stephen. "Towards a Post-Modern Wagner." Review of Abbate, *Unsung Voices*. *Wagner* 13, no. 3 (1992): 108–21.
McClelland, Ryan. "Sequence as Expressive Culmination in the Chamber Music of Brahms." In *Expressive Intersections in Brahms: Essays in Analysis and Meaning*, edited by Heather Platt and Peter H. Smith, 147–85. Bloomington: Indiana University Press, 2012.
McCreless, Patrick. "Roland Barthes's *S/Z* from a Musical Point of View." *In Theory Only* 10, no. 7 (1988): 1–29.
McDonald, Matthew. "Silent Narration? Elements of Narrative in Ives's *The Unanswered Question*." *19th-Century Music* 28 (2004): 263–86.
McFarland, Thomas. *Romanticism and the Forms of Ruin: Wordsworth, Coleridge, and Modalities of Fragmentation*. Princeton, NJ: Princeton University Press, 1981.
McGann, Jerome. *The Romantic Ideology: A Critical Investigation*. Chicago: University of Chicago Press, 1985.
McGeary, Thomas. "Schoenberg's Brahms Lecture of 1933." *Journal of the Arnold Schoenberg Institute* 15, no. 2 (1992): 5–99.
McKee, Eric. "Alternative Meanings in the First Movement of Beethoven's String Quartet in E♭ Major, Op. 127: Emergence and Growth from Stagnation and Decline." *Theory and Practice* 24 (1999): 1–27.
McQuillan, Martin. "Aporias of Writing: Narrative and Subjectivity." Introduction to *The Narrative Reader*, edited by Martin McQuillan, 1–33. London: Routledge, 2000.
Metz, Christian. *Film Language: A Semiotics of the Cinema*. Translated by Michael Taylor. Chicago: University of Chicago Press, 1991. Originally Metz, Christian. *Essais sur la signification au cinema*. Paris: Klinksieck, 1968.
Meyer, Leonard B. *Explaining Music*. Chicago: University of Chicago Press, 1973.
———. "A Pride of Prejudices; or, Delight in Diversity." In *The Spheres of Music: A Gathering of Essays*, 262–80. Chicago: University of Chicago Press, 2000.
Micznik, Vera. "Music and Narrative Revisited: Degrees of Narrativity in Beethoven and Mahler." *Journal of the Royal Musical Association* 126, no. 2 (2001): 193–249.
Monahan, Seth. "'Inescapable' Coherence and the Failure of the Novel-Symphony in the Finale of Mahler's Sixth." *19th-Century Music* 31, no. 1 (2007): 53–95.
———. "Mahler's Sonata Narratives." PhD diss., Yale University, 2008.
———. "'I Have Tried to Capture You . . .': Rethinking the 'Alma' Theme from Mahler's Sixth Symphony." *Journal of the American Musicological Society* 64, no. 1 (2011): 119–78.
———. "Success and Failure in Mahler's Sonata Recapitulations." *Music Theory Spectrum* 33, no. 1 (2011): 37–58.
———. "Action and Agency Revisited." *Journal of Music Theory* 57, no. 2 (2013): 321–71.
Monelle, Raymond. "Music and the Peircean Trichotomies." *International Review of the Aesthetics and Sociology of Music* 22, no. 1 (1991): 99–108.

———. *Linguistics and Semiotics in Music*. Chur, Switzerland: Harwood Academic, 1992.
———. "The Temporal Image." In *The Sense of Music: Semiotic Essays*, 81–114. Princeton, NJ: Princeton University Press, 2000.
———. *The Musical Topic: Hunt, Military, and Pastoral*. Bloomington: Indiana University Press, 2006.
Monroe, William. *Power to Hurt: The Virtues of Alienation*. Urbana: University of Illinois Press, 1998.
Montgomery, Kip James. "Cyclic Form in the Music of Brahms." PhD diss., State University of New York at Stony Brook, 2002.
Morgan, Robert P. "The Delayed Structural Downbeat and Its Effect on the Tonal and Rhythmic Structure of Sonata Form." PhD diss., Princeton University, 1969.
Müller, Gunther. "Erzählzeit und erzählte zeit (1948)." Reprinted in Müller, Gunther. *Morphologische Poetik: Gessamelte Aufsätze*. Edited by Helga Egner and Elena Müller, 247–68. Tübingen, Germany: Niemeyer, 1968.
Murdoch, William. *Brahms: With an Analytical Study of the Complete Pianoforte Works*. New York: AMS Press, 1978. First edition London: Rich and Cowan, 1933.
Musgrave, Michael. *The Music of Brahms*. London: Routledge and Kegan Paul, 1985.
———. "Schoenberg's Brahms." In Bozarth, George S. *Brahms Studies: Analytical and Historical Perspectives*, 123–37. Oxford, UK: Clarendon, 1990.
———. *A Brahms Reader*. New Haven, CT: Yale University Press, 2000.
Nelson, Thomas K. "The Fantasy of Absolute Music." PhD diss., University of Minnesota, 1998.
Neuwirth, Markus. "Joseph Haydn's 'Witty' Play on Hepokoski and Darcy's Elements of Sonata Theory." Review of *Elements of Sonata Theory*, by James Hepokoski and Warren Darcy. *Zeitschrift der Gesellschaft für Musiktheorie* 8, no. 1 (2011). Retrieved December 31, 2013 (http://www.gmth.de/zeitschrift/artikel/586.aspx).
Newcomb, Anthony. "Those Images That Yet Fresh Images Beget." *The Journal of Musicology* 2, no. 3 (1983): 227–45.
———. "Once More 'Between Absolute and Program Music': Schumann's Second Symphony." *19th-Century Music* 7, no. 3 (1984): 233–50.
———. "Sound and Feeling." *Critical Inquiry* 10, no. 4 (1984): 614–43.
———. "Schumann and Late Eighteenth-Century Narrative Strategies." *19th-Century Music* 11, no. 2 (1987): 164–74.
———. "The Polonaise-Fantasy and Issues of Musical Narrative." In *Chopin Studies* 2, edited by John S. Rink and Jim Samson, 84–101. Cambridge, UK: Cambridge University Press, 1994.
———. "Action and Agency in Mahler's Ninth Symphony, Second Movement." In *Music and Meaning*, edited by Jenefer Robinson, 131–53. Ithaca, NY: Cornell University Press, 1997.
———. "The Hunt for Reminiscences in Nineteenth-Century Germany." In *Music and the Aesthetics of Modernity*, edited by Karol Berger and Anthony Newcomb, 111–35. Cambridge, MA: Harvard University Press, 2005.
Newman, William S. "Some Nineteenth-Century Consequences of Beethoven's 'Hammerklavier' Sonata, Op. 106 (Part One)." *The Piano Quarterly* 67 (1969): 12–18.
———. "Some Nineteenth-Century Consequences of Beethoven's 'Hammerklavier' Sonata, Op. 106 (Part Two)." *The Piano Quarterly* 68 (1969): 12–17.
———. *The Sonata since Beethoven: The Third and Final Volume of A History of the Sonata Idea*. 2nd ed. New York: Norton, 1972. First edition Chapel Hill: University of North Carolina Press, 1969.

Neytcheva, Svetlana. "The Timeless Present: On Two Modes of Distorting the Illusion of Time in Music." *Tijdschrift voor muziektheorie* 6, no. 2 (2001): 101–14.
Notley, Margaret. "Discourse and Allusion: The Chamber Music of Brahms." In *Nineteenth-Century Chamber Music*, edited by Stephen E. Hefling, 242–86. New York: Schirmer, 1998.
———. *Lateness and Brahms: Music and Culture in the Twilight of Viennese Liberalism*. New York: Oxford University Press, 2007.
Nowick, Wojciech. "Fryderyk Chopin's Scherzo in B Minor Op. 20: Form and Thematic Process." Translated by Katharine Tylko-Hill. In *Chopin Studies* 5 (1995): 174–89.
———. "Chopin's Sonata Counter-Type: Error of Construction or Innovative Idea." In *Chopin and His Work in the Context of Culture*, edited by Irena Poniatowska, 334–39. Krakow, Poland: Musica Iagellonica, 2003.
Parakilas, James. *Ballads without Words: Chopin and the Tradition of the Instrumental Ballade*. Portland, OR: Amadeus Press, 1992.
Parmer, Dillon. "Brahms, Song Quotation, and Secret Programs." *19th-Century Music* 19, no. 2 (1995): 161–90.
———. "Brahms and the Poetic Motto: A Hermeneutic Aid?" *The Journal of Musicology* 15, no. 3 (1997): 353–89.
———. "Musical Meaning for the Few: Instances of Private Reception in the Music of Brahms." *Current Musicology* 83 (2007): 109–30.
———. "Musicology as Epiphenomenon: Derivative Disciplinarity, Performing, and the Deconstruction of the Musical Work." *Repercussion* 10, no. 1 (2007): 8–56.
———. "'Come, Rise to Higher Spheres!': Tradition Transcended in Brahms's Violin Sonata No. 1 in G Major, Op. 78." *Ad Parnassum* 7, no. 13 (2009): 129–52.
Pascall, Robert. "Some Special Uses of Sonata Form by Brahms." *Soundings* 4 (1974): 58–63.
Peirce, Charles Sanders. *The Philosophy of Peirce: Selected Writings*. Edited by Justus Buchler. London: Kegan Paul, 1940.
Petty, Wayne. "Chopin and the Ghost of Beethoven." *19th-Century Music* 22, no. 3 (1999): 281–99.
———. "Brahms, Adolph Jensen, and the Problem of the Multi-Movement Work." *Music Analysis* 22, nos. 1–2 (2003): 105–37.
Phelan, James. *Experiencing Fiction: Judgments, Progressions, and the Rhetorical Theory of Narrative*. Columbus: Ohio State University Press, 2007.
Polheim, Karl K. *Die Arabeske: Ansichten und Ideen aus Friedrich Schlegels Poetik*. Paderborn, Germany: Schöningh, 1966.
Rabinowitz, Peter J. "Truth in Fiction: A Reexamination of Audiences." *Critical Inquiry* 4, no. 1 (1977): 121–41.
———. "The Click of the Spring: The Detective Story as Parallel Structure in Dostoyevsky and Faulkner." *Modern Philology* 76, no. 4 (1979): 355–69.
———. "Rats behind the Wainscoting: Politics, Convention, and Chandler's *The Big Sleep*." *Texas Studies in Literature and Language* 22, no. 2 (1980): 224–45.
———. "Fictional Music: Toward a Theory of Listening." *Bucknell Review* 26, no. 1 (1981): 193–208.
———. "Pleasure in Conflict: Mahler's Sixth, Tragedy, and Musical Form." *Comparative Literature Studies* 18, no. 3 (1981): 306–13.
———. "Circumstantial Evidence: Musical Analysis and Theories of Reading." *Mosaic* 18, no. 4 (1985): 159–73.
———. "The Turn of the Glass Key: Popular Fiction as Reading Strategy." *Critical Inquiry* 11, no. 3 (1985): 418–31.

———. *Before Reading: Narrative Conventions and the Politics of Interpretation*. Ithaca, NY: Cornell University Press, 1987.
———. "Whiting the Wrongs of History: The Resurrection of Scott Joplin." *Black Music Research Journal* 11, no. 2 (1991): 157–76.
———. "Chord and Discourse: Listening through the Written Word." In *Music and Text: Critical Inquiries*, edited by Steven Paul Sher, 38–56. New York: Cambridge University Press, 1992.
———. "'With Our Own Dominant Passions': Gottschalk, Gender, and the Power of Listening." *19th-Century Music* 16, no. 3 (1993): 242–52.
———. Review of *Wagner Androgyne: A Study in Interpretation: A Study in Interpretation*, by Jean-Jacques Nattiez. *The Opera Quarterly* 11, no. 2 (1995): 157–62.
———. "On Teaching *The Story of O*: Lateral Ethics and the Conditions of Reading." *Journal of Literary Theory* 4, no. 1 (2010): 157–66.
———. "Shakespeare's Dolphin, Dumbo's Feather, and Other Red Herrings: Some Thoughts on Intention and Meaning." *Style* 44, no. 3 (2010): 342–64.
Ratner, Leonard. *Classic Music: Expression, Form, and Style*. New York: Schirmer, 1980.
Reddick, Carissa. "Formal Fusion and Rotational Overlap in Sonata Forms from the Chamber Music of Brahms, Dvořák, Franck, and Grieg." PhD diss., University of Connecticut, 2009.
———. "Becoming at a Deeper Level: Divisional Overlap in Sonata Forms from the Late Nineteenth Century." *Music Theory Online* 16, no. 2 (2010). Retrieved December 31, 2013 (http://www.mtosmt.org/issues/mto.10.16.2/mto.10.16.2.reddick.html).
Reich, Nancy B. "Clara Schumann and Johannes Brahms." In *Brahms and His World*, rev. ed., edited by Walter Frisch and Kevin C. Karnes, 57–71. Princeton, NJ: Princeton University Press, 2009.
Reynolds, Christopher. "A Choral Symphony by Brahms?" *19th-Century Music* 9, no. 1 (1985): 3–25.
———. *Motives for Allusion: Context and Content in Nineteenth-Century Music*. Cambridge, MA: Harvard University Press, 2003.
Richardson, Brian. "The Implied Author: Back from the Grave or Simply Dead Again?" *Style* 45, no. 1 (2011): 1–10.
Ricoeur, Paul. *Time and Narrative*. 3 vols. Chicago: University of Chicago Press, 1984.
Rink, John. "Chopin's Ballades and the Dialectic: Analysis in Historical Perspective." *Music Analysis* 13, no. 1 (1994): 99–115.
———. "'Structural Momentum' and Closure in Chopin's Op. 9, No. 2." *Chopin Studies* 5 (1995): 82–104.
———. "Opposition and Integration in the Piano Music." In *The Cambridge Companion to Brahms*, edited by Michael Musgrave, 79–97. Cambridge, UK: Cambridge University Press, 1999.
Rivers, Marie. "Johannes Brahms, Gustav Nottebohm, and Beethoven's 'Hammerklavier' Sonata." *Arietta: Journal of the Beethoven Society of Europe* 5 (2005): 4–11.
Robinson, Jenefer, and Robert S. Hatten. "Emotions in Music." *Music Theory Spectrum* 34, no. 2 (2012): 71–106.
Rosand, Ellen. "The Descending Tetrachord: An Emblem of Lament." *The Musical Quarterly* 65 (1979): 346–59.
Rosen, Charles. *The Classical Style: Haydn, Mozart, Beethoven*. Expanded ed. New York: Norton, 1997. First edition New York: Norton, 1971.
———. *Sonata Forms*. Rev. ed. New York: Norton: 1988. First edition New York: Norton, 1980.

———. *The Romantic Generation*. Cambridge, MA: Harvard University Press, 1995.
Rothstein, William. *Phrase Rhythm in Tonal Music*. New York: Schirmer, 1989.
Sacks, Sheldon. *Fiction and the Shape of Belief: A Study of Henry Fielding, with Glances at Swift, Johnson, and Richardson*. Chicago: University of Chicago Press, 1964.
Said, Edward W. "The Poet as Oedipus." Review of *A Map of Misreading*, by Harold Bloom. *New York Times Book Review*. Retrieved January 5, 2014 (http://www.nytimes.com/books/98/11/01/specials/bloom-misreading.html).
Samarotto, Frank. "A Theory of Temporal Plasticity in Tonal Music: An Extension of the Schenkerian Approach to Rhythm with Special Reference to Beethoven's Late Music." PhD diss., City University of New York, 1999.
———. "Multiple Voices and Metrical Dramas in Beethoven's Goethe-Songs, Op. 83." *Beethoven Forum* 12, no. 2 (2005): 151–75.
———. "Determinism, Prediction, and Inevitability in Brahms's Rhapsody in E♭ Major, Op. 119, No. 4." *Theory and Practice* 32 (2007): 69–99.
———. "Fluidities of Phrase and Form in the 'Intermezzo' of Brahms's First Symphony." *Integral: The Journal of Applied Musical Thought* 22 (2008): 117–43.
———. "'Phantasia subitanea': Temporal Caprice in Brahms's Op. 116, Nos. 1 and 7." In *Expressive Intersections in Brahms: Essays in Analysis and Meaning*, edited by Heather Platt and Peter H. Smith, 186–216. Bloomington: Indiana University Press, 2012.
Samson, Jim. *The Music of Chopin*. London: Routledge and Kegan Paul, 1985.
———. "Chopin and Genre." *Music Analysis* 8, no. 3 (1989): 213–31.
———. "Chopin and the Structures of History." In *Chopin and His Work in the Context of Culture*, edited by Irena Poniatowska, 47–57. Krakow, Poland: Musica Iagellonica, 2003.
Sanguinetti, Giorgio. "La scala come modelo per la composizione." *Rivista di analisi e teoria musicale* 15, no. 1 (2009): 66–94.
Satyendra, Ramon. "Conceptualising Expressive Chromaticism in Liszt's Music." *Music Analysis* 16, no. 2 (1997): 219–52.
———. "Liszt's Open Structures and the Romantic Fragment." *Music Theory Spectrum* 19, no. 2 (1997): 184–205.
Schachter, Carl. "The First Movement of Brahms's Second Symphony: The Opening Theme and Its Consequences." *Music Analysis* 2, no. 1 (1983): 55–68.
———. "Review of *The Music of Chopin*, by Jim Samson, and *The Music of Brahms*, by Michael Musgrave." *Music Analysis* 8, nos. 1–2 (1989): 187–97.
Schlegel, Friedrich. *Die Griechen und Römer: Historische und krittische Versuche über das klassische Altertum* (1797). In *Studien des Klassischen Aletertums*, vol. 1 of *Kritische Friedrich Schlegel Ausgabe*, edited by Ernst Behler, with the cooperation of Jean-Jacques Anstett and Hans Eichner, 203–368. Munich, Germany: Schöningh, 1979.
———. *Athenäum Fragmente*. In *Charakteristiken und Kritiken I* (1796–1801), volume 2 of *Kritische Friedrich Schlegel Ausgabe*, edited by Ernst Behler, with the cooperation of Jean-Jacques Anstett and Hans Eichner, 165–255. Munich, Germany: Schöningh, 1967.
———. *Fragmente zur Literatur und Poesie*. In *Fragmente zur Poesie und Literatur*, volume 16 of *Kritische Friedrich Schlegel Ausgabe*, edited by Ernst Behler, with the cooperation of Jean-Jacques Anstett and Hans Eichner, 83–190. Munich, Germany: Schöningh, 1981.
Schlegel, August Wilhelm. *Vorlesungen über dramatische Kunst und Literatur*. In August Wilhelm Schlegel, *Kritische Schriften und Briefe*, volume 6, edited by Edgar Lohner. Stuttgart, Germany: Kolhammer, 1967.

Schmalfeldt, Janet. "Cadential Processes: The Evaded Cadence and the 'One More Time' Technique." *The Journal of Musicological Research* 12, nos. 1–2 (1992): 1–52.
———. "In Search of Dido." *The Journal of Musicology* 18, no. 4 (2001): 584–615.
———. *In the Process of Becoming: Analytical and Philosophical Perspectives on Form in Early Nineteenth-Century Music*. New York: Oxford University Press, 2010.
———. "One More Time on Beethoven's 'Tempest,' from Analytic and Performance Perspectives: A Response to William E. Caplin and James Hepokoski." *Music Theory Online* 16, no. 2 (2010). Retrieved December 31, 2013 (http://www.mtosmt.org/issues /mto.10.16.2/mto.10.16.2.schmalfeldt3.html).
Schoenberg, Arnold. "Brahms the Progressive." In Arnold Schoenberg, *Style and Idea*, edited by Leonard Stein, translated by Leo Black, 298–441. London: Faber & Faber, 1975.
Schubring, Adolph. "Five Early Works by Brahms (1862)." Translated by Walter Frisch. In *Brahms and His World*, rev. ed., edited by Walter Frisch and Kevin C. Karnes, 195–215. Princeton, NJ: Princeton University Press, 2009.
[Schubring, Adolph.] "Schumanniana Nr. 8: Die Schumann'sche Schule IV. Johannes Brahms." *Neue Zeitschrift für Musik* 56 (1862): 93–96, 101–4, 109–12, 117–19, 125–28.
Schumann, Robert. "Sonaten für das Klavier." *Neue Zeitschrift für Musik* 10, no. 34 (1839): 134–35.
———. "Neue Bahnen." *Neue Zeitschrift für Musik* 39, no. 18 (1853): 185–86.
———. *Gesammelte Schriften über Musik und Musiker*. Vol. 3. Leipzig, Germany: Georg Wigand, 1854.
Scott, Ann Besser. "Thematic Transmutation in the Music of Brahms: A Matter of Musical Alchemy." *The Journal of Musicological Research* 15 (1995): 177–206.
Seaton, Douglass. "Narrativity and the Performance of Beethoven's 'Tempest' Sonata." In *Beethoven's "Tempest" Sonata: Perspectives of Analysis and Performance*, edited by Pieter Bergé, coedited by Jeroen D'hoe and William E. Caplin, 273–92. Leuven, Belgium: Peeters, 2009.
Shauffler, Robert H. *The Unknown Brahms: His Life, Character and Works, Based on New Material*. Westport, CT: Greenwood Press, 1972. First edition New York: Dodd, Mead, 1933.
Sholes, Jacquelyn Elizabeth Coran. "'Transcendence,' 'Loss,' and 'Reminiscence': Brahms's Early Finales in the Contexts of Form, Narrative, and Historicism." PhD diss., Brandeis University, 2008.
Sisman, Elaine. "Brahms's Slow Movements: Reinventing the 'Closed' Forms." In *Brahms Studies: Analytical and Historical Perspectives*, edited by George S. Bozarth, 79–103. Oxford, UK: Clarendon, 1990.
———. "The Music of Rhetoric." In *Musicology and Sister Disciplines: Past, Present, Future*, edited by David Greer, with Ian Rumbold and Jonathan King, 169–78. Oxford, UK: Oxford University Press, 2000.
Smith, Peter H. "Liquidation, Augmentation, and Brahms's Recapitulatory Overlaps." *19th-Century Music* 17, no. 3 (1994): 237–61.
———. "Brahms and the Neapolitan Complex: ♭II, ♭VI, and Their Multiple Functions in the First Movement of the F-Minor Clarinet Sonata." In *Brahms Studies* 2, edited by David Brodbeck, 169–208. Lincoln: University of Nebraska Press, 1998.
———. "Brahms and Subject/Answer Rhetoric." *Music Analysis* 20, no. 2 (2001): 193–236.
———. *Expressive Forms in Brahms's Instrumental Music: Structure and Meaning in His Werther Quartet*. Bloomington: Indiana University Press, 2005.

———. "The Drama of Tonal Pairing in Chamber Music of Schumann and Brahms." In *Expressive Intersections in Brahms: Essays in Analysis and Meaning*, edited by Heather Platt and Peter H. Smith, 252–90. Bloomington: Indiana University Press, 2012.
Smith, Raymond R. "Motivic Procedure in the Opening Movements of the Symphonies of Schumann, Bruckner, and Brahms." *The Music Review* 36, no. 2 (1975): 130–34.
Steblin, Rita. *A History of Key Characteristics in the Eighteenth and Early Nineteenth Centuries*. Ann Arbor: UMI Research Press, 1983.
Stewart-MacDonald, Rohan H. "'Developmental Recession' and Large-Scale Teleology in the Sonata-Type Movements of Felix Mendelssohn Bartholdy." *Ad Parnassum: A Journal of Eighteenth- and Nineteenth-Century Instrumental Music* 7, no. 14 (2009): 71–113.
Straus, Joseph N. *Remaking the Past: Musical Modernism and the Influence of the Tonal Tradition*. Cambridge, MA: Harvard University Press, 1990.
———. "The 'Anxiety of Influence' in Twentieth-Century Music." *The Journal of Musicology* 9, no. 4 (1991): 430–47.
Street, Alan. "Superior Myths, Dogmatic Allegories: The Resistance to Musical Unity." *Music Analysis* 8, nos. 1–2 (1989): 77–123.
Suurpää, Lauri. "The Undivided Ursatz and the Omission of the Tonic Stufe at the Beginning of the Recapitulation." *Journal of Schenkerian Studies* 1 (2005): 66–91.
Swafford, Jan. *Brahms: A Biography*. New York: Knopf, 1998.
Tarasti, Eero. *A Theory of Musical Semiotics*. Bloomington: Indiana University Press, 1994.
Taruskin, Richard. "Speed Bumps." Review of *The Cambridge History of Nineteenth-Century Music*, edited by Jim Samson, and of *The Cambridge History of Twentieth-Century Music*, edited by Nicholas Cook and Anthony Pople. *19th-Century Music* 29, no. 2 (2005): 185–295.
Thompson, Christopher K. "Brahms and the Problematizing of Traditional Sonata Form." PhD diss., University of Wisconsin, 1996.
———. "Re-Forming Brahms: Sonata Form and the Horn Trio, Op. 40." *Indiana Theory Review* 18, no. 1 (1997): 65–95.
Tovey, Donald. "Brahms's Chamber Music." In Donald Tovey, *The Main Stream of Music and Other Essays*, collected and with an introduction by Hubert Foss, 220–70. New York: Oxford University Press, 1949. Originally in *Cobbett's Cyclopedic Survey of Chamber Music*, vol. I, edited by W. W. Cobbett, 158–82. Oxford, UK: Oxford University Press, 1929.
Vande Moortele, Steven. "Form, Program, and Deformation in Liszt's *Hamlet*." *Dutch Journal of Music Theory* 11, no. 2 (2006): 71–82.
———. "Beyond Sonata Deformation: Liszt's Symphonic Poem *Tasso* and the Concept of Two-Dimensional Sonata Form." *Current Musicology* 86 (2008): 41–62.
———. "The First Movement of Beethoven's 'Tempest' Sonata and the Tradition of Twentieth-Century 'Formenlehre.'" In *Beethoven's "Tempest" Sonata: Perspectives of Analysis and Performance*, edited by Pieter Bergé, coedited by Jeroen D'hoe and William E. Caplin, 293–314. Leuven, Belgium: Peeters, 2009.
———. *Two-Dimensional Sonata Form: Form and Cycle in Single-Movement Instrumental Works by Liszt, Strauss, Schoenberg, and Zemlinsky*. Leuven, Belgium: Leuven University Press, 2009.
———. "Sentences, Sentence Chains, and Sentence Replication: Intra- and Interthematic Formal Functions in Liszt's Weimar Symphonic Poems." *Intégral* 25 (2011): 121–58.

von Goethe, Johann Wolfgang. *Faust: Ein Fragment*. Leipzig, Germany: Göschen, 1790. Reprinted as von Goethe, Johann Wolfgang. *Faust: Ein Fragment*. Deutsche Litteraturdenkmale des 18. Jahrhunderts, no. 5, edited by Bernhard Seuffert. Stuttgart, Germany: G. J. Göschen, 1882.

Webster, James. "Schubert's Sonata Form and Brahms's First Maturity." *19th-Century Music* 2, no. 1 (1978): 18–35.

———. "Schubert's Sonata Form and Brahms's First Maturity (II)." *19th-Century Music* 3, no. 1 (1979): 52–71.

———. "Brahms's *Tragic Overture*: The Form of Tragedy." In *Brahms: Biographical, Documentary, and Analytical Studies*, edited by Robert Pascall, 99–124. Cambridge, UK: Cambridge University Press, 1983.

———. "The Alto Rhapsody: Psychology, Intertextuality, and Brahms's Artistic Development." In *Brahms Studies* 3, edited by David Brodbeck, 19–45. Lincoln: University of Nebraska Press, 2001.

———. "Comments on James Hepokoski's Essay 'Sonata Theory and Dialogic Form.'" In *Musical Forms, Form, and Formenlehre*, edited by Pieter Bergé, 96–100. Leuven, Belgium: Leuven University Press, 2009.

Wellek, René. "The Concept of 'Romanticism' in Literary History: I: The Term 'Romantic' and Its Derivatives." *Comparative Literature* 1, no. 1 (1949): 1–23.

———. "The Concept of 'Romanticism' in Literary History: II: The Unity of European Romanticism." *Comparative Literature* 1, no. 2 (1949): 147–72.

Wheelock, Gretchen. "*Schwarze Gredel* and the Engendered Minor Mode in Mozart's Operas." In *Musicology and Difference: Gender and Sexuality in Music Scholarship*, edited by Ruth A. Solie, 201–21. Berkeley: University of California Press, 1992.

Wimsatt, William K. Jr. "The Structure of Romantic Nature Imagery." Reprinted in *Romanticism and Consciousness: Essays in Criticism*, edited by Harold Bloom, 77–88. New York: Norton, 1970.

Wingfield, Paul. "Beyond 'Norms and Deformations': Towards a Theory of Sonata Form as Reception History." Review of *Elements of Sonata Theory: Norms, Types, and Deformations in the Late-Eighteenth-Century Sonata*, by James Hepokoski and Warren Darcy. *Music Analysis* 27, no. 1 (2008): 137–77.

Wintle, Christopher. "The 'Sceptered Pall': Brahms's Progressive Harmony." In *Brahms 2: Biographical, Documentary, and Analytical Studies*, edited by Michael Musgrave, 197–222. Cambridge, UK: Cambridge University Press, 1987.

———. "Wotan's Rhetoric of Anguish." Review of Abbate, *Unsung Voices*. *Journal of the Royal Musical Association* 118, no. 1 (1993): 121–43.

Wordsworth, William. "Preface" (1802, rev. 1802). Reprinted in R. L. Brett and A. R. Jones, eds., *Wordsworth and Coleridge: Lyrical Ballads*, 286–314. London: Routledge, 2005.

Wunder, Heide. *He Is the Sun, She Is the Moon: Women in Early Modern Germany*. Translated by Thomas Dunlap. Cambridge, MA: Harvard University Press, 1998. Originally *Er ist die Sonn, sie ist der Mond: Frauen in der Frühen Neuzeit*. Munich, Germany: C. H. Beck'sche Verlagsbuchhandlung, 1992.

Zenck, Martin. "Classicism vs. the 'New German School': About the Political Codes 'Conservative'-'Progressive' in the Music of the Second Half of the 19th Century, with Regard to Brahms's Op. 1 and Liszt's *Piano Sonata in B Minor*." In *Quellenstudium und musikalische Analyse: Festschrift Martin Just zum 70. Geburstag*, edited by Peter Niedermüller, Cristina Urchueguía, and Oliver Wiener, 243-52. Würzburg, Germany: Ergon, 2001.

Index

Page numbers in italics refer to illustrations and musical examples. Works by composers are arranged in the order of the opus number. Opus numbers have been set in italics for clarity.

Abbate, Carolyn, 41, 58
action spaces, 39
arabesque, 26–27, 29
Arcadia topic: Classical norm as, 151–152, 170–172, *171*, 174–175; in development sections, 156–157, 159; gateway passages and, 77–78; in *Gesangsthema* S-themes, 82, 85, 113, 134–140, *136–137*, 141, 144–146; in interpolated interjections, 102; major/minor binary opposition and, 133–135; overview, 21–22, 30–31n13; recapitulation of, 107; Romantic pastoral narrative type, 65, 77–78, 126–128, 130, 134–140; suppression/mocking of, 140–143, 144–145, 147

Bach, Johann Sebastian, 172, *173*
Bakhtin, Mikhail, 42–43
bardic style, 169–170
Baroque aesthetic, 55
Barthes, Roland, 42
Beethoven, Ludwig van: Brahms references to, 56, 130, 139, 141–142, *142*, 145, 168–170; cadential events in, 148; Chopin references to, 94; development sections, 160; fate motive, 56, *92*, 94, 130, 138, 145, 160; narrative conflict in, 178; parenthetical enclosures, 80n19; sonata development by, 6; structural discontinuities in, 41; tragic-to-triumphant plots in, 133. Works: Piano Sonata in C minor, *op. 13* ("Pathétique"), 141–142, *142*; Symphony no. 3 in E♭ major, *op. 55* ("Eroica"), 160, 178; Overtures to *Coriolan*, *op. 62*, 134; Symphony no. 5 in C minor, *op. 67*, 56, 133; Symphony No 6 in F major, *op. 68* (Pastoral Symphony), 21; Piano Concerto No. 5 in E♭ major, *op. 73* ("Emperor"), 168–170, *169*; *Egmont*, *op. 84*, 134; Piano Sonata no. 30 in E major, *op. 109*, 120n11
Berger, Karol, 34–35, 44, 46n22
Bloom, Harold, 25
Booth, Wayne C., 13–15, 30n10, 39–40, 149
Bozarth, George, 68–69, 69, 75, 80n24, 120n15
Brahms, Johannes: dimensional counterpoint in, 114–116; early piano sonatas, historical context of, 123; fragmented recapitulation in, 162–165; hypothetical S-theme proposals, *117*, 126, 129, 137, 147, 157–162, 160; major/minor binary opposition and, 133; narrative strategies in, 41; "Rückblick" intermezzo of, 104
Piano Sonata in C major, *op. 1*: ambiguous transitions in, 114–118; conflated atemporality in, 143; development section, 155–158; development sections, 177; disruption of narrative flow, 53, 57–58, 101; dissolving-restatement TR-type, 126; durational atemporality in, 58–66, *58*, *62*, 85–86; expressive motivation in, 56–57, *57*, 93–94; external narrating agents in, 58–61; narrative motivation in, 85–91, *88–89*; narrative voice in, 52–53, *54–55*, 55–56; recapitulation in, 162–164; Romantic fragment aesthetic in, 12; as "Verstohlen geht" setting, 51–53, *52*, 67–69, 74, 78nn1, 2
Piano Sonata in F♯ minor, *op. 2*: Brahms biographical correlations in, 146–147; Classical form in, 69–70, *70*; conflated atemporality in, 143; development sections, 158–159; diegetic coda in, 171–172, *172*; diegetic shifts in, 168–169; dissolving-restatement TR-type, 125–126; durational atemporality in, 70–71, 70–76, 73–74; medial caesura in, 125–126, *126*; as "Mir ist leide" setting, 67–73, *68–69*; narrative strategies in, 41, 67, 87, 91; poetic slow movements, 51; recapitulation in, 162–165; Romantic fragment aesthetic in, 12, 135–140; ruptured atemporality in, 76–77, 107, 127, 136–140, 145; S-theme fragmentation in, 135–140, 144–146, *144*, 177; transition in, 4–6, *5–6*; unconventional structure of, 11
Piano Sonata No. 3, *op. 5*: Brahms biographical correlations in, 146; conflated atemporality in, 103–108, *105–106*; development sections, 160, 177; diegetic coda in, 172–175; narrative motivation/longing in, 120n16; narrative voice in, 106–107; post-MC interpolation in, 128–131, *129*; recapitulation in, 165–166; Romantic fragment aesthetic in, 12; ruptured atemporality in, 116, 118, 160; sonata structure of, *117*; spatiality in, 106–107; S-theme fragmentation in, 140–143; transition in, 125–126, 129, 131n1
Violin Sonata in A major, *op. 100*, 161–162
Violin Sonata in D minor, *op. 108*, 161–162

199

British Romanticism, 27
Brooks, Peter, 14
Bruckner, Anton, 12, 151, 178
Byron, Lord (George Gordon), 27

cadences: ambiguous transitions and, 4, 94, 114–118; door closing/opening with, 80n16; expanded cadential progressions, 66, 80n22; historical context and, 148, 151–152; as narrative devices, 53–54, 75; as normative devices, 11; suppressed cadences, 61, 65–66, 174; in temporal layering, 60
Caplin, William E., 66, 84
Cervantes, Miguel de, 26–27
Chicago School of literary criticism, 20–21
Chopin, Frédéric: Arcadia topic in, 30–31n13; influence on Brahms, 123; major/minor binary opposition and, 133; nocturnes, 3–4
　Ballade No. 1 in G minor, *op. 23*, 133, 135, 170
　Ballade No. 4, *op. 52*, 133, 135, 152n11
　Piano Sonata in B minor, *op. 58*: chromatic disturbances in, 1–4, 91–96, *92–93*, 101–102, 120n11; developmental themes, 161; disruption of narrative flow, 11, 101–103, 138; dissolving TR-type, 91, *97*, 98, 113, 126; mm. 1–45, *2–3*; pre-MC interpolation in, 125; recapitulation in, 166; ruptured atemporality in, 91–92, *92–93*; sonata structure of, 6
chromatic harmony: chromatic disturbances, 57, 74–75, 91–96, *92–93*, 120n11; chromatic transitions, 1, 11; enharmonic equivalences, 93, 107
chronotopes, 42–43, 108
cinematic narrative, 47n32, 79n13
Classical aesthetic: atemporal narrative structure in, 62; in Brahms *op. 2/i*, 126–128; in Brahms's developmental sections, 160–161; four-bar phrases in, 63, 70–72, 82, 91, 96–98, 120n12; influence on Romantic literature, 19, 22–28; major/minor binary opposition, 132–133; narrative conflict in, 178; normative sonata temporality, 44; normative "subdominant recapitulations," 162, 166–167n6; *partimento* tradition and, 170, *171*; piano sonata influences in, 12; rotational ordering, 155–156, 166n1; in Schuman *op. 11/iv*, 108
codas: deflected codas, 145–146; diegetic codas, 171–175, *172*; as extrastructural, 140; introduction-coda frames, 170–171; narrative motivation and, 66, 80n24, 104, *117*, 120n16; recapitulation-coda complexes, 163; violent coda in Brahms *op. 2*, 147
Coleridge, Samuel Taylor, 27
concertos, 19
Cone, Edward T., 30n10

Darcy, Warren, 12, 38–39, 62, 80n16, 169–170. *See also* Sonata Theory
Daverio, John, 26–27, 41
deformation theory, 46n25, 148–151
description vs. narration, 47n32
development sections: Brahms hypothetical S-theme proposals, *117, 126, 129, 137, 147, 157–162, 160*; Classical norms and, 160–161; developmental P-themes, 4, 155–156; dissolution of, 147; Romantic aesthetic and, 155; stalled development, 42; temporality of, 152n8
dialogism, 42
Dickensheets, Janice, 41, 152–153n13, 153n18, 169–170
Diderot, Denis, 23
discourse, 14, 41–42
dramatic genre, 34–35, 39–40, 42

emplotment, 14, 45n5, 146
Enlightenment: piano sonata influences from, 12; progress theme in, 22; Romantic borrowings from, 19, 23; Romantic rejection of, 20, 25–26
epic genre, 34–35, 39–40, 42
Essential Expositional Closure (EEC): Arcadia and, 85; atemporal digression/rupture and, 135; attenuated EEC, 138–139, 143, 153n14; cadential events and, 80n16, 82, 119, 136, 142–145, *144*; Classical sonata structure and, 39, 125, *126*; false EEC, 159; harmonic movement and, 102; historical context and, 148; narrative trajectory and, 137–140; reimagined EEC, 160; as S-theme closure, *112*, 113–114. *See also* recapitulation
Essential Structural Closure (ESC), 39, 135, 140, 148, 173–174. *See also* recapitulation

Fenaroli, Fedele, 170, *171*
Forte, Allen, 15
Foucault, Michel, 20
fragmentation: in the arabesque, 29; in development sections, 155–158; enclosing gestures and, 63; fragmented recapitulation, 162–165; of narrative themes, 59, 70, 91; pedal point projection of, 112; pedal tones as projected fragments, 112; Romantic fragment aesthetic and, 12, 26–29, 28–29, 135–141; in Romantic vs. Classical sonatas, 27–28, 44, 70; S-themes and fragmentation, 135–140, 140–143, 144–146, *144*, 177
Frye, Northrop, 22, 24–25

gateway passages: Arcadia topic and, 77–78; in development sections, 156; external anachrony and, 115; framing of interpolations by, 77, 102–103, *103*,

107, 118–119, 160; narrative agency in, 92–93, 96, 99, *99–100*, *110–111*, 112–113; S-openings as, 87; tonal disengagement as, *105–106*, 106–107
gender, 134, 152n11, 153n21
Genette, Gérard: on anisochrony, 37, 40, 58–59, 72; categories of anachronies, 35–39, 114, 119; on first narrative temporality, 43–44; on *mood* (*mode*), 53–54, 65, 67, 73; on narratology, 13–14; on normative narrative chronology, 44; on the *pause*, 64, 108, 155; on the *summary* (*sommaire*), 76; on *voice* (*voix*), 52–53; zero reference point, 37, 58, 61
genre, 35
German Romanticism, definitions of, 27–28
Gesangsthema: Classical origins of, 133; as common Romantic S-type, 82–83, *83*; normative functionality of, 127–128, 130–131, 135–137, 141; proposal register of, 160; in P-theme/S-theme contrasts, 177; suppression/mocking of, 144–146
Gifford, Terry, 22
Goethe, Johann Wolfgang von, 27

Hatten, Robert, 30–31n13, 41–42, 116, 120n11, 133
Haydn, Joseph, 6
Hepokoski, James, 12, 38–39, 46n25, 62, 80n16, 134, 169–170. *See also* Sonata Theory
heteroglossia, 42
Hoffman, E. T. A., 41
Homer, 36–37
Hume, David, 23

Iliad, 36–37
implied author, the, 20–21, 30n10, 59, 79n14, 147, 149–150
interpolation: atemporal interpolation, 63–64, 96, 103, 113–114, 155–156; gateway entrances/exits, 77, 103, 107, 118–119, 160; interpolated analepsis, 112–113; interpolated interjections, 102; interpolated pauses, 108; overview, 40; parenthetical enclosures, 41, 63, 80n19, 96, 107–108; post-MC interpolation, 125, 127–131, 139, 141; pre-MC interpolation, 125
Iser, Wolfgang, 46n25
isochronous (isochrone) narrative, 60

Jean Paul (Johann Paul Friedrich Richter), 41
Jena School Romanticism, 27–28

Keats, John, 27
Kinderman, William, 41, 63
Klein, Michael, 30–31n13, 133, 135, 152n11
Kramer, Lawrence, 153n21
Kretzschmer, August, 51, 53, 78nn1, 2

landscape painting, Romantic, 21, 28, 30n5, 33n46, 133, 157
Liszt, Franz, 11, 12, 161
Lovejoy, Arthur, 23
lyric genre, 34–35, 46n22, 133

Mahler, Gustav, 12, 135, 161, 170, 178
markedness, 40–42, 46n25
Marx, Adolph Bernhard, 134
McGann, Jerome, 31n20
medial caesura (MC): ambiguous transitions and, 4, 6, 11, 86–91, *88*, 93–95, *97*, 98, *99–101*, 114, *117*; cadential events and, 3, 11, 102–103, 108–109; narrative motivation in, 125; normative functionality of, 39, 109, 125; post-MC interpolation, 125, 127–131, 139, 141; pre-MC interpolation, 125, 166
Mendelssohn, Fanny, 12
Mendelssohn, Felix, 12, 170
Metz, Christian, 45n8, 47n32
minus functions (Iser), 46n25
Mozart, Wolfgang Amadeus: atemporality in, 62; cadential events in, 148; narrative conflict in, 178; Schumann references to, 82; sonata development by, 6

narrative: arabesque as strategy in, 29; biographical correlations in, 146; chronotopes, 42–43, 108; cinematic narrative, 47n32, 79n13; diegetic agency in, 127, 130; disruption of narrative flow, 26–27, 53, 57–58, 98–99, *99–101*; emplotment, 14, 45n5, 146; fragmented development sections and, 155–158; implied author, the, 20–21, 30n10, 59, 79n14, 147, 149–150; implied prototypes, 72; implied readers/listeners/audiences, 60, 79n14, 91, 149–151; interiority of the narrator, 61, 64–65, 73–74; interjections, 73; isochronous (isochrone) narrative, 60; literary *pause*, 64, 74, 108; longing as motivation in, 22, 66, 86–91, 112–113, 118–119, 120n16, 157–158; lyric agency, 40–42, 53, 55–56, 130, 145; lyric compared with, 34–35, 46n22; modality of narrative representation, 53; *mood* (*mode*), 53–54, 65, 67, 73; musical-narrative agents, 39; narrative discourse, 14; narrative voice in, 39–41; *per aspera ad astra* plot archetype, 133; quest narratives, 25; Romantic musical narratives, 13–15, 20–21, 177–178; sentence replication and, 72, 81n31, 98, 113; structural narratology, 35–38; *summary* (*sommaire*) in, 76; temporal structure in, 35–38; tragic-to-triumphant expressive genre, 30–31n13, 132–133; zero reference point in, 37, 58, 61
Neapolitan harmony, 3, 57, 60–61, 65, 72, 74, 144, 146

Newcomb, Anthony, 41
nocturnes, 3–4, 95, 152n11
Novalis (George Philipp Friedrich Freiherr von Hardenberg), 27–28, 41
novel: Bakhtin on, 42; Brahms *op. 1/ii* as, 58–59; as multidimensional work, 13; novelistic S-space, 152–153n13; pastoralism in, 21; *Roman* structural tendencies, 26–27, 34, 41

opera, narrative voices in, 41

parabasis, 26–27
pastoralism: Arcadia topic in, 21–22, 30–31n13, 65, 77–78, 135–142; Clara Schumann account and, 146–147; interior themes and, 135, 152n11; *partimento* tradition and, 170, *171*; Romantic pastoral narrative type, 21–22, 77–78, 133–135; S-space relationship with, 130–135; in untexted music, 82
pedal tones, 1, 3, 71, 73, 75, 112, 143
Picasso, Pablo, 150–151
Plato, 34
primary themes (P-themes): Brahmsian P-themes, 4; developmental P-themes, 4, 155–156; fragmented recapitulation in, 162–165; P-theme/S-theme binary opposition, 133–135, 177–178; Schumann sentence format, 6; in Sonata Theory, 39; as transition substitute, 3–4; transitions from, 1
Prokofiev, Sergei, 178

Rabinowitz, Peter J., 149–151
Rachmaninoff, Sergei, 12, 178
Ravel, Maurice, 178
recapitulation: atemporal digression/rupture in, 139–140, 145; correspondence measures and, 153n20; ESC role in, 39; fragmented recapitulation, 162–165; narrative trajectory and, 147, 151; recapitulatory S-themes, 128, 132, 139, 172–175; subdominant recapitulations, 158, 162, 166–167n6. *See also* Essential Expositional Closure; Essential Structural Closure
rhetoric: diegesis-mimesis distinction, 34, 42, 79n13, 136, 143, 156, 161, 168–169; rhetorical gestures, 40–42, 46n25; rhetorical narrative theory, 13–15, 15n12; in Sonata Theory, 39–40; tonal/motivic dissolution, 1
Ricoeur, Paul, 45n5
Riemann, Hugo, 11
Romantic aesthetics: atemporality, 38, 44, 61–66, *62*, 119; biographical correlations in, 146–148; Brahmsian lyrical S and, 4; Brahms's early piano sonatas and, 123; cadential events in, 148; Classical literary influence in, 19, 22–28; development sections, 155, 160–161; discursive shifts in, 91, 95–96; disruption of narrative flow, 26–27, 53, 57–58, 98–99, *99–101*; as epistemic system, 20; essential expressive opposition of, 177–178; fragments in, 12, 26–29, 28–29, 135–141; *Gesangsthema* as normative in, 144; major/minor binary opposition, 132–135; narrative motivation/longing in, 22, 66, 86–91, 112–113, 118–119, 120n16, 157–158; organicism/unity expectations, 6; pastoralism and, 21–22, 77–78, 133–135; piano sonata influences in, 12; post-MC interpolation and, 125, 127–131, 139, 141; *Roman* (novel) relationship with, 26–27, 34, 58–59; Romantic musical narrative, 13–15; spatiality as component in, 24–26; staged conflict in, 77
Rosen, Charles, 120n12
Rothstein, William, 72
Rousseau, Jean-Jacques, 23

Sanguinetti, Giorgio, 172, *173*
Schlegel, August Wilhelm, 25, 27–28
Schlegel, Friedrich: on arabesque, 29; on Classical form, 19; Classical fragments in, 27–28; on Classical spatiality, 29n1; disruption of narrative flow, 26–27; on the *Roman* (novel), 34, 41, 42; Romantic aesthetic environment and, 12; spatiality in, 25–26
Schmalfeldt, Janet, 85, *86*
Schubert, Franz, 54
Schumann, Clara, 146–147, 153n21
Schumann, Robert: on Classical form, 19; influence on Brahms, 123, 147; narrative strategies in, 41; progressive vs. normative style, 11; sentence chain (*Satzkette*) gesture of, 81n31, 113; sentence P-theme format, 6
Piano Sonata in F♯ minor, *op. 11*, 6–11, *7–10*: cadence effects, 83–85, *86*; conflated atemporality in, 108–113, *110–112*; disruption of narrative flow, 98–99, 98–103, *99–101*, 138; dissolving TR-type, 96–98, *99–101*, 113, 126; durational atemporality in, 82, 112–114; pre-MC interpolation in, 125; recapitulation in, 166; ruptured atemporality in, 112–113, 118
Piano Sonata in G minor, *op. 22*: recapitulation in, 166
secondary themes (S-themes): biographical correlations in, 146–148; Brahms hypothetical S-theme proposals, *117*, *126*, *129*, *137*, *147*, 157–162, *160*; in Chopin nocturnes, 3, 11; *Gesangsthema* type of, 82–83, *83*, 127–128, 130–131, 133, 135–136, *160*, 177; lyrical S-theme, 3, 4, 11, 34–35, 82, 109,

152n8; MC relationship with, 86–87; narrative motivation in, 86–91, 125, 151–152; normative Romantic S-themes, 11, 133–135; novelistic S-space, 152–153n13; P-theme/S-theme binary, 133–135, 177–178; Romantic fragmentation in, 135–141; in Sonata Theory, 39, 132
slow introductions, 96, 146
Smith, Peter, 114–116, 133, 135
Sonata Theory: as analytical tool, 12–13; atemporal narrative structure and, 38–39; cadence effects, 83–85, 148, 151–152; cadence failure in, 66, 80n23; compound basic ideas, 84; correspondence measures, 145, 153n20; deformation theory, 46n25, 148–151; dissolving TR-type, 91, 98, 99–101; Essential Expositional Closure (EEC), 39, 80n16, 82, 85, 102, 113–114, 135, 137–140, 145; Essential Structural Closure (ESC), 39, 135, 140; expanded cadential progressions (ECP), 66, 80n22; narrative voicing and, 39–41; normativity in, 46n25; "one more time" technique (OMT), 85, 86; rhetoric and, 39–40; S-space considerations, 132–133
sonatas: atemporal narrative structure in, 38–39; Chopin struggles with, 3–4, 11; countermelodies as indexical signifiers, 54–55, 79n9; medial caesura structural role, 125; as multidimensional works, 13; normative Classical temporality, 44; pastoralism and, 133–135; road chronotope and, 43–44, 108; as Romantic genre, 12, 24, 177–178
spatiality: chronotopes, 42–43, 108; interiority of the narrator, 61, 64–65, 73–74; pastoral interior themes, 135, 152n11; Romantic interiority, 20, 24–27, 59; Schlegel on Classical spatiality, 25, 27, 29n1; spatial projection, 24, 106–107, 118
Strauss, Richard, 12, 178
style hongrois folk dance, 144–145, 153n18
symphonic poems, 169–170
symphonies, 19, 169–170

Tchaikovsky, Pyotr Ilyich, 12, 134, 170, 178
temporality: achronies, 37, 64; anachronies, 37, 64, 113–114, *115*; *analepsis* (flashback), 36–37, 64, 79n13, 96, 112–114, 119, 131; anisochronies, 37, 40, 58–61, 72, 107; Classical atemporality, 62; conflated atemporality, 103–108, *105–106*, 108–113, *110–112*, 143; durational atemporality, 58–66, *58, 62, 70–76, 85–86, 103–104, 112–114, 118, 135–137*; first narrative temporality, 43–44; isochronous (isochrone) narrative, 60; multiple temporal streams, 14, 44, 75, 93, 98–99, 113–115; in narrative structure, 35–38, 38–41, 57–58; normative structure of, 40–41; *prolepsis* (flash-forward), 37, 40, 44, 77, 96, 130–131; resetting-the-clock gestures, 61, 74, 76, 80n16, 85, 107–108, 109, 129; ruptured atemporality, 64, 73–74, 76–77, 91–92, 92–93, 103–104, 112, 112–113, 118, 127, 136–140, 160; temporal disruptions, 42; temporal duality in narrative, 45n8; time vs. temporality, 36, 45n10, 59. *See also* interpolation
texts, 42
Tieck, Ludwig, 27–28
Todorov, Tzvetan, 13
Toggenburg, Kraft von, 67
Tolstoy, Leo, 150–151
tragedy, 30–31n13
transitions (TR): ambiguity in Brahms, 4; chromatic disturbances and, 91–96, *92–93*, 120n11; chromatic transitions, 1; dissolving TR-type, 6–7; dissolving-consequent TR-type, 129; dissolving-continuation TR-type, 157, 159; dissolving-restatement TR-type, 125–126; recapitulatory telescoped TR, 162–165; in Sonata Theory, 39, 120n8

untexted Romantic music: atemporality and, 63–64, 66, 86; discursive shifts marked by, 85, 91, 95–96; narrative rhythm and, 71; slow movements in Brahms as analogous, 82; texted/untexted opposition, 70

Virgil, 30–31n13
voice, narrative: in Brahms *op. 1/ii*, 52–53, 55–56, 58–61; in Brahms *op. 5/v*, 106–107; diegetic subjective agency in, 127, 130; external narrating agents, 58–61; as narrative/sonata component, 39–41

Wackenroder, Wilhelm Heinrich, 27–28
Wagner, Richard, 134
Weber, Carl Maria von, 134
Wellek, René, 23
Wilhelm, August, 23
Wordsworth, William, 19, 20, 23–24, 25

Zuccalmaglio, Anton Wilhelm, 51, 53, 78nn1, 2

Musical Meaning and Interpretation
Robert S. Hatten, editor

A Theory of Musical Narrative
Byron Almén

Approaches to Meaning in Music
Byron Almén and Edward Pearsall

Voicing Gender: Castrati, Travesti, and the Second Woman in Early Nineteenth-Century Italian Opera
Naomi André

The Italian Traditions and Puccini: Compositional Theory and Practice in Nineteenth-Century Opera
Nicholas Baragwanath

Debussy Redux: The Impact of His Music on Popular Culture
Matthew Brown

Music and Embodied Cognition: Listening, Moving, Feeling, and Thinking
Arnie Cox

Music and the Politics of Negation
James R. Currie

Il Trittico, Turandot, and Puccini's Late Style
Andrew Davis

Neil Young and the Poetics of Energy
William Echard

Psychedelic Popular Music: A History through Musical Topic Theory
William Echard

Reconfiguring Myth and Narrative in Contemporary Opera: Osvaldo Golijov, Kaija Saariaho, John Adams, and Tan Dun
Yayoi Uno Everett

Interpreting Musical Gestures, Topics, and Tropes: Mozart, Beethoven, Schubert
Robert S. Hatten

Musical Meaning in Beethoven: Markedness, Correlation, and Interpretation
Robert S. Hatten

Intertextuality in Western Art Music
Michael L. Klein

Music and the Crises of the Modern Subject
Michael L. Klein

Music and Narrative since 1900
Michael L. Klein and Nicholas Reyland

Musical Forces: Motion, Metaphor, and Meaning in Music
Steve Larson

Is Language a Music? Writings on Musical Form and Signification
David Lidov

Pleasure and Meaning in the Classical Symphony
Melanie Lowe

Breaking Time's Arrow: Experiment and Expression in the Music of Charles Ives
Matthew McDonald

Decorum of the Minuet, Delirium of the Waltz: A Study of Dance-Music Relations in ¾ Time
Eric McKee

The Musical Topic: Hunt, Military, Pastoral
Raymond Monelle

Musical Representations, Subjects, and Objects: The Construction of Musical Thought in Zarlino, Descartes, Rameau, and Weber
Jairo Moreno

The Rite of Spring at 100
Severine Neff, Maureen Carr, and Gretchen Horlacher, with John Reef

Meaning and Interpretation of Music in Cinema
David Neumeyer

Deepening Musical Performance through Movement: The Theory and Practice of Embodied Interpretation
Alexandra Pierce

Expressive Intersections in Brahms: Essays in Analysis and Meaning
Heather Platt and Peter H. Smith

Expressive Forms in Brahms's Instrumental Music: Structure and Meaning in His Werther Quartet
Peter H. Smith

Music as Philosophy: Adorno and Beethoven's Late Style
Michael Spitzer

Death in *Winterreise*: Musico-Poetic Associations in Schubert's Song Cycle
Lauri Suurpää

Music and Wonder at the Medici Court: The 1589 Interludes for *La pellegrina*
Nina Treadwell

Reflections on Musical Meaning and Its Representations
Leo Treitler

Debussy's Late Style: The Compositions of the Great War
Marianne Wheeldon

ANDREW DAVIS is Dean of the Kathrine G. McGovern College of the Arts at the University of Houston and author of *Il Trittico, Turandot, and Puccini's Late Style* (Indiana University Press, 2010).

www.ingramcontent.com/pod-product-compliance
Lightning Source LLC
Chambersburg PA
CBHW041311240426
43661CB00065B/2903